Evaluation

EVALUATION
A CULTURAL SYSTEMS APPROACH

MARY ODELL BUTLER

Left Coast Press inc.

WALNUT CREEK, CALIFORNIA

LEFT COAST PRESS, INC.
1630 North Main Street, #400
Walnut Creek, CA 94596
www.LCoastPress.com

ISBN 978-1-62958-082-1 hardback
ISBN 978-1-62958-083-8 paperback
ISBN 978-1-62958-084-5 institutional eBook
ISBN 978-1-62958-085-2 consumer eBook

Library of Congress Cataloging-in-Publication Data

Butler, Mary Odell.
    Evaluation : a cultural systems approach / Mary Odell Butler.
        pages cm
    Includes bibliographical references and index.
    ISBN 978-1-62958-082-1 (hardback : alk. paper)
    ISBN 978-1-62958-083-8 (paperback : alk. paper)
    ISBN 978-1-62958-084-5 (institutional ebook)
    ISBN 978-1-62958-085-2 (consumer ebook)

    1. Social sciences—Research—Evaluation.   2. Evaluation—Methodology.
3. Anthropology—Methodology.   4. Educational evaluation.   I. Title.
    H62.B88 2015
    300.72—dc23
                                                                    2015012880

Printed in the United States of America

∞ ™ The paper used in this publication meets the minimum requirements of American National Standard for Information Sciences—Permanence of Paper for Printed Library Materials, ANSI/NISO Z39.48–1992.

CONTENTS

ACKNOWLEDGMENTS

Like many of us who reach this point in a book, I am overwhelmed by the number of friends who supported me at every step of the way in writing this book and, more importantly, helping me learn the things I needed to know to do it. It forms a mighty crowd, and if I leave your name out here, please accept my apologies and my gratitude.

I would like to extend my thanks to James Hersey who opened the door to evaluation and invited me in. To Susan Squires and Lenora Bohren, who helped me see evaluation within the framework of anthropology. To Eve Pinsker, who, as head of the Evaluation Anthropology Working Group within the National Association for the Practice of Anthropology, kept me focused on the fit between anthropology and evaluation and provided lots of technical support. And to my colleagues and clients over the years, who provided the space for me to learn evaluation and create new ways of doing it.

I am grateful to my editors at Left Coast Press, Inc.: Jack Meinhardt and, before him, Jennifer Collier, both of whom assured me that this was a feasible undertaking. And to Mitch Allen, the Big Man at Left Coast, who first convinced me this book was a good idea.

I acknowledge my debt to my classes in evaluation anthropology at the University of Maryland and the University of North Texas. Much of what is in this book they either taught me or helped me to teach myself.

Finally, thanks to all of my relatives and friends who listened over and over to my trials and perils in putting all of this together. Your patience knows no end.

CHAPTER ONE

INTRODUCTION

This book is about how to link evaluation and anthropology into a dynamic and flexible approach that brings out the vitally human nature of the ways people organize themselves to accomplish their goals. I present an approach to evaluation that merges anthropology and evaluation to make something new, an approach to valuing from the perspective of both the insiders who generate the things being evaluated and the outsiders who will use the evaluation. Evaluation anthropology, alone or in combination with other approaches, can generate explanations of human activities in ways that are both rigorous in their ability to explain and adaptable to changing circumstances. As we will see in the chapters that follow, evaluation is a large field and one requiring many different kinds of abilities.

Evaluation teams go far beyond anthropology. But anthropology has something important to contribute. By using anthropology, evaluators can tease out the multiple perceptions of the thing being evaluated—the evaluand—from the various kinds of people who are influenced by it, untangle the complex dynamics of communities in which programs are embedded, qualify the contextual influences coming from outside of programs yet affecting them often profoundly, and integrate large amounts of information to build descriptions of both individual implementations and widespread programs.

So what are we talking about here? What is it that can help us map diversity on diversity, relationship on relationship, in such a way that we get a three-dimensional view of what kinds of processes generate modern life? Capturing and translating the "inside" of human communities to the "outsiders" who observe them is the time-honored task of the ethnographer (Harris 1968; Stake 2006).[1] Ethnography too must be re-interpreted and disciplined to meet the scientific demands of evaluation. This volume will explore how the two disciplines—anthropology and evaluation—can move together to help us see how people organize to get the jobs of living done in the complex systems in which all of us must function.

I will argue here that anthropology, as refined and used in this century, enables us to layer reality upon reality in human activity in such a way that the evaluator can assemble what can be known and map program activities onto it. In this way the value of a program in the natural community can be inferred. Evaluation adds the perspectives, the methods, and the science needed to do this in a way that is credible to those who rely on evaluation to make decisions.

WHY EVALUATION?

I chose to write about evaluation because evaluation is what I have done with myself for the past twenty-five years. Evaluation is a scientific endeavor conducted for the purpose of describing the worth, value and/or effectiveness of some activity directed to serving a human need or solving a human problem. Evaluations may be focused on programs, projects, products, media campaigns, curricula—almost anything that is delivered to communities of humans. I will focus on program evaluation in this volume because it is what I know best. However, the same approach can and has been used to evaluate projects, policies, and products.

One of the most important things about evaluation, however it is done, is the need for clear thinking and methodological rigor to protect the credibility of results. Decisions about policies, careers, and funding often rest on evaluation results. Evaluations can protect the public good while alerting authorities to things that aren't working as they should. The scientific demands of evaluation require that anthropologists incorporate into their methods the safeguards needed to protect their results' validity, reliability, and credibility.

I did not find evaluation; evaluation came to me because some people knew I could do ethnography and believed that ethnography would be helpful to their efforts to understand programs. In the early years I don't think my clients cared whether I was an anthropologist—although they all said it must be interesting! Instead, they wanted program evaluation and knew that they couldn't understand how a program worked unless they could ask the people involved with it. They were pretty sure I could do that.

I knew nothing about evaluation when I started twenty-five years ago. Fortunately my colleagues were better informed. I quickly learned that evaluation has a body of method and theory of its own, not deducible from any other discipline. To become an evaluator, I had to take courses, read the literature, and attend and participate in professional meetings. But once I discovered the field, evaluation became the arena in which I do anthropology. I was impressed with the rigor of evaluation and its flexibility as a way of understanding why the things that people try to do—programs, projects, product development—succeed or fail. I discovered that people doing programs can and will explain to me in great detail what they are trying to do if I ask the right questions and listen carefully to what they are telling me. It was a familiar set of skills, one I had learned as I became an anthropologist.

I used to say to anyone who would listen that "I landed on my feet as an anthropologist when I began doing program evaluation." Evaluation is a wonderful career choice for anthropologists. In this era, when the traditional ways of doing ethnography become less accessible to us, evaluation provides a strategy to investigate human life that is connected to our own time, deepens our understanding of what people are about, and produces something useful. I have tried to teach anthropologists to be evaluators for the past fifteen years. Recently I have reversed the arrow and begun to teach ethnography to evaluators. As teaching so often does, this has helped me see evaluation from many different sides. Evaluation—all evaluation—is very applied research, although some people distinguish between evaluation (doing it) and evaluation research (developing and testing ways to do it.)[2] Evaluation is defined by usefulness to a client. It is oriented to action and generates knowledge for decision making.

Thus, evaluation is a scientific study of something—an actual or planned program, process, or product—to determine whether it can or does achieve what it sets out to do. The goal of evaluation is to assess something. This can be contrasted with studies in which the purpose of the research is, for example, to test a theory. People normally do not pay for evaluations because they are curious about a theory; they commission evaluations because they need to know how to do something for some purpose or reason. They need to plan a program, discover how people relate to a problem, and determine whether what they are doing is working.

The research problem is developed by working with users and/or stakeholders to understand and articulate what they need to know. Stakeholders are people with some kind of interest or "stake" in the outcome of the evaluation. Stakeholders can have very diverse interests in the outcome of the evaluation. For example, I once evaluated a program to support families in which the project officer (in this case, the "client") hoped the program would fail because staff disagreed with the political agenda implicit in the program's design. Of course, the client didn't tell us that at the first meeting.

It took time, skilled interviewing, and several meetings before this information emerged. In evaluation, as in ethnography, good research depends on building trust with stakeholders.

The product of evaluation may be knowledge or recommendations for action or both. Sometimes what clients want is the summary and conclusions only. Sometimes they want the evaluation to go beyond that to build recommendations on how they should proceed given the results of the evaluation.

Who are evaluators? Right now an evaluator is someone who evaluates. Evaluators are defined by their use of evaluation methods and theories and by their participation in an evaluation community. Obviously there are better and worse evaluators based on training and experience. The American Evaluation Association debates the issue of building credentials for those who can call themselves an evaluator, but there is no formal credentialing at the present time. Regardless of the issue of credentials, evaluation has its own body of method and theory. You will not succeed as an evaluator unless you learn evaluation. You will need to take courses, read up, go to evaluation meetings, and get smart. I will try to help you do that in this book. However, this will be the merest introduction. Throughout your career you will continue to build your knowledge and understanding of evaluation.

Evaluation is multidisciplinary. Evaluation of programs and projects originated in educational psychology in the 1930s, but it is now done by people with many kinds of scientific preparation. It is very often done in teams with people from various backgrounds. Anthropologists fit well into these teams because of our holistic perspective and tendency to systems thinking. To function effectively on teams, however, we must commit to lifelong learning. It is wise to acquire enough understanding of the various skills that may be called on in evaluation designs. I would strongly recommend, for example, a working knowledge of statistics and scientific design from a general social sciences perspective. Learn the meaning of things like experimental and quasi-experimental designs, validity, and reliability that come up constantly in evaluation. It is very difficult to work with your teams if you can't think in these terms.

Who buys evaluations? People who make decisions and administer efforts to meet human needs and solve human problems make up most of the clients for program evaluations. For all evaluations within the scope of this book, the viewpoints of human beings are central to collecting and using information from evaluations. Clients are the funders and supervisors of evaluations. They define the scope of the evaluation and the information the evaluation should provide. Much success in evaluation comes from a cumulative understanding of your clients and their needs. A nonexhaustive list includes private business, government agencies, international development organizations, nonprofit agencies, nongovernmental organizations (NGOs), health care organizations, and educational organizations. You will probably discover other examples. Private businesses often do product evaluation. These seek to find out how people interact with products like computer systems and drugs. For example, Susan Squires conducted several projects assessing the needs of consumers for communications technology in the global market (Squires 2005).

Some evaluators look at programs—that is, organized sets of activities that are trying to achieve some specific benefits in a defined group of people.[3] Government is probably the biggest consumer of program evaluations. Government agencies are often required to be accountable for the programs they are mandated to deliver. Legislative bodies assess programs for compliance with goals of legislation. Government evaluations can be domestic or international. Sometimes they are completed by agencies themselves; other times government agencies develop contracts with outside companies to complete evaluations. Charity Goodman and her colleagues at the US Government Accountability Agency provide an example of an evaluation done by a government agency. In this case they incorporated ethnography into GAO's investigative audit techniques to understand clinicians' adherence to patient safety measures in Veterans Administration hospitals (Goodman, Trainor, and Divorksi 2005).

If you have your heart set on a career in an international arena, you can do this easily as an evaluator. Many of us work for agencies, NGOs, foundations, and universities that are building and evaluating programs and projects to alleviate social, health, and economic problems all over the world. International development organizations of various kinds commission or perform evaluations. For example, USAID does evaluation using their own specialized set of methods. If you plan to pursue a career in international development organizations, you are well advised to look for a job—at least your first job—with an organization or a company that has an established track record in doing this so that you can become familiar with this evaluation paradigm. It is extremely difficult for companies to break into the USAID arena for the first time. Be skeptical if a potential employer tells you in a job interview that their company plans to get into international development work—you may not live long enough for this to happen!

Health care organizations—hospitals, managed care organizations, and other health care providers—conduct evaluations to see whether people are using services the way they should or to ascertain the needs in the community for services. With changes due to the Affordable Care Act, the demands for these kinds of evaluations can be expected to grow in the immediate future. Large health organizations often have internal evaluators on staff. This is a good job for an anthropologist because health care is a culturally sensitive domain requiring community ethnography.

Educational organizations—school systems and universities—evaluate curricula, educational programs, and special programs for designated population subgroups. Like health care evaluations, these are often directed to community-based programs. Also, large educational organizations and school districts often have their own evaluators. As we'll see, evaluation originated in educational settings and is still very important in education.[4]

WHY ANTHROPOLOGY?

I have chosen to bring in anthropology because I am an anthropologist by both training and inclination. Anthropology is, of course, many different things. There are three anthropological ideas that I have built this volume around: the use of culture to orient ourselves to human life, the method-theory nexus that is ethnography, and the concept of the community as the arena in which people do things. Many of the tools we have built as anthropologists can make important contributions to the field of evaluation. The methods and skills evaluators use are important to anthropology as well. It is important to note that many of the concepts used here are in no way unique to anthropology. Ethnographic methods, for example, are part of the tool kit of other disciplines. The fact that they are not unique to anthropologists in no way diminishes the value of an anthropological perspective for evaluators. They are important to the way we present ourselves as evaluation anthropologists. If we present ourselves to potential employers and clients as anthropologists who evaluate, we enhance our value in the workplace for ourselves and those who come after us.

Some of the perspectives that anthropologists can bring to evaluation are:

- The ethnographic method—critical to understanding human activity in the world—is the core of what cultural anthropologists do. Ethnography supports us as we solicit the diverse perspectives of stakeholders and bring them to our thinking about evaluation design. And it is often a method for structuring data collection and data analysis.

- Systemic/holistic thinking—We are trained to see wholes and the fit of parts into them. Whole human experiences are our subject matter. It always surprises me that this is not intuitive to some people from other disciplines who are trained to understand things in terms of economics or epidemiology or genetics. My career as an evaluator has brought home to me over and over again the variety and legitimacy of different perspectives on the world. I learned this, of course, as an anthropologist. But I understand it from my experience as an evaluator working on interdisciplinary teams.

- Participatory philosophy—For traditional anthropological fieldwork the first step is building rapport with people in the field site and bringing them into the research as soon as is feasible. This trust-building process is equally important in evaluation. It also suits us to conduct participatory evaluations that we often find intuitive. We are comfortable with participation. From evaluation I learned the critical need not to over-identify with participants because to do so risks bias.

- Relativism and the ability to withhold judgment—Because we seek to work with culture, we must detach ourselves from judgments about what may be very strange or even practices we consider immoral. Female infanticide springs to mind. The very idea of killing infants because they are a less preferred gender is appalling to most people coming from a European and American background. But it has its own logic to those who practice it. As anthropologists, we learn to listen with suspended judgment to what people tell us. This allows us to see unexpected things rather than screening them out.

- Understanding of language and the workings of symbol systems— Language is the major way in which culture is expressed; however, people don't usually say what they mean and mean what they say. An understanding of the arbitrary linkage of symbols to the symbolized helps us distinguish the meanings of utterances from speech habits and differences in word usage.

I have observed that when people come looking for an anthropologist to help with an evaluation, they are looking for someone to help them figure out what questions are important to one or more constituencies they serve. This usually involves, in whole or in part, the use of ethnography, the core methodological and theoretical concept in which much of anthropology is embedded. The ethnography that anthropologists do is part of a worldview that is not unique to anthropology but remains the philosophical stance in which anthropologists are grounded.

Anthropology—at least wearing its sociocultural hat—is the study of human life as seen through the concept of culture. Culture has always been a difficult thing for anthropologists to describe. The uncertainty of anthropology about exactly what comprises culture is visible in the numerous definitions of culture that appear in the anthropological literature.[5] We all know it when we see it, but that, of course, isn't good enough. In the end most of us define it as we will use it so that we can go about our work of describing its manifestations. This has to be good enough for most of us. Supported by tradition, I will define *culture* as "the learned, shared ideas and behaviors that people have because they live in a particular group of human beings." Culture can be distinguished from ideology (beliefs), society (relationships among people and groups of people), and technology (material things), yet all of these things are cultural. The same ideas, social organizations, and technologies may have different meanings in different groups of people. I guess this is why there is a whole discipline, anthropology, that is trying to figure out what culture is.

Many of the interesting things that people do happen in some kind of community, whether it is an agricultural village, Wall Street, or the virtual world of Facebook. Multiple players in multiple communities connect for some purpose, only to break into new constellations as new realities emerge and mature. Increasingly communities can be identified as sets of linkages in overlapping networks. In daily life this pleases us or intimidates us or maybe does a lot of both. But for our purposes here—the evaluation of human activities—the concept of communities elaborates the context in which our research must be located. It is no longer useful to pretend that we can somehow hold context aside and have much left to say about what remains. Please note that communities are not necessarily based on geographic continuity. Communities can be based on kinship, social or economic bonds, professional or religious associations, and anything else that ties people together so they can achieve some purpose or function.

Another important thing that anthropologists bring to evaluations is their training in ethnography. Ethnography is an approach to investigating some kind of human community by seeking to understand cultural events as they are experienced by the insider. There may be many kinds of "insiders."

In evaluation they are usually the stakeholders identified in the early stages of the process. Methodologically ethnography relies on multiple data sources and data-collection methods, but the key strategies are open interviewing and careful observation of what is happening in the community. To the extent possible, we try to use participant observation, in which we participate in events along with the "natives." For example, we may attend coalition meetings, walk the environment with engineers, and observe products' usage patterns in domestic settings. The purpose of all of this is to move closer to an insider understanding of what is happening before our eyes. Direct or participant observation of events provides us with an independent point from which we can assess what people tell us. It helps counter bias in informants' accounts.

The concept of culture operating in communities of people and the grounded approach of ethnography help anthropologists to uncover the armature of the sociocultural systems around which things operate. Evaluation supports the rigorous methodologies and the scientific orientation needed for evaluations to be credible, valid, and reliable. Ethnography, at least as it is used in evaluation, is an empirical exercise. It goes beyond chatting with people about what's happening. As is the case in any evaluation, its purpose is to build a corpus of evidence that can be used by agencies, organizations, and individuals to maintain, reinforce, and improve social responses to problems, needs, and special situations. No body of data is intrinsically evidence; evidence is built by clear specification of questions to be asked, well-managed data collection, and careful control of data analysis. To do good evaluation—and to do good evaluation with ethnography—one must do good science.

Ethnography focuses on the things that groups of people consider worth doing and why. What outcomes are desirable and what are people willing to do to achieve them? Do people agree on what matters and how to achieve it? Are agreements and disagreements crystallized around substantial differences in worldview, or are they differing perspectives on the same things? How is any intervention embedded in a community that includes those who deliver it, those who pay for it, and those who receive it?

Ethnography is not the only way to find out these things, but it is often the easiest way. The inductive and grounded theories and methods underlying ethnography effectively address questions like these. The ethnographer can tease out the definitions of issues and responses to them from the perspective of multiple stakeholders, condense them, and map them onto a single programmatic understanding. They can fill out the diverse perspectives of insiders and outsiders and weave them into a single story. Many other current approaches to evaluation use ethnographic methods, at least in part.[6] This is further discussed in Chapter 2.

My assertion that evaluation must be science is not an uncontroversial one. There is a vast body of literature in both anthropology and evaluation that argues for naturalistic approaches that are not scientific but are instead grounded in participants' experience rather than an a priori research design. Embedding things in experience, of course, is what ethnography does, but to build credibility in evaluation, the ethnographer must have respect for the linkage of evidence to conclusions and recommendations made from evaluations. Failure to do this undermines their own credibility and that of other anthropologist-evaluators as well.

WHY EVALUATION ANTHROPOLOGY?

Why make this thing called evaluation anthropology? Many anthropological concepts—culture, cultural context, and ethnography—are already part of evaluation. So why merge evaluation and anthropology into a single framework for program evaluation? A new approach to evaluation—in a field already replete with branded approaches—requires thoughtful justification for adding yet another.

The idea for evaluation anthropology came out of a discussion at the 2002 annual meeting of the American Anthropological Association (AAA) in which a group of twenty-five anthropologists who were also evaluators met to discuss how our background in anthropology had influenced our approaches to evaluation. We began to build toward an integrated approach theoretically grounded in the embeddedness of program efficacy and effectiveness in dynamic cultural systems that are unstable in time and space. As we refined the concept, we presented sessions both at AAA and in the meetings of the American Evaluation Association. In the years since then, we have built a network of anthropologists and others who do evaluations of cultural systems. For the past decade, we have presented sessions at the American Evaluation Association meetings and the American Anthropological Association meetings. In 2005 Jacqueline Copeland Carson and I co-edited a volume, *Creating Evaluation Anthropology: Introducing An Emerging Subfield*, with participation of both evaluators and anthropologists (Butler and Copeland-Carson 2005).

Evaluation anthropology is stronger than its parts. Evaluators may not have the training or the instincts needed to do ethnography in a complete way. Anthropologists may not have an adequate knowledge with or experience of evidence-based approaches to evaluation. The usefulness of the concept of evaluation anthropology is that it draws attention to and systematizes an approach that many of us use but without an explicit knowledge of the strength of consciously merging the two in our approach to evaluations. The concept of culture helps anthropologists describe the armature of the sociocultural systems in which things operate. Evaluation supports the rigorous methodologies and the scientific orientation needed for evaluations to be credible, valid, and reliable. Anthropology cannot be an effective evaluation tool unless the scientific perspective of evaluation is incorporated into our efforts every step of the way. In addition, the anthropological part of evaluations must articulate seamlessly with other components of the evaluation. We design and implement evaluations with the goal of bringing all of the evidence we can find to bear on a single set of evaluation questions. Both anthropology and evaluation are part of the equation. Each gains from the other. In this volume I will describe a broad range of theories and methods in both evaluation and anthropology because we must be acquainted with the range of issues considered in both disciplines. But for most of us, our practice tends to fall somewhere within the overlap between the two.

A key issue in both evaluation and applied anthropology is linking method, theory, and practice so that they reinforce each other. For me, the practice of anthropology in any context has always been an enterprise in which certainty and truth are elusive and context dependent. We combine method and theory to focus in on what is important given the circumstances. This is much less comfortable than the world of the .05 significance level, a very important orientation to many evaluators.

But it is also less comfortable than the theoretical certainties anthropologists are fond of. We all have them, and often we must unlearn them to be effective as practitioners of anthropology or, in fact, anything else. Here are the ones I had to unlearn. Yours may be different, but I guarantee they will be there.

- Marxism—the belief that all truth lies in material conditions of life and in political economics. I was trained as a cultural materialist. I had to walk away from this formulation to understand the complex world of programs, although the orientation to political and economic influences on programs has been very useful.
- A belief in the supremacy and fixity of power relations. The first thing I used to ask of social situations is who can tell who else what to do. To

some extent this is important, but it isn't congruent with official power relations or with what people tell you. It requires cross-checking and triangulation to figure out how power flows in organizations. And the power dynamics may be, well, dynamic. It may depend on context and specific events.

- Positivism—the belief that there is an external truth out there that is knowable and testable. Many evaluators think this way. I did too for a long time. I was trained as a biologist. This idea works fine there—as long as you don't get too up close and personal with the animals. It doesn't work as well in programs where so much of what happens is in the eye of the beholder.
- An aversion to eclecticism. Eclecticism is technically the use of different theories in different situations. I grew up in science believing it was a bad thing to do because if you were free to select a theory depending on the situation, you could never be wrong. I have discovered in practice that different theories are differentially useful depending on the circumstances. It's a very contingent and a very relative world.

I believe that evaluation must be scientific. There is a lot of discussion in anthropology and in evaluation about the relevance of science to human problems, but for the purposes of evaluation, we need to resign from this debate. No one is going to pay a half-million dollars (or even $50,000) to support a decision about programs, funding, or staffing based solely on people's thinking about things. This does not mean that ethnography is not important—it is a powerful evaluation tool—but it does mean that it needs to be embedded in a scientific approach that combines ethnographic data with other material to reach conclusions about how people *act* in specific settings.

So what are the necessary conditions for applying scientific theories to social problems? I think there are three:

- Respect for the rules. Honor your evidence; don't throw any out to make it come out right. Be diligent in your search for your own bias.
- Skepticism. Be a little doubtful about what you believe to be true. If you don't maintain a little doubt, you won't question your own perceptions when you should.
- Flexibility. Be open to alternative hypotheses, new evidence, and new questions. Be alert and willing to incorporate new insights into your work.

Often in doing science we do what we do from instinct, but it is instinct based on training, experience, and respect for evidence. It is also intrinsically dependent on transparency and the scrutiny of our work by clients, peers, and the people we study. You need to go out into left field to keep yourself honest.

No matter what your discipline or your intellectual background, it has left in your thinking theoretical orientations that you may no longer recognize as such. It is very enlightening if you can uncover these underlying orientations and make them explicit, as they are part of what makes you define problems the way your do. Sometimes these will be helpful in evaluation; sometimes they will not. Either way, knowledge is power.

To give you an example of my own baseline thinking, the theory of natural selection as I learned it in undergraduate biology, refined it in graduate school, and taught it in Introduction to Cultural Anthropology still governs my first pass at defining problems. Things—biological or cultural—are not alike even if they are related or part of a common pattern; that is, there is variation in groups of anything. A lot of these are neutral, not affecting what you are seeing at all. However, some variants are in some way "better" (or worse) *in a specific context at a given time.* The biological criterion is genetic variability being adaptive in specific ecologies. In culture there an analogous relationship between variants of—say, agriculture or marriage rules—and the cultural ecology in which they are used. Finally, the variants that achieve the greatest success in the specified environment will tend to become more prevalent than those that are less effective. There is selection such that some traits increase in frequency while others decrease, leading over time to a change in the characteristics of the population. Good simple biology and anthropology.

This model often works for evaluation too and is how I unconsciously structure my thinking when I define evaluation questions and come up with designs.

- There are multiple ways to do anything,
- They are not all of equal value in a given context.
- The ones that work best will tend to be used more often than competitors, all things being equal (which, of course, they never are).

This analogy—and remember that it is an analogy—breaks down somewhat in the last step vis-à-vis evaluation. Although theoretically the fit should survive, this is seldom the case with programs because other factors are often more important than the fit or absolute "success" of an evaluand. Political interests, for example, may be central in maintaining programs that work less well than others might.[8] And economic considerations may doom effective programs. The point is that making this kind of intrinsic tendency in my thinking protects me from a kind of biological reductionism that is very common in social science.[7] It forces me to examine my problem solutions for the places where I have used this theory correctly and those where I have misused the analogy.

A FEW DETAILS ABOUT THIS BOOK

I have written this book for people like those who have attended my courses and workshops in evaluation or whom I have mentored directly. They are students, beginners in evaluation, and people who for one reason or another have made midcareer transitions into evaluation. Some of them are students of either ethnography or evaluation. Others are professional evaluators or users of evaluation results in academic or nonacademic settings.

Although I tried to be faithful to the scholarship around specific issues, I do not intend this to be primarily a scholarly work. It is designed to be useful to those who are contemplating evaluations or careers in evaluation. I envision it as a text to support classes for applied anthropologists or ethnographic evaluators, a kind of resource that I have not yet found for my own teaching. I hope it also will help those involved in self-study of these topics, although I caution you that you cannot build capacity to evaluate from any one book alone. I see it as useful for anyone who works in "qualitative evaluation" and would like some ways to think about it. Finally, to those who evaluate, I hope it will provide a new view of how it may be done and will generate ideas that will enrich or correct the material presented here.

I have tried as much as possible to stick to what I know well. This imposes a couple of limitations on the scope of this work.

- I talk about program evaluation rather than product evaluation, cost-effectiveness analysis, or curriculum evaluation. A program is an organized set of activities that is conducted to obtain some kind of social objective. The majority of evaluations I have done have been program evaluations, and I trust my experience here. The work of my colleagues as well as the evaluation literature have shown me that most of what I say here applies broadly to any kind of evaluation that involves people making choices. However, it is grounded in the evaluation of programs.

- I have directed my attention in this volume to those who practice evaluation regardless of whether they are anthropologists. The ideas and the methods here can be used by any evaluator who is trained or experienced in doing face-to-face work with people and who is comfortable with the culture concept.
- Evaluation as discussed here is virtually always interdisciplinary. Evaluation teams usually consist of members from several disciplinary backgrounds. This is a strength of evaluation. You may not know your teammates yet or even what disciplines they will come from, but I guarantee you that they are out there and that you will work with them in the future. In this sense discussions of evaluation almost always stray across disciplinary boundaries. Even if you aren't the "anthropologist" on an evaluation team, you will still do a better evaluation if you understand the ethnographic parts of the evaluation design and implementation.
- I tend to orient my examples to health because health is what I know. I have made an effort to include other examples, but you will probably notice this bias. Once again, it is a matter of what I know well and where my own experience has been.
- Some of the examples used here are of very sensitive evaluations. Where this is the case, I have modified agencies, names, and places to protect individuals' confidentiality.

This book cannot be all things to all evaluators or to all anthropologists. A few things this book is not:

- It is neither a theoretical tome nor a methodological treatise. The dichotomy in our thinking about theory and method has entangled us in debates for years, and in the end the question is, if you will pardon the pun, academic. To approach anything scientifically, you need all of the pieces of solution—the why, the what, and the how.
- Nor is it a cookbook. I hope to provide you with some tools you can use to help you create good evaluations using ethnographic thinking. But it would be an abuse of this volume to use it to generate the specifics of any project. You will have to do the rest yourself. You will need to unearth and investigate each evaluation question on its own terms and

in its own context. That's where the challenge comes in. But I hope this book will give you some ideas about what to take into consideration and where to start.

- Finally, it is not the last word on anything. Because the world is so uncertain from moment to moment here in the first part of the twenty-first century, ideas that haven't been thought yet will impinge on the usefulness of the things proposed here.

This is an especially interesting time to dive into the deep end of the social pool, the spot where new things are constantly emerging from old. I hope the ideas here will mature over time as some of you work to build on this volume. In this way our work will become ever more adapted to the exciting moment in which we live and more versatile in helping us understand what does and doesn't doesn't work in human life.

CHAPTER TWO

EVALUATION: AN ORIENTATION FOR ANTHROPOLOGISTS

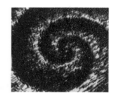

In this chapter we will look at the development of evaluation as a scientific approach to understanding how people interact with regard to processes and programs. We will begin by looking briefly at how evaluation works and defining some terms that are important in the vocabulary of evaluation. We will review some developments in evaluation that will help us understand the undercurrents that affect practice of the discipline today.

THE SCOPE OF EVALUATION

Evaluation is a huge field. It incorporates many different schools of thought, each with its own vocabulary. It took me years to get the jargon down. I am accreting a glossary that continues to grow over time.[1] I define an *evaluation* as a study that seeks to scientifically determine the value of something for some kind of utilization. Three critical words in this definition are science, value, and utilization.

Evaluators can evaluate almost anything that people do. They evaluate programs that are organized sets of activity that seek to serve some social good. Project evaluations look at specific implementations of program designs to discover an array of effective processes and to estimate the variation and effectiveness of modes of intervention. Product evaluations are conducted to assess the interaction between people and products and to determine what makes products more or less effective. There are other kinds of evaluation that you may encounter from time to time. The important thing about them all is that they aim to assess some human endeavor. These kinds of evaluations come from similar intellectual foundations. They share their methods and many of their theories. The distinctions among them often structure people's jobs and the kinds of clients or organizations they work for. But much of what is said in this book will apply to them all.

Evaluation: A Cultural Systems Approach, by Mary Odell Butler, 25–47. © 2015 Left Coast Press, Inc. All rights reserved.

I tend to talk about program evaluation because this is what I have done. Conditions governing a successful program are developing a program that can work (efficacy), implementing it correctly (implementation fidelity), delivering it to the right people (as specified in the program plan), and determining whether it achieves what it was supposed to achieve in the short and long run (outcome and impact evaluation).[2] Some kinds of program evaluation include:

- *Evaluability assessment* asks whether the program is well-enough designed and coherent enough so that it can be implemented correctly. If it isn't, there is no sense in evaluating it because you cannot determine whether success or failure has anything to do with the design of the program or its correct implementation.
- *Process evaluation* seeks to discover whether the program is being implemented correctly and completely. Part of this may be regular monitoring of implementation. Without effective process evaluation, you cannot attribute the outcomes that you observe to the program.
- *Outcome evaluation* seeks to assess, given evaluability and a favorable process evaluation, whether the program achieves its desired outcome. What did it achieve in the short and long term?
- A *cost-effectiveness study* tends to appear as an element in other kinds of evaluation. It is used to estimate the worth of the evaluated thing, given merit. Put another way, even if the program is a good one, is it worth what it costs? There are many measurement issues in cost-effectiveness studies. Cost effectiveness is a fairly crude measure of program's costs-per-unit outcome (e.g., the cost of an intervention per client served). Cost-benefit analysis is a much more rigorous measure that assumes estimators of direct (monetary) and indirect (opportunity costs, lost income, etc.) costs. This is an important distinction that clients often don't understand. Cost-effectiveness studies are more feasible and are usually enough for what is needed.

Formative and summative evaluations are important terms you will often encounter. The concepts come from the work of Michael Scriven to distinguish evaluations that provide input to programs and those that demonstrate their effectiveness (Scriven 1967). *Formative evaluation* is done to improve the program and may be done in the early days of implementation. *Summative evaluation* is done to determine the merit of the program in light of its outcomes. To quote from Robert Stake, another evaluator: "When the cook tastes the soup, that's formative; when the guest tastes the soup, that's summative" (Scriven 1991:19).[3]

Evaluation is used by organizations to support program planning. In fact, program planning and evaluation are often in the same office in government agencies. It is—at least theoretically—this feedback of evaluation into organizations that governs the fate of programs. In practice, the role of evaluation tends to be much more politicized than that. There are results that don't permit action, even if they are accurate. For example, cost-effectiveness data compiled as part of evaluations may tell you to eliminate crucial public health programs (like immunizations) or close schools that aren't showing good enough test results for what they cost. This kind of thing is not usually feasible.

Funding mechanisms for evaluations can be grants or they can be contracts. Under a contractual mechanism you act as an agent of your client. Grants are much more open to your choice of problem and method and much less collaborative than contracts. Not surprisingly, most evaluations are done under contract as part of the management of programs. Their link to planning means that evaluation and, especially, the results of evaluations are management tools for the client. They can strongly affect the programs evaluated.

PARADIGMS IN PROGRAM EVALUATION

One of my professors used to say that everyone was born either a little Aristotelian or a little Platonist and that they never change the way they think. This comment reflects one of the fundamental splits in how people view the conditions of knowledge over the past few centuries. There are the positivists (Aristotelians) who believe that there is an objective reality (or at least a reality that can be known) and that reality can be explored empirically using a set of rules encoded in the scientific method. And there are the other people (postpositivists, constructivists, interpretivists, naturalists[4]) who believe that reality is constructed by observers and participants in a situation that it is context sensitive and can only be discovered by exploration and cross-checking with those who live the situation. The distinction between these two paradigms is one of the key themes in evaluation.

Paradigms are frameworks within which we think. They contain within them concepts, assumptions about how the world works and how we know about this, the questions that are appropriate to ask, and what answers are useful. They underlie how we study things, but they are seldom directly examined. They just seem "right" to those who have been educated within the community that uses them. Paradigms become obvious only when they are pushed to the surface in opposition to competing paradigms (Kuhn 1962:170).[5]

Paradigmatic positions on this positivist-constructivist dichotomy have methodological implications that are important to evaluation. The positivists believe that knowledge is built by direct observation of the world that is then tested against hypotheses about how the world operates. Positivist science focuses on uniformity of methods and questions and is often quantitative in approach. The application of the scientific method to social problems, as to those of the natural sciences, produces an ever-more accurate description of reality. Quantitative evaluations usually try to infer the properties of populations from a subset of respondents chosen to be representative of a larger population.

Those of the constructivist school believe that knowledge is indirect, filtered through the observer. Therefore, understanding is built up by inference from observation grounded in emergent properties of situations. Constructivist thinking is concerned with methods and questions that are context and case specific and are usually qualitative. Constructivists see social science as a different kind of inquiry, requiring a different epistemology from that used in the natural sciences. In qualitative work the investigator tries to surface an understanding of the relations among elements in a specific case or situation. The validity of qualitative research is assessed by such methods as agreement of multiple observers, triangulation across data sources, and consistency of findings across multiple cases.

Social scientists in particular tend to have lots of emotion invested in paradigmatic positions. They are so fundamental to the way we think about how we think that it is often difficult to bring these differences to the surface. Anthropologists are usually the most familiar with the constructivist position, but many of the people you work with will come from the other side of things. Evaluators are found hotly arguing both positions.

The reason this matters to us here is that a lot of discussion about the utility or superiority of qualitative and quantitative approaches is basically an argument that proceeds from these basic epistemological positions. In evaluations that combine quantitative and qualitative methods, positions on this issue can bring up theoretical misunderstandings because members of the team from alternate positions may be trying to do different things. You are unlikely to change anyone's mind, but sometimes you can simply side-step the issue if you are aware that this minefield is at the table. For all practical purposes paradigm differences matter less than collaboration around results.

Most evaluators understand that you don't need to choose between qualitative and quantitative approaches and that it all depends on the needs of the evaluation and the stakeholders. Still, you will deal with this difference for the rest of your career, especially if you come from the qualitative side of the room. Qualitative research is sometimes accused of being unscientific and anecdotal because bad qualitative studies are compared with good quantitative studies. This is why it is so important for us on the qualitative side to do what we do as well as we can.

There are patterns in what gets done qualitatively and what gets done quantitatively. Generally speaking, nationwide evaluations concerned with impact or outcome are very likely to be at least partly quantitative. In the contracting world they tend to be done by large companies, often with an economic slant. These are normally led by evaluators with well-established reputations in doing big outcome evaluations. These evaluations are usually multi-million-dollar undertakings. They take a long time. But they are very profitable, and they mean that the qualitative-quantitative debate stays open if for no other reason than the desire to maintain or obtain access to the big projects.

State and local evaluations or small program evaluations concerned mostly with process and immediate outcomes—was the program delivered and did people get it and how did it work for them?—are often qualitative and conducted by smaller companies or in-house evaluators. Academics sometimes do these evaluations on a consulting basis. These are much less costly and usually take two years or less to complete.

Neither is intrinsically more or less rigorous or empirically sound in its argument. The basic scientific requirement for each is definition of an evaluation question, developing evidence for the question using a clear and technically sound method, and analysis that grounds findings in evidence.

Integrated approaches are growing in importance in evaluation. Integration is often organized around the content of the program being evaluated. These mixed-method evaluations utilize strengths of both kinds of methods. For example, focus groups and surveys combine to provide data that are both wide and deep. These are very gratifying evaluations to do but are often quite costly. It is also important to note that there are considerations of data comparison for mixed methods that go beyond simple additive analysis. The study must be integrated so that all methodologies used address a single set of questions and are conducted and analyzed in such a way that data from multiple sources can reinforce each other in terms of triangulation and determining data quality.

I do not believe that a preference for qualitative or quantitative methodologies should govern evaluation design. When it comes to selecting research methods, I think evaluation is a matter of identifying the best possible methods and then implementing them in an interdisciplinary fashion. However, largely "quantitative" evaluations have a long and distinguished history in evaluation and are part of the armature of evaluation as it is practiced today. I want to spend some time trying to clarify these methods because it is important to many people's thinking about what evaluation should be. You will run into this conception of evaluation repeatedly in your careers if you become a doer of evaluations, a purchaser of evaluations, or a runner of programs that are evaluated. You can't really be any kind of an evaluator without an acquaintance with these approaches.

DEVELOPMENT OF EVALUATION

In this section we will review the emergence of evaluation as a field of investigation. In a field as large as evaluation, there are many ways to approach this question. For our purpose here, I will distinguish three major streams in evaluation: (1) experimental and quasi-experimental, (2) qualitative or mixed-method evaluations, and (3) evaluation for accountability.

For a long time qualitative work was the "handmaiden" of quantitative evaluations. People did qualitative studies to support the design and instrumentation of quasi-experimental evaluations. Then in the 1960s came the War on Poverty, Lyndon Johnson's effort to eliminate the causes of poverty in the United States. The War on Poverty produced many programs in employment, housing, health, and social services that were directed to the poor. The context in which programs were implemented was critical for understanding the potential effectiveness of these programs. It was not to be expected that programs implemented in urban zones would operate in the same way when introduced to rural communities. Moreover, they were quite varied. It was hard to think in terms of quasi-experimental designs.

Qualitative and mixed-method evaluations began to come into their own at this time, eventually culminating in the kinds of evaluation that anthropologists are well qualified to do. This philosophy of evaluation depends on the application of scientific methods—adapted from the natural sciences—to the evaluation of social programs.

QUANTITATIVE EVALUATIONS

Quantitative evaluation approaches are grounded in hypothesis-testing and measurement of the evaluand in order to demonstrate results statistically. Many of them are experimental and quasi-experimental designs. Not all quantitative evaluations are experimental in design, but these other quantitative evaluations all assume that they are getting an adequate understanding of a truth "out there" by virtue of logical design and statistical methods.

The use of experimental and quasi-experimental evaluation designs is a standard in much evaluation conducted by the federal government, less for health programs than for educational and substance abuse programs.[7] It is also the standard for clinical trials of medical interventions.

Evaluation originated in the 1930s in projects to assess the merit of innovative education approaches. At that time there was a lot of experimentation with more open, flexible ways of delivering education and great interest in seeing whether these new educational forms were effective. John Dewey's work in the early twentieth century had moved educators away from the authoritarian models to new kinds of thinking about education based on experimentation and practice (Gouinlock 2014). The growth of new ways of doing things built interest in ways to understand if and how these new models were effective.

The beginning of evaluation as it is practiced today is usually linked to the work of Ralph Tyler in the Eight-Year study of New York City Schools begun in 1934 (Tyler 1991). The Eight-Year Study set out to evaluate the effectiveness of more open, student-driven activities on educational outcomes. Tyler was an educational psychologist and thought in terms of experimental uses of evaluation that could show measurable quantitative outcomes. However, he was aware of the role of socioeconomic differences on education outcomes. He either used this information impressionistically or as categorical variables. In one example, he evaluated open classrooms in Nebraska and discovered quite serendipitously that the program did well in schools where students came from working-class backgrounds and poorly for poor students. He explained this in terms of the relative amount of structure at home. Working-class students came from more ordered homes and were able to take advantage of the more open school. Poor students were alarmed by the chaos of open classrooms that resembled their chaotic homes. However, he tested none of these socioeconomic factors.

Experimental and quasi-experimental evaluation became important in the 1960s and early 1970s. People have gone on to improve and solidify this approach over the thirty-five years since it first emerged, and it is still critically important today. But the basic lineaments of this approach came from a particular intellectual context and were set out before about 1975.

Many evaluators are involved in developing methods and theories for these "hard science" evaluations. Two of them have been very important in developing evaluation as a scientific enterprise: Michael Scriven and Donald Campbell. Although not everyone would have chosen these two, I feel that they are so important that even those who disagree with them must take their work into account. Both of these scientists worked out their basic approach to evaluation in the 1960s, a time when there were several important historical trends that supported their work.

First of all, there was a widespread belief that all social problems could be solved by rational social programming. This was the time of the Great Society. Social programming was never again as important and well funded as it was under Johnson and in the succeeding Nixon administration. There were a lot of pilot programs and demonstration programs to evaluate. The federal government was focused on developing programs in housing, education, and employment to meet the needs of the poor. These are easier to assess using experimental methods because demonstration projects are implemented under ideal conditions—lots of money, plenty of staff, and the time to incorporate evaluations as part of program design.

This was also the time when the capacity of a rational scientific approach to accomplish almost anything was a central cultural tenet in the United States. The first moon landing occurred in 1969. Computers were put into widespread use in the 1960s, and people were just beginning to glimpse their potential for use in social research. The microprocessor was invented in 1973. People believed in science. It was a time of great optimism and idealism.

MICHAEL SCRIVEN: PERSPECTIVISM AND THE ASSESSMENT OF VALUE

Michael Scriven is an Oxford-trained philosopher who has written extensively on the philosophy of science. He began doing program evaluation when his attention turned to practical things. A major goal of Scriven's work was to ensure validity of evaluation by working very hard to eliminate as many sources of error as possible from observation (Scriven 1967).

Scriven's way of thinking is less foreign to anthropology than might appear from the very quantitative nature of his work. He described himself as "postpositivist," believing that there is a reality out there, but it cannot be directly observed because it always comes to us through mediating theories and perceptual distortions. He spoke of perspectivism, the idea that everyone sees the world through biased filters. He believes that there's a reality out there that can be described, but you can't really trust people to describe it because of the bias inherent in human perceptions.

For Scriven, evaluation is about the interpretation of value, period. It is not concerned with utilizing findings or policy development or anything else. Evaluation, he argues, should be goal-free and not be governed by the needs of managers or others who manage programs being evaluated. Values have empirical reality and can be investigated scientifically just like anything else. Programs are evaluated to determine whether they're "good" or "bad" relative to objective criteria of merit. Value is not based on the goals that program managers have for their program—it can only be assessed relative to needs; that is, a program (or anything else) is only valuable if it meets a need of some group. He has no interest whatsoever in what program staff think. In fact, he argues that you shouldn't talk to them at all, as doing so will bias the evaluator's perspective on what's going on.

Scriven believes that evaluation is conducted in the "public interest," defined as the interests of all people who are consumers of the thing being evaluated. The criteria of merit are the dimensions on which the program must do well to be "good" and comes from needs assessment of the population to be served. Standards of merit are how good the program has to be based on criteria that are established by comparison to alternative modes of doing the same thing. Once you have these two things, you measure and assess the merit of the program. There is no need for program theory in Scriven's scheme; all you need to establish is whether the program succeeds in meeting standards of performance. It doesn't matter how it works as long as it does (Shadish, Cook, and Leviton 1991, 77–88).

Much of Scriven's work aims to build a set of rules to generate statements of value that are as unbiased as possible, to structure evaluations in a way that could be a standard, replicable approach to evaluation. For example, he developed a Key Evaluation Checklist (KEC) that he argued could be used in any kind of evaluation—process or outcome (Scriven 2012). The function of the KEC, from Scriven's perspective, is to control bias coming from program designers, implementers, and even recipients. The KEC is a matrix of guidelines for moving through evaluation from the first meeting with the person who requested the evaluation to dissemination of the final report. It contains very specific definitions of the steps to be done, the things to be understood, the evidence to be compiled. It has been widely recognized in evaluation (Davidson 2005).[8]

DONALD CAMPBELL: DEMONSTRATING CAUSE AND EFFECT IN EVALUATION

Donald Campbell is the leading exponent and arguably the "father" of the use of the experimental method in program evaluation. Campbell was educated as a psychologist and taught for many years at Northwestern, where he trained a generation of experimental and quasi-experimental evaluators. He focuses on establishing the best possible description of reality by controlling both known and unknown biases. He does this using the experimental method.

Campbell also describes himself as a postpositivist; that is, there is a knowable world out there. However, it is hard to discern reality because of observational bias. Put another way, all measurement is theory laden in the sense that it is filtered through the observer. Therefore, objective knowledge is impossible. The best you get is intersubjective verification of observations (Campbell 1974).

For Campbell, evaluation is about establishing causation—that is, demonstrating causal links between a program intervention and outcomes. Causation means that a change in variable X produces a measurable change in Y. He emphasizes experimental methods because he believes this can rule out threats to establishing causes (Campbell and Stanley 1963; Cook and Campbell 1979).

Campbell considers experimental evaluation to be a deductive approach to assessing a program's value in a controlled way. The ideal experiment involves the same assumptions that are part of laboratory experiments. Two groups of subjects are defined. Some of them receive the "treatment" (i.e., program being evaluated); the others do not. It is critical that the "treatment" and "control" groups are assembled before the programs begin and that neither experimenters nor chosen individuals know which group they are in (the "double-blind" design). These methods are used to avoid contamination of the experiment because of experimenter error such as failure to randomly assign groups for some reason or because of inadvertent contact between members of and control groups, leading to bias in outcomes. Measures of program effectiveness are derived from a theory of how the program should achieve its outcomes and are applied to both treatment and control groups. The effectiveness of the program is determined by comparison of values on variables defined to indicate success between treatment and control groups.

Random assignment to treatment and control groups promotes internal validity because it eliminates the problem of different initial states by randomizing them out. Campbell is especially distrustful of program implementers and staff, feeling that they manipulate programs for political gain and that their perception has little to do with whether or not the program works. This was a very dark vision of bureaucrats.

Experimental evaluations require enough units of analysis to support statistical analysis, which becomes very costly if the unit is a community, a school, or some other group. Moreover, contamination of the design is hard to avoid, especially if the double-blind assumption is violated (which it almost always is because the experiment relies on cooperation from managers and even members of the sample). So sometimes you need to do a quasi-experimental evaluation. In this case, known experimental units are matched to control units based on characteristics that may affect program outcome (demographics, poverty, test scores, etc.) Outcomes are then measured in both groups and analyzed statistically for significant similarities and differences.

For Campbell (and most people in this school of evaluation), the true experiment is greatly superior to the quasi-experiment, which is a distant second because of the difficulty of obtaining a truly matching comparison group. Experiments are designed to provide protection against threats to the internal and external validity of an evaluation. Internal validity refers to the accuracy of the data collected—that is, the question of whether this the way the program "really" works. External validity touches on the issue of generalization to other cases not part of the experiment.

Campbell's vision of evaluation takes into account that quantitative measures rest on qualitative judgments of what is worth measuring. He stresses the need for critical comment on measures, use of multiple measures, and measuring process. There is a great deal of negotiation about measures and testing them for adequacy prior to the evaluation.

Campbell has a vision of the "Experimenting Society," in which experimental approaches to program development and evaluation would improve the quality of everyone's life. Campbell was very idealistic in his ideas of how society should function around evaluation. In a 1969 article "Reforms as Experiments," he argues for an experimental approach to social reform in which evaluated programs are demonstrated to be effective by rigorous evaluations. He felt that social progress would rest on "hardheaded evaluation" of proposed programs for effectiveness. His is a model for a rational society (Campbell 1969).

THE LIMITATIONS OF EXPERIMENTAL AND QUASI-EXPERIMENTAL METHODS

Experimental and quasi-experimental methods come from a strongly academic position. Their goal is scientific validity. They do not take into account the ways in which evaluations are used by consumers of evaluation. Their methods are applied to evaluation design, but there are almost always compromises to deal with the real needs of agencies requesting evaluations. For example, funding and timing almost never permit a priori designation of treatment and control groups. Program managers usually need results sooner rather than later. And there are almost always budget limitations. It's really no surprise that quasi-experimental evaluations are much more common than are true experiments.

The practical methods proposed by members of this school of evaluation are constrained by factors that have little to do with science. Perhaps more fundamentally, they assume that programs as implemented are more rational than they are. Political factors are often of overriding importance in the success of programs. And there is always a random element in what gets implemented and evaluated. Moreover, the experimental evaluators have a low level of concern with the process of program implementation that damages replicability of the experiments. Effective programs should be replicated, but you can't replicate anything unless you understand how it works. Failure to document how programs are implemented, how they are received, and by whom limits how useful an evaluation can be as applied in practice.

QUALITATIVE EVALUATION

Qualitative research is about description rather than enumeration. The basic assumption is that if you describe things in detail (*thick description*), you can infer relationships among elements based on logical rather than on statistical inference. Most qualitative research is context dependent. Evaluations using qualitative methods are important when the context is part of the thing being evaluated. In these cases, if you "control out" context, you will alter the fundamental operations of the thing being evaluated. Qualitative evaluations seek understanding by carefully compiling information on attributes or characteristics of some unit of analysis—a program, a phenomenon, a population, an individual—and producing details based on observations and discussions with people. The unit of analysis for a qualitative study must be operationally defined—that is, specified in such a way that everyone can tell what is is not included in the study. Analysis of data is conducted using some kind of content analysis or other method permitting characterization and synthesis of findings across units of analysis included in the study.

In this section I present several schools of evaluation that rely on qualitative methods. None of them specify a priori what methods should be used, and quantitative methods are used commonly in each of them. They are characterized by designs that are governed by the needs of the evaluation and the outcome of the evaluation process itself. These include Michael Quinn Patton's work on utilization-focused evaluation, Robert Yin's and Robert Stake's approaches to case-study evaluation, and the empowerment evaluation approach developed by David Fetterman. These are certainly not the only approaches to qualitative evaluations, but taken together, they exhibit the characteristics and issues that arise in this kind of work.

MICHAEL QUINN PATTON: UTILIZATION FOCUSED EVALUATIONS

Michael Quinn Patton developed this approach over the past twenty-five years (Patton 2008). He likes anthropologists and anthropological approaches, as is clear in the article he did in the NAPA Bulletin 24 on Evaluation Anthropology (Patton 2005). This is so because one of the most important parts of his thinking about evaluation has to do with his belief that people are the most important thing in making any program run.

Utilization-focused evaluations are evaluations that have a user focus built in. Potential users participate in the design, implementation, and reporting of evaluation results in such a way that the results will be utilized because users have ownership of the evaluation from the beginning. Patton identifies those who are likely to be primary users of evaluation and engages them in negotiation about the evaluation questions, the evaluation design, and the kind of process and information that will be useful to them. Patton's is a very politically conscious approach. He is articulate on the manifest and hidden political impact of evaluation and insists that these political contexts be unearthed.

Patton argues that "reality testing" is part of evaluation design; that is, primary users must be induced to look at programmatic and organizational reality if evaluation is to be effective in engendering program change. What is perceived as real is real, but getting to the perception is difficult. One way it is done is by getting people to focus on evaluation questions that will be meaningful for them.

CASE-STUDY EVALUATIONS

I have used this approach more than any other in evaluations I have done for federal clients, both the CDC and others. The strength of case studies in evaluating programs comes from their ability to provide deep, testable descriptions of programs in situations in which it is very difficult to distinguish programs from their context. For example, substance abuse prevention programs, no matter how faithfully implemented, are dependent on where they are implemented. It is seldom possible to argue that context is constant across multiple implementations. This approach treats context as a variable, a characteristic of the program.

There are two principal evaluators who have developed this approach, although many others have participated. They both use mixed-method approaches, but Robert Yin is a sociologist and comes from a more positivist position. Robert Stake, a psychologist, is much more on the constructivist side.

Case-Study Evaluation: Robert Yin

Robert Yin is perhaps the leading proponent of case-study methodology for evaluation (Yin 1993). According to Yin, a case study is (1) an empirical inquiry that (2) investigates a contemporary phenomenon within its real-life context (3) using multiple sources of evidence. Case studies can be exploratory, descriptive, explanatory, or hypothesis testing using logical inference—that is, conclusions based on systematic comparison of findings and deduction. It is the research plan (the design of the evaluation) that specifies the logical model of proof—that is, the circumstances in which hypotheses will be tested. Yin distinguishes case studies from, for example, historical phenomena from which you can't triangulate the data. He doesn't disrespect historical studies; it's just not what he's doing relative to evaluation (Yin 2006).

Yin is insistent on utilizing case-study methods that protect the empirical basis of the evaluation in such a way that all findings can be unequivocally linked to evidence. The reader must be able to view the link of evidence to conclusions for themselves. Analysis matrices that lay out the evidence in tables that link them to evaluation questions are an important part of this approach.

Case studies are derived from multiple sources of evidence and are not intrinsically qualitative or quantitative. In fact they are usually mixed method. The idea is to triangulate in on the "truth" about programs—that is, verify observations in as many different ways as possible. So, for example, there will often be a focus group, a survey, individual interviews, analysis of existing documents, databases, and so forth.

To protect the empirical quality of the case study, the evaluator must use at least some kind of case study protocol—that is, a written document that guides the researcher in adhering to the design and the methodology consistently over the course of the data collection and data analysis. If multiple staff are working on the project, they must be trained in the protocol prior to initiating work. Deviations from the protocol will happen, because, well, stuff happens. All deviations from the protocol must be documented and used in report writing to qualify findings.

Case-Study Evaluation: Robert Stake

Stake is an important evaluation theoretician who has made many contributions to the field. Possibly his most important contribution to evaluation is the development of *responsive evaluation,* an approach that concentrates on the perceptions of those who participate in the program as guides to evaluation design, implementation, and interpretation (Abma and Stake 2001; Shadish, Cook, and Leviton 1991).

The focus in responsive evaluation on participant perceptions means that evaluation begins with the local rather than national evaluations. The local perspective created a dilemma in evaluating programs with multiple implementations of a single national program model. To resolve this, Stake developed an approach to case-study evaluation that incorporates the variability of multiple exemplars of programs (Stake 2006).

For Stake, the case is a noun, not a function or an activity. It is defined by "organic systemicity"; that is, it has working parts that are brought together to achieve some purpose. Stake argues that all cases are at least implicitly "multiple case studies." Cases are studied as exemplars of a wider universe of similar cases with the same purpose. Stake captures this in a distinction between a "case" and a "quintain." A case is a single instance of something; a quintain is the broader set of similar entities from which the case is drawn. For example, the case might be the Drug-Free School activities in your own high school. The quintain from which this case is drawn is all Drug-Free School Programs in New York City, or New York State, or the entire United States. Stake says that we study the similarities and differences in cases in order to understand the quintain better. Even if the scientist has not made the quintain explicit, cases are chosen because they represent something.

The case/quintain distinction focuses attention on the generality and specificity of findings. Science in itself places more emphasis on the generalizable, whereas professionals and practitioners often prefer more particular findings on which they can act. We must, of course, do both. But with a finite budget and finite time, we must often choose where to put the emphasis. We must negotiate a balance between paying attention to the things that tie the quintain together with the situationality of individual cases. In designing the evaluation one would start by identifying what needs to be known about the quintain, study each case in terms of its own circumstances, interpret patterns within each case, and then analyze patterns across cases to arrive at general findings about the quintain.

The distinction also gives us a way to look at the fact that programs with multiple implementations (which is just about all programs) are embedded in their own contexts and have their own characteristics, many of which may be idiosyncratic. The case-quintain allows us to vary the questions asked of individual cases while still addressing the larger issues driving the evaluation.

EMPOWERMENT EVALUATION: DAVID FETTERMAN

Empowerment evaluation was developed by David Fetterman, an anthropologist who was president of the American Evaluation Association in 1994. It was the theme for his presidency, got a lot of attention then, and, largely because of Fetterman, has ever since. Fetterman has published book after book on this topic and has promoted it in every way he can. The theory and methods behind empowerment evaluation have shifted somewhat in the last ten years.

"Empowerment evaluation," Fetterman writes, "is the use of evaluation concepts, techniques and findings to foster improvement and self-determination" (Fetterman 2013:305). Control of the evaluation is vested in the community affected by the thing being evaluated. Community members design, implement, analyze, and make recommendations based on their own needs. The evaluator is there as a facilitator and technical expert.

Empowerment evaluation is usually directed to poor, disenfranchised people or to programs serving them. They are almost always conducted with a single program in a single location. At worst there may be a program administered by a single group of people and implemented in a few locations. The face-to-face nature of empowerment evaluation limits how much can feasibly be done if the program is too large or complex.

Fetterman (2005) describes, using a specific example, what empowerment evaluation looks like. The evaluated project was one to assist eighteen American Indian tribes and two African American communities to plan for improved access to and use of computer resources in their communities. The role of the evaluator in each of these projects was as a "coach or critical friend" as the community worked through the process of specifying what it was trying to do (its mission), mobilizing the resources it already had to support the mission, and planning future activities to obtain new resources and achieve the mission. The program communities—defined as those who run or are affected by the program in some way—have complete control over evaluation design, implementation, and use of evaluation results.

Jean Ann Linney and Abraham Wandersman (1991) (Wandersman is Fetterman's most important collaborator in developing this material) have identified ten characteristics that mark empowerment evaluation. These can be lumped into things having to do with inclusive participation (community ownership, inclusion, democratic participation, social justice), knowledge development (community knowledge, evidence based), and capacity building (capacity building, improvement, organizational learning, accountability).

In inclusive participation the evaluator must be sure everyone important is at the table or else the benefits of the empowerment approach in community building may be lost. Search to be sure you get all stakeholders especially poor and disenfranchised clients. Try to bring them all under the umbrella of fostering social justice for the disenfranchised.

Capacity building and fostering self-determination is a key goal of the empowerment evaluation process. The idea is to give participants the tools, knowledge, and skills they need to become advocates for themselves not only in the evaluation context but, more broadly, in promoting programs to serve them and to lead to social justice. Empowered stakeholders will be able to be accountable for what they do because they are enfranchised to control their own destiny.

Knowledge development uses participants to capture community knowledge of problems and solutions: they know best. Once you have community knowledge, link this to evidence from other sources to ensure credibility.

The Critique of Empowerment Evaluation

There has been substantial critique of this approach. Smith and other critics of this approach argue that it is *not* the role of evaluators to support social agendas. If they do this, they lose their value as evaluators. Bradley Cousins (2005) argues that empowerment evaluation is appropriate in the context of program development but should not be used where "tough-minded" decisions about program continuation and funding because empowerment evaluation (and other participatory approaches) have an inherent self-serving bias.

Important criticisms of empowerment evaluation come from both the policy and the evaluation. The policy questions are: Does it work as advertised? Does empowerment evaluation really empower? Miller and Campbell (2006) analyzed forty-seven examples of empowerment evaluation (as identified by evaluators using Fetterman's approach (Fetterman 1994, 1999, 2001a, 2001b, 2002, Fetterman, Kaftarian and Wandesman 1996, Fetterman and Wandesman 2005). They distinguished three modes of doing empowerment evaluation: (1) Socratic coaching (evaluator stays out of it, only providing requested guidance), (2) structured guidance (evaluator designs and uses a set of steps for implementation by stakeholders), and (3) participatory evaluation (evaluator designs and implements study with stakeholder feedback). They found that the goals of inclusive participation were the least used principles and that the goal of empowering beneficiaries of programs was far less important in these evaluations than facilitation of program staff. On this basis Smith (2007) argues that empowerment evaluation doesn't result in significant empowerment, concluding that it does not perform as advertised because it is not implemented as envisioned.

Some evaluators argue that empowerment evaluation is not evaluation but rather something else entirely. Evaluation is about assessing merit or worth, not advocating for social change. This definition is at the core of evaluation. It raises the question of whether empowerment evaluation can evaluate in the sense of determining whether a community effort is effective in either meeting goals or achieving any outcome whatsoever. So is it a good thing to do? You bet! Is it evaluation? This is more questionable. I have never encountered a government-funded evaluation that was at all interested in empowering people with no consideration of accountability. However, I have seen such evaluations come from foundations. And the approach might be useful in development projects.

RAPID ASSESSMENT

Those who do qualitative studies, especially ethnographers, are often invited in to do rapid ethnographic studies directed to a relatively narrow but urgent need. This methodology has emerged as the need for ethnographic data was recognized by funders who seldom had time to wait for the results of traditional ethnographies (Beebe 2001). In the effort to develop as complete a description of a culture as possible, ethnography requires substantial input from those who live the culture. Thus, it often takes more time than alternative approaches. For this reason ethnography may not be chosen, even if it is the best approach to an evaluation problem. Fortunately there are a number of methods that can speed up the process while maintaining the quality of the results.

Rapid assessment means more than doing an assessment quickly. There are methodological principles that guide rapid assessments and safeguard the quality of the data that they produce. These studies generate quick answers to highly focused questions in a short time period. Usually these are done when you need results for immediate program action, such as disaster relief, or you are waiting for results in order to implement a health or welfare program with considerable benefits. These evaluations are very often community oriented. They are common in international development work.

Rapid assessment comes in a wide variety of styles with lots of different names (McNall and Foster-Fishman 2007). These methods reflect different historical developments, but basically they all involve interviews with program staff and program clients, focus groups, and reviews of existing databases. They are often iterative in that a question is addressed to one set of stakeholders, revised, and used with another set. Because these are done quickly and are implemented rapidly, technical control of method is especially important. The question can be broad, but it must be clear; that is, it must specify what you want to know. Method must be chosen carefully and used faithfully. Results are provided in an easily accessible format. A big challenge in rapid assessment evaluation is requiring good evaluation methodology to protect quality while maintaining the focus needed for rapid assessment. Rapid assessment requires people who are experts in describing and interpreting culture and usually involves some participation of local people. The time constraints demand that the evaluator already has this expertise to connect with insiders to tap *their* expertise. Ethnography fits really well in this context.

PARTICIPATORY EVALUATION

You have probably observed that there is a bewildering plethora of approaches to participatory evaluation. How do you decide and how do you control participation? In trying to pull this together I came up with some pictures. Although ethnographic approaches are used with all of the evaluation types presented here, the role of the "native perspective" varies across a continuum from relatively small at one end to dominant at the other. This is shown in Figure 2.1.

By traditional evaluation, I mean evaluations driven by the scientific method, that privilege the authority of the professional evaluator and the client. Ethnography may be used in traditional evaluations if, for some reason, the culture of the people affected by programs or products is of prime importance. But the interpretation is translated to be comprehensible to outside users in the report.

A good example of the use of ethnography in traditional evaluations is interpretation of "cultural competence" or "cultural sensitivity" in programs directed to minorities. An ethnographic component is used to assess (1) what is considered unproblematic by the population served, and (2) how the program meets or addresses cultural needs. These are then used to develop an explanation of cultural competence (or the lack thereof) that makes sense to program administrators and staff.

Figure 2.2 provides a series of continua based on several dimensions that structure the degree of participation by program staff and clients.

Utilization-focused approaches are located a little more toward the insider end of the scale because they focus on the perceptions of stakeholders; however, these are usually program staff or policy makers rather than populations served. The assessment of stakeholder needs often utilizes ethnography to try to understand the place of the program and various components in the cultural system of administrators and to identify points of conflict among various subgroups administering the program as well as between programmers and populations served. Ethnographic expertise serves quality utilization-focused evaluation well.

Participatory evaluations vary a lot in their approach and in their position on the continuum. They are defined by some kind of reciprocity or

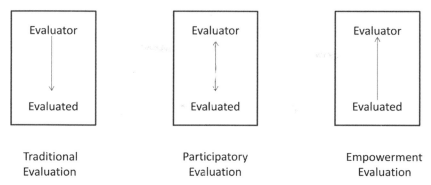

Figure 2.1 **Relationship between Evaluator and Evaluated**

partnership between the evaluator and stakeholders (which may include program administrators, program staff, affected populations, and program recipients). In participatory evaluation one or more of these groups participates in, contributes to, and blesses the evaluation design, implementation, and interpretation. Sometimes these evaluations are controlled by the client through the evaluator with advice from stakeholders; other times stakeholders are evaluators and/or have veto power.

I once worked on a participatory evaluation to assess a project designed to facilitate tracking and treatment of tuberculosis-infected people who migrated across the US-Mexico border. The project was a binational one, with

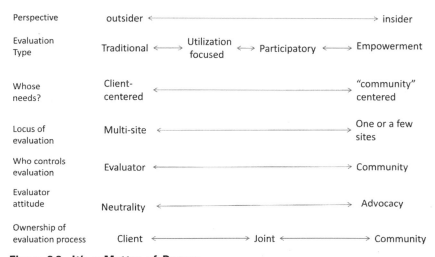

Figure 2.2 **It's a Matter of Degree**

local health agencies in both the United States and Mexico cooperating to move information between health agencies on both sides of the border. The project was very politically sensitive because of different understandings of how health care should be delivered and difficult history of power relations along the border that complicates all binational efforts.

The evaluation could only be participatory. There was a council of about thirty people from two countries as well as the CDC and us, as evaluators. As outside evaluators, my colleagues and I were there mostly to provide evaluation expertise and to implement data collection and data analysis plans approved by this group. I drafted evaluation questions, the CDC revised them, and then they went to the working group, who often completely rewrote them, throwing some out and adding some of their own. The group wrote the instruments that I revised for technical reasons in conference with them. They told us what kind of data collection was feasible and acceptable to them and what kind of information they needed. They assisted with analyzing quantitative data, although, for reasons of confidentiality, we did the qualitative analyses. The results were delivered to them in a briefing. I did a lot of ethnographic work for this evaluation in interviews in the field and by telephone. The detailed description of various kinds of stakeholders' perceptions on the evaluation was an important outcome because it taught stakeholders what communication barriers had to be overcome.

However, it was not an efficient evaluation. It took three years to complete and cost $700,000. We went up a lot of blind alleys, developed pieces of information that turned out to be pretty useless, and couldn't use some of the information we had because of politics. In this case, because it was a binational project being conducted in two countries with very different health systems, comparison of various "insider" perspectives was crucial. Even in retrospect, however, it was worth it. But this isn't always the case (Butler 2012).

It is always wise to ask yourself whether the participatory approach is worth what it costs. Alternatively you can, for example, conduct a case-study evaluation with an advisory panel.

EVALUATION FOR ACCOUNTABILITY

Evaluation for accountability is a third stream of evaluation. These evaluators believe that the function of evaluation is to help bureaucracies be accountable for the outcome of their activities. An early theoretician in this area is Joseph Wholey, who worked closely with the federal government for his entire career both as an insider and as a contractor. He developed a model of evaluation as part of performance-based management of federal programs based on the achievement of program goals. He argued that evaluators should, "when appropriate, recommend or provide options for redesigning agency management systems ... to focus on program goals ... [and] assist in redesigning agency management systems to focus on results" (Wholey 2010:666).

The role of evaluation in accountability achieved high visibility in the Clinton administration when Al Gore came up with the National Partnership for Reinventing Government. This effort was specified in the Government Performance and Results Act of 1993.[9] GPRA's aim was to link funding to performance of government agencies. Agencies were required to develop quantifiable indicators of their performance and identify means to track these indicators, then report to Congress on the progress and achievements of their programs. Funding for agencies would be linked to performance. The federal budget process doesn't really work in such a manageable fashion, however, and the results of GPRA have been mixed. Nonetheless, GPRA is still there in every federal agency. And it often consumes the lion's share of evaluation resources.

CHAPTER THREE

ANTHROPOLOGY: AN ORIENTATION FOR EVALUATORS

W hen I am at some kind of social event, the question of "What do you do?" comes up sooner or later. "I'm an anthropologist," I say. "Wow, that must be interesting!" There was a time when I would have smothered them with a lot of information about why it's so interesting—more than they ever wanted to know and probably forgot immediately after they moved on to the next topic. I suspect that even today these people don't have much idea about what anthropology is and why it's so interesting. It conjures up images of digging for early man and living with people in foreign villages. But most people are unaware of the depth and breadth of anthropology.

Anthropology ranges across all of the domains of human life and human experience, from Neanderthals to kinship studies to the general nature of language to the philosophy of knowledge. It even ventures into human genetics and the behavior of nonhuman primates. It is a good field of study for those who could never stick with a single major, which is a problem because anthropologists can have some difficulty focusing on a single question. Because we're into everything, we tend to get drawn into everything. But to use anthropology for evaluation—or for anything else for that matter—we need to be clear about what kind of anthropology we are talking about and how we plan to use it.

This chapter tries to pull together what you need to know to understand the anthropological underpinnings of evaluation anthropology. I have tried to write this for the curious social scientist who is not necessarily an anthropologist, who tend to form the core of evaluation teams. If you are an anthropologist, you should read this anyway, forgiving my restatement of what you may already know. To use anthropology for evaluation you need to understand something of the ways in which anthropology and evaluation can support each other. We need to establish how anthropology is applied in order

Evaluation: A Cultural Systems Approach, by Mary Odell Butler, 49–70. © 2015 Left Coast Press, Inc. All rights reserved.

to resolve problems that people encounter when living and working together. Both anthropology and evaluation are concerned with this set of issues.

In order to orient both anthropologists and nonanthropologists, I will begin with a discussion of the currents underlying the development of anthropology as practice, parallel to the history of evaluation as outlined in Chapter 2. We will move on to concepts that are so fundamental to anthropology that most anthropologists treat them as basic assumptions. Some of these are culture, ethnography, and community—things we don't think of defining until we find that members of our team are all using them a little differently. Others are trends in anthropology that are critical to the application of anthropological thinking to current dilemmas, like systems thinking and the meaning of globalization for culture and community, and include the role of science in exploring how people function in social systems. Finally, I will conclude by addressing the theory and method nexus in anthropology and how we can transcend the arguments about what is most important when thinking about evaluation.

Before going any further with this discussion I would like to define "applied" and "practicing" anthropology as I use the terms in this book. The two terms are often used interchangeably. Although there is certainly overlap between these categories, applied anthropologists and practicing anthropologists are not exactly the same thing. *Applied anthropology* is that branch of the discipline that uses anthropology to address real-world problems. *Practicing anthropology* is used by those anthropologists who apply the theories and methods of anthropology outside of academia, either part or full time. Both of these concepts include academic and nonacademic anthropologists. For example, they may be people with academic jobs who practice anthropology for outside clients. Many anthropologists would assign themselves to both categories, but to be a practitioner, one must have a professional stake outside of the academy. All practitioners are applied anthropologists, but not all applied anthropologists are practitioners; some applied anthropologists are full-time academics.

DEVELOPMENT OF APPLIED ANTHROPOLOGY

As evaluation was developing in government and in education, the applied focus was emerging in anthropology. There are a number of similarities in both the course and the timing of their emergence from contemporary trends in social science in the United States and elsewhere.

Conrad Arensberg's (1947) definition of applied anthropology, developed for the Society for Applied Anthropology (SfAA), still works well. Applied anthropologists (1) study living cultures and contemporary peoples, (2) are "problem oriented" based in needs rather than purely abstract interests, and (3) reach across disciplinary boundaries to investigate problem.

Applied anthropology is defined by its central concern with contemporary problems. This would make a lot of people "applied anthropologists" who probably don't identify themselves as such. There is a perception among some that applied anthropologists are concerned primarily with the application of methodologies to practical problems, whereas theory about how culture operates remains the purview of the academy. Applied anthropology does not mean atheoretical. Like evaluation, it is defined by usefulness. The aim of theory in applied anthropology is to understand the dynamics of the human response to crisis and change. This is in fact the role of all scientific theory (Kuhn 1962:170).

Efforts to understand contemporary cultures became very important in the 1930s, but at that time anthropology was a result of anthropology's concerns in its early days at the end of the 1800s and in the early 1900s. Anthropology emerged as the study of the primitive, human origins, and elementary forms of human experience (kinship, families, religion, political systems, economies). There was a fascination with the progress of humans from primitive roots to the pinnacle of civilization, which was, of course, thought to be occupied by white Anglo-Saxons. Much of the anthropology conducted in the early days was "armchair" anthropology based on travelers' accounts, letters from missionaries, and other secondary sources (Stocking 1987).

Franz Boas turned all of this around. Boas began doing anthropology in 1898 with studies of the physical characteristics of Eskimos and, eventually, immigrants to establish that physiognomy was not destiny. He was trained in Germany and held a PhD in physics. He came to anthropology with a kind of radical inductivist paradigm typical of his training. Boas felt that no generalization or comparison about human beings was appropriate; rather, the task of the anthropologist was to perform punctilious data collection and written description, usually in great detail. Boas's write-up of his work with the Northwest Coast Indians contained numerous ways to prepare blueberries and detailed instructions on how to smoke salmon (Boas 1925, 1974, Harris 1968).[1] Boas also viewed ethnography as salvage work: civilizations were disappearing on all sides; it was critical that we write down everything about them before they disappeared. This reinforced the concern of anthropology with primitive forms, unpolluted by contact with Americans, Europeans, or even with other "primitive" societies.

Boas trained an entire generation of American anthropologists during his long tenure at Columbia University, including Margaret Mead, Ruth Benedict, Alfred Kroeber, Robert Lowie, Edward Sapir—many of the founders of anthropology as we know it today (Harris 1968, 251). Boas's students gave rise to an empiricist school in anthropology that produced a rich body of ethnographic data from the Americas, Asia, and the Pacific. Margaret Mead, one of Boas's more noted students, began her fieldwork in 1925. She always believed that the appropriate grist for anthropology was in developing solutions for contemporary problems. Her special interest was enculturation and intergenerational relations, a topic that she pursued for the rest of her life (Mead 1970).

There was a separate stream of development in Europe arising from social anthropology, especially in England. British social anthropology focused on the operation of sociocultural systems. The social anthropologists did much of their work in various parts of the British Empire. Among the theoretical schools that supported ethnographic approaches to applied questions was British structural-functionalism, headed by A. R. Radcliffe-Brown and other British social anthropologists, many of whom worked in Africa. Radcliffe-Brown spent several years in Chicago in the early 1950s, where he exerted a strong influence on the development of applied anthropology in the United States.[3] The structural-functional approach he developed was important in the development of both sociology and anthropology, moving beyond the concern with static description that had been the norm for social science up to his time. Structural-functionalism focuses attention on the ways in which social structures are shaped by the task that they accomplished in their society—that is, their functions. This approach has now been largely replaced with more dynamic systems thinking. Yet during my practice I used this theoretically outmoded approach often because it is simple, useful, and easily comprehended by clients. Much of the development of logic models for evaluation depends on this flexible approach to culture.

In the United States in the 1930s applied anthropologists were brought in to work with the US Bureau of Indian Affairs (BIA). These anthropologists tried to document the lives of the tribes in support of BIA policy and tended to "describe the tribes as if the Europeans had never crossed the

Atlantic" (Eddy and Partridge 1978). US-applied anthropology was given a tremendous boost during World War II when mainstream anthropologists came out of the academy temporarily to aid in the war effort. The nature of the war and the emergence of the United States as a world power required perspectives on contemporary peoples encountered during the war, and as a result, anthropologists participated in a number of commissions, offices, and activities, such as conducting national character studies of participants in the war (the most notable Ruth Benedict's study of Japan, Benedict 1946). They developed methods and instruments for interviewing educated members of other cultures for insight and explored conditions underlying the effectiveness of food programs, health services, training programs, and many other things the war brought to public attention.

During the late 1940s and into the 1950s anthropologists became part of a social-action stream in the United States. This took applied anthropologists away from the previous position of anthropologists as detached observers and to a new emphasis on their responsibility to provide studied peoples with information and technical assistance needed to improve their lives.

Action anthropology, first conceived by Sol Tax, Robert Redfield, and others in the University of Chicago Department of Anthropology, directed anthropologists to a focus on contemporary societies dealing with the effects of modernization. Tax began his action anthropology in a project in which a team of investigators worked with the Fox Indians in Iowa to help them develop constructive ways to communicate and negotiate with their non-Indian neighbors. Tax did not view action anthropology as anthropological practice; instead, he argued that the action anthropologist must be a member of the academic community because he can "have no master," and he must be a theoretical anthropologist because he must constantly develop new knowledge (Tax 1975:516).

Action anthropology became a movement as anthropologists moved into the development work of the 1950s both in the United States and internationally. International work in action anthropology includes the work of George Foster in Mexico (1962) and Alan Holmberg in Vicos, Peru (Holmberg and Dobyns 1965), both concerned with helping local communities modernize their agricultural practices. In the United States W. L. Warner was an anthropologist who participated in the "Bank Wiring Observation Room Study" of fatigue among office workers, conducted in the Hawthorne Plant of the Western Electric Company. Among other things, this study gave rise to the famous *Hawthorne effect*—that observation alters behavior. W. L. Warner also collaborated with Robert and Helen Lynd on the Middletown study that demonstrated that the United States had a culture just like everyone else (Whyte 1978).

The use of anthropological theories and methods to facilitate technological and cultural change was a theme that would resonate within anthropology up to the present, although its theoretical and practical underpinnings have evolved considerably over time as the interface between anthropologists and communities dealing with technological and social change has become ever more controversial (Schensul and Butler 2012).[2]

The relationship of these emerging forms of applied anthropology to the rest of anthropology, especially the professional associations, was not a problem during the war, when everyone was doing their best to contribute to the war effort. And most applied anthropologists at that time weren't practitioners; they were academicians dealing with contemporary problems as part of their academic careers. After the war most of them went back to the academy and seldom collaborated again with anthropologists working outside of universities.

The American Anthropological Association debated for some time about incorporating applied anthropology and practicing anthropologists into the then completely academic association. Should there be a place for them at all? Were they scholars, or were they something else? Eventually the applied anthropologists left AAA and founded their own organization, the Society for Applied Anthropology (SfAA) in 1941 to give voice to the professional goals of those concerned with the specific problems of consequence to living people and the relevance of anthropology for policies and programs that affected them. At that time the entire concept of using anthropology to support public and private agendas was somewhat questionable. The founders of SfAA needed their own voice, separate from the more abstract academic views represented by the AAA.[4]

The relationship of applied and practicing anthropologists to more traditional anthropology is still a tension within SfAA and AAA. For practitioners—that is, those who work outside of the academy—there wasn't much support in anthropology for any kind of practice until the formation of the National Association for the Practice of Anthropology (NAPA) in 1981. Practitioners have grown in strength and numbers since this time. The precise number of practitioners is uncertain, but it is estimated that more than half of the US anthropologists with graduate degrees practiced outside of the academy.[5]

Today there is debate between some academics and practitioners about how anthropologists should be trained for participation in the labor force. Can an anthropologist work in the nonacademic labor market and still maintain their ethical integrity as anthropologists? What rules should govern the collection of proprietary data? How is practical work to be scrutinized by disciplinary bodies in the profession for moral, ethical, and anthropological quality? Things are changing in anthropology relative to practice, and some of these issues have workable alternatives to manage data, protect confidentiality, and ensure ethical soundness. The improvement in the status and understanding of practice as anthropology has been partly because of the presence of practitioner-academics in the community to educate anthropologists for practice.

CONCEPTS IN ANTHROPOLOGY

Any discipline has terms that are so central to its core that they assume everyone understands what they are, an assumption that can lead to considerable confusion, as often the common-sense meanings of these words may be misleading vis-à-vis their professional usage. Moreover, different disciplines may define the same terms differently and/or different terms the same. I hesitate to get into debates about the subtleties of meaning here, but we will need some of these terms later. So I will define culture, ethnography, and community as I will use them here. I have also added two terms that are useful enough to this discussion to give them a place in this chapter—emic and etic, which refer to the insider-outsider perspective in studying human activities. Finally, there is a discussion of the role of systems and context in interpreting what we observe in evaluations or any other anthropological enterprise.

CULTURE

Anthropologists have wrestled with the concept of culture for the past 150 years. Is culture ideas or social organizations, thought or behavior, concepts or material conditions of life, or all of the above? What is the effect of culture on individuals, societies, economic behaviors, religious beliefs? What is its relationship to other parts of people's lives? How do you know culture when you see it? Are fine arts any more cultural than anything else? The boundaries of culture—what it is and is not—is the grist of the study of anthropology.

In this book we aren't directly concerned with the debate over what culture is and is not; what we need is a good working definition so that we can move on to other things.

Therefore, we will use the concept of *culture* to refer to the learned, shared ways of thinking and behaving that people have because they were born into a particular society at a particular time in a particular context. Culture is acquired by all humans as a part of normal development. You cannot keep a normal human being from acquiring and using culture. We all spend our entire lives living in culture and seldom seeing it.

Culture is dynamic, more like a kaleidoscope than portrait. Its elements are always changing in relationship to each other and to other cultures with which people come in contact. We incorporate cultural traits that we acquired as part of our life experience. In that way we are living in a culture matrix that is accumulated over time. However, different individuals living within communities may have somewhat different assemblages of cultural elements. People can combine pieces of many cultures into new ways of life. You can see this readily in the United States by traveling from one locality to another. Populations in Massachusetts have ways of life that are distinct from Mexican populations in Texas or urban factory workers in Detroit. People combine cultural pieces from their shared and their unique experiences. And culture changes continuously. The dynamic and mutable nature of culture confronts us almost every day in the twenty-first century as we face the communications revolution and globalization.

Culture—at least big parts of it—is often invisible to insiders. It is such a fundamental basis for what we perceive that it comes to be viewed as "truth" by those who live it. In practicing evaluation anthropology, it is crucial to understand this attribute of culture because very often in evaluation the individuals who are affected by evaluation have different kinds of cultural expectations. For example, a major concern of many service delivery programs is the issue of cultural competence. Have we designed and presented this program in such a way that the members of the recipient population understand what it does? Are our goals of value to them and our ways of delivering the program acceptable to them?[6] The important thing to understand here is that culture—the shared understandings and behaviors that we have because we grew up, live, and work where we do and not somewhere else—is the raw material from which we build our ways of relating to the world and to each other. It is also the context in which evaluation anthropologists do their work.

Sensitivity to varying cultural perspectives is very important even within single programs in single communities, especially if we are trying to engage cultures not our own. Some years ago I did an evaluation of a community health promotion program in a city in Texas that had both African American and Latino participants. For some reason the program was not popular with the Mexican American communities in which it was introduced, although the African American populations liked it just fine. A little ethnographic interviewing by people not directly associated with the project showed that Latinos were offended by the business-like approach of the African Americans who were running the program. We were told that if you wanted something to take off in their community, you needed to sit down with people, have coffee, and establish a social relationship before anything else could happen. Of course, this was not the only reason for this program's limitations; there was a lot of history between African Americans and Latinos in this city. But without establishing a community basis for the project, nothing could happen and no progress could be made toward resolving other issues. This demonstrates that important cultural factors affecting programs may go unspoken and generate resistance to an intervention that has little to do with the intervention itself. The culturally mandated ways of getting acquainted with outsiders was a small piece of culture but one with ramifications to acceptability of the program to the entire Latino population.

There are a number of cultural factors that affect our lives profoundly and are often problematic in designing and delivering any service to a population. Some of these are:

- *Cultural variability,* as suggested above, must be acknowledged and explored in building interventions and doing evaluation. There is great variation in beliefs and values within any community. When you've talked to one person, you've only talked to one person. Before you build your program or try to evaluate it, you need a broader perspective in order to surface common cultural ideas that are appearing in what you see.

- *Human racial and ethnic diversity is a recurrent issue that is almost always there but seldom talked about.* This diversity may profoundly affect what happens on the ground when you implement an evaluation. There are a lot of classifications of people by race or ethnicity. Race and ethnicity are cultural things that are often very sensitive. The patterning and nonpatterning of human biological and cultural diversity must be incorporated in designing, implementing, and evaluating programs, projects, or products. Failure to explore the meaning of Latino, Asian American, or African American in the communities where people live is a major cause of nonacceptance. Just understanding what meaningful groups are requires a lot of finesse.

- *Communities must be defined to understand the cultural context of interventions.* Communities are interacting groups of people bound together by a common purpose or job. We use this phrase most often to refer to approximately geographically contiguous groups of people. However, this isn't the only way to use this concept. In complex societies like ours, people live in multiple, overlapping professional communities, religious communities, political communities, and many others. People's position in communities has a lot to do with how they perceive innovations. In the immortal words of Tip O'Neill former Speaker of the US House of Representatives, "All politics are local." This may result in acceptability of a program in one locality and rejection of an identical program in another. Your job as an evaluator is to find out why there is the difference in the two communities.

- *Assume that people acting from culture are rational.* Sometimes people seem to be acting against all reason. If people appear to be behaving perversely relative to their own health and welfare, it often has to do with cultural incentives. In a study I participated in we discovered that American Indian women were comfortable with mammograms and very uncomfortable getting pap smears. One reason for this problem was that men didn't like their wives going to male physicians for what they perceived as a very invasive procedure. The problem was resolved by staffing the screening program with female practitioners. When many people respond in the same way to an intervention, there is always a reason.

ETHNOGRAPHY

Ethnography is more than a method for anthropologists; it is one of the most important theory-method nexuses that defines cultural anthropology as a discipline. The theoretical basis of ethnography is that there is a cultural system that is used by "natives" of a society to negotiate their daily lives. Cultural things may or may not be visible to the participant; they may or may not be visible to the outsider. It is the job of the ethnographer to tease out culture using ethnographic theories and methods to investigate ideas and behaviors of individuals in groups.

Ethnography is very important to anthropological evaluation because people who develop, implement, and receive products and programs can have overlapping but somewhat different cultural ways of doing things. Most problems that arise in program implementation come from misperceptions of what someone else was saying or doing and, most especially, from thinking that you understand what's happening when you don't.

This difficulty with perspective is one of the things we try to resolve when we identify "stakeholders"—that is, people who have an interest in the outcome of the evaluation. An explicit understanding of the ethnographic approach helps you make sure that you have the right ones and that you have all of the important ones, even if you don't intend to use an ethnographic approach to your evaluation. We will discuss this issue more completely in Chapter 6.

Ethnography uses a variety of social science methods for the study of some human society with the goal of producing or uncovering the cultural system that generates what we observe. It is this central purpose—of constructing a cultural system—that defines the approach for anthropologists. The effort to do this requires that we compile information from people who live inside a cultural system, however we do it—surveys, interviews, observation, participant observation, and so forth. The usefulness of ethnography in evaluation is that it produces *thick description,* in the words of Clifford Geertz—that is, a very detailed cultural description. Although ethnography aims to be thick description, not all "thick description" is ethnographic (Geertz 1973). Detailed description of this type can deal with many topics. What makes it ethnographic is the focus on culture.

Traditional ethnographies attempted to portray entire cultures in as much detail as possible. The genealogy of anthropology is replete with such ethnographies. For the first half of the twentieth century these were pretty much all there was. Early ethnographers considered culture to be a pattern that underlay what we were looking at, one that we were trying to find as ethnographers. Essentially culture was static, and culture change was viewed as a stressor that the culture struggled to adapt to or as pathology due to culture contact.[7]

The traditional definition of ethnography as the study of ethnically defined people who live together in a closed community and presumably sharing a common culture became less and less useful with the application of anthropology to real-world problems during World War II and after. The result of all of this was a shift in focus to the study of plantation laborers, urban laborers, and farmers, groups of individuals who had a shared culture but also showed significant diversity in subcultural responses, especially to change. The vision of anthropology broadened beyond the closed community, and the use of ethnography to solve problems gave rise to the idea that anthropological ideas could be applied to achieve useful results.

Ethnographic work is by its nature focused on individual communities. Multisite investigations produce multiple ethnographies that are in some sense idiosyncratic. So what is the logic that we use to develop findings across multiple sites and even to sites that were not part of our study? This has been a challenge from the earliest days of anthropology. There have been attempts to address this issue in the development of culture areas, the comparative method. In the twentieth centuries anthropologists defined culture areas geographically and culturally. Anthropologists themselves clumped into groups defined by areas (e.g., Latin Americanists, Africanists, Asianists). Peoples living in a culture area were usually geographically contiguous and shared a core set of cultural traits. When one goes to the field in New Guinea, we know that it will be different from going to the field in Peru. And we have a rough roadmap of how to proceed in specific culture areas.

As ethnography has matured, it has become clear that a more focused approach dealing with specific questions in cultural context provides more useful answers than the effort to describe whole cultures. Ethnography is now oriented to more specific questions and collects data in a more organized fashion. We are now less likely to lose the forest because there are too many trees.

COMMUNITY

All interventions take place in some kind of community. A *community* is a group of people who are linked together by some common attribute—residence, kinship, religion, profession, baseball team—that makes them candidates for some kind of action. As you will discover over and over (if you haven't already), the apparently straightforward idea of community is hard to describe on the ground. Communities show wide variability that makes it hard for us to say what is and is not a proper community. Most of us know community when we see it but would be hard-pressed to come up with a definition that would work in all situations.

Communities vary in the number and strength of their interconnections. Some are just groups sharing some common characteristic that give them a common interest in something, at least in someone's minds (e.g., employed women between twenty and forty, middle school students). These kinds of communities are often the "target populations" for programs or projects. Other communities are defined by connections between people for some shared purpose (e.g., members of the American Evaluation Association, staff of the Midtown Hospital, undergraduate students at Ohio State University). Still others are groups who interact on a daily basis—families, coworkers, members of the Reno Nevada Rotary Club.

Although historically anthropologists have defined communities in terms of shared locality and sometimes shared ethnicity, communities may or may not be geographically specific. Families in the United States are an example of a more-or-less closely interacting community that may be quite widely dispersed geographically. School districts are less intensely connected communities defined by geographic location. Communities may have sharp or "fuzzy" boundaries. In the first case you can identify everyone, whether they are part of your research unit or not, as being either "in" or "outside" of the community. In the latter case people can be part members, or the community may be temporary, or people may move in and out of communities. People attending the Super Bowl are a temporary community with a sharp boundary—you were either there or you were not. Members of the First Baptist Church of Tulsa is a community with a fuzzy boundary. At any given day the group may include new members, lifetime members, people who are thinking of joining, and people who are leaving.

So how do we get to a useful way to define communities? The best way to go about this is to come up with a core description that has wide applicability and leave the description of the kind of community we are talking about—its members, its openness, the things that connect it—to the empirical process undertaken as part of our evaluation.

I will define community for our purpose here as groups of people connected by a common interest so that they interact in some common way with the societies in which they function. I omit from this definition groups of people defined solely on the basis of shared characteristics with no mechanism for connecting members in some kind of activity—for example, Ohio State undergraduates, Unitarians, French teenagers. It is not that these kinds of "communities" are not important; statisticians use them all the time. But for the purpose of evaluation, communities must have some kind of functional process in order to be defined well enough to be evaluable. It is not part of evaluation to assess the status of "immigrants in America," although we may well evaluate programs, projects, and products directed to immigrants' needs.

Difficult though it may sometimes be, a first step in building any evaluation is to identify the community in which the evaluation will take place. This may be an entire community exposed to the evaluand, or it may be a subset of geographic loci chosen as representative of all communities implementing an intervention. It may be a community purposely chosen because it is a good example of process ("best practice" communities), or it may be chosen as a worst-case scenario, although I do not recommend this.[8]

EMICS AND ETICS

Anthropology can also provide methodological advantages to the study of global changes by using tools of ethnography to understand how people define membership and nonmembership in groups. One element of our stock in trade as anthropologists is identifying and making intelligible the multiple understandings of events that participants in activities bring to the table. The etic-emic distinction is one way to do this that many of us have used at one time or another (Harris 1968; Pike 1954). *Emic* is the interpretation of culture from the perspective of the insider. The test for goodness of fit is the agreement of the native that this is an accurate explanation of what they are doing with a particular piece of cultural behavior. You get this perspective by asking the participant "What is happening here?" or "What would you do in this situation?" *Etic* is the interpretation of culture from the perspective of the outsider, normally the community from which the ethnographer comes. Traditionally explanation is in anthropological terms. In evaluation the relevant outsider is often the client. The test for goodness of fit is the agreement on the part of the outsider (scientific) community that this is what is in fact occurring.

As an example, think about that quintessential American holiday, Halloween. You are a visiting ethnographer who knows nothing about this. What do you see? People, mostly children, walking around dressed like Batman and princesses of various kinds, going from door to door, uttering a chant (trick-or-treat), and getting gifts of food in return. And just when you think this is a holiday for children, you see some adults oddly dressed and going into each other's houses. Mysterious, huh? How do you explain it to yourself? What would be the emic perspective? What might be an example of an etic perspective?

This example is a fairly obvious one. I have just given you the etic perspective. You can provide the emic one. But to further explore the use of these concepts, let's look at another scenario. You are vacationing with your family in the Southwest. One day you visit a Pueblo. The clerk at your hotel told you there was a ceremony there and you don't want to miss it. When you arrive, people are standing around in a central area—eating, socializing, calling to their children. All of a sudden drums start beating and people start chanting. Then, between two buildings come two lines of marchers. They are wearing colorful costumes and huge masks and look kind of frightening. They march into the plaza, dancing in a pretty repetitive way, and chanting. Some people dance with them; some just stand there and watch. Both adults and children are involved, although the masked dancers are all adults. They seem to be in a pretty good mood. What on earth is going on?

At first you might think that this is something like our holiday of Halloween—masks, costumes, chants, everybody eating, having a good time, socializing. But you would be wrong. You ask around to see whether you can figure it out. You ask someone what's going on, and he tells you that this is a Kachina dance, widespread among Pueblo peoples in the Southwest of the United States. This is not a party but a religious ritual designed to maintain the order of the universe. The dancers are members of sacred societies that have the duty to perform these dances in the interest of everyone. The beliefs of the Indians hold that the Kachina dancers are the gods themselves, come to help the people. A far cry from ghosts, goblins, and tricks.

The definition of insiders and outsiders is, of course, relative to the perspective of the investigator. In program evaluation the "native" is a member of a group of people in need of some kind of service or product. The "outsider" is all too often the person who is trying to provide the service (the program). Sometimes program recipients or even local service providers do not consider outside personnel to be members of their "tribe," an attitude that can drastically hinder the implementation of interventions.

It is in brokering the communication across cultural, social, and economic boundaries that anthropology makes one of its most important contributions to evaluation. Anthropological research teaches us how to transcend these kinds of barriers by fostering collaboration between different kinds of people, building rapport with those who run the programs and those who are expected to use them. Anthropologists are trained to enter communities as outsiders and negotiate access to the insider perspective. Most evaluations have some explanations of each type. Often emic interpretation forms the basis of analysis, which is then translated to etic perspective for reporting. Ethnographic evaluation—and, arguably, all ethnography—is an act of translation from one culture (in this case the program, people, or service providers or recipients) to another (the client).

SYSTEMS AND CONTEXT

Anthropologists are taught to understand the embeddedness of local happenings in state and national political and economic systems. We are not, of course, the only people who do this, but we do it well. We are permitted to bracket "our people" for purposes of description, but any explanation of what we see requires us to link our observation to conditions impinging from the outside. This perspective on the embeddedness of human life in larger systems is especially critical when considering many social programs because discontinuities in policies and commitments between the national and the local level can have dire consequences for the poor at the bottom of the hierarchy. For example, anthropologists have frequently pointed out situations in which national policy was far removed from the needs of those who are vulnerable to the worst ravages of infectious disease. The assumption that goodwill and dedication on the part of local staff will lead to a positive outcome in terms of peoples' lives is wishful thinking at best in the absence of good national policy and the staff and funding needed to implement it.

New approaches to multisite ethnography promise to enhance our ability to model general processes in localities by embedding several communities in a single research inquiry. While acknowledging macro-level systems, this emergent form of ethnography traces cultural constructions across time and space rather than confining the inquiry to a single site embedded in a world system (Marcus 1995). Considering cultural meanings and objects as the subject of study rather than localities, the ethnographer becomes open both to variations in the manifestation of the thing observed and to the connections that are built across sites by shared understandings and challenges. Thus, we can build ethnographies of migrants that are grounded in multiple sites connected by the presence and movement of people in systems (Rouse 1991). This is a far cry from the traditional ethnographic focus on conceptually static communities embedded in larger constructs such as nation-states, capitalism, developing economies, and many others. This new conceptualization of the ethnographic endeavor provides a flexible means to understand the subjective experience of people in a global environment where the conditions of life change rapidly across time and space.

POWER AND PROSPECTIVE IN ANTHROPOLOGY

You often hear that the winners write the history of things. Anthropology has a long—and often questionable—history as the agents of governments in learning how to administer populations brought into their jurisdiction by colonialism, conquest, trade, and exploitation during the past few centuries. Over the past several decades there has been great concern over the issue of inequalities in power between the anthropologists and those with whom they work.

Anthropology traces its beginnings to early contacts between European and American powers and the "savage" peoples of the Americas, Africa, and Asia. The relationship between emissaries of the West and the people they found as they expanded around the world has been subjected to criticism from anthropologists in the past two decades. In the United States anthropologists worked with the Bureau of Indian Affairs in developing and implementing Indian policy, and British social anthropologists informed colonial administrations in Africa and Asia to understand and manage local populations. This has focused attention within anthropology on the role of institutionalized power as it affects the welfare of those with whom we work.[8]

Most of what we do as evaluators and as anthropologists involves at least an implicit power differential between us as observers and the people who we study. This is certainly one of the most basic dilemmas of anthropology and one that is inescapable in evaluation, where our job is to establish the worth of someone else's work. Do anthropologists and others actually create or modify culture when we write ethnography? What are the implications of power differentials for what we perceive and report? These issues matter in evaluation because, as you will discover again and again if you do this, there is a power differential built into the role of evaluator, so much so that the word itself elicits a negative response from people whose work is to be evaluated.[9] There is no way to avoid this. It's one of the conditions of being an evaluator. It's important to be aware of this both in interviews and analyses. It can require some reassurance about precisely what is being evaluated and for what purpose. Most of the evaluations I do for federal agencies are not evaluations of individual implementations but are instead concerned with the effectiveness of the federal programs of which the individual projects studied are exemplars. However, no matter how many times I explain this, they seem to not quite get it. Many of them remain skeptical of our intentions.

This concern means that we need to be explicit about perspectives and interpretations of what we see. There are multiple perspectives in any situation. It is the job of the ethnographer to try to untangle them and present them in such a way that differences in perspective are clear to the people who use our research. This is a critical consideration because clarity and consistency on this dimension is crucial to the interpretability and stability of ethnographic evaluation results.

METHODS IN APPLICATION OF ANTHROPOLOGY TO EVALUATION[10]

We have been discussing the theoretical underpinnings of evaluation anthropology coming from anthropology. In this section we turn to methods. In doing any social science, theories imply methodological choices.[10] They are closely related to each other. It is for this reason that the design of evaluations requires vigilance to ensure that the methods chosen can address the theoretical challenges of the project. Some of the contexts in which anthropological approaches are appropriate are:

- Formatively when there isn't enough information about the subject to be evaluated to know what kinds of questions to ask.
- When the desired information is why something happens rather than what happens.
- When there are diverse stakeholders and many perspectives that must be teased out of the data.

Other situations will emerge in practice, but the above ones are, in my experience, the most common.

In doing the anthropological side of evaluation, I have found that the methods I use are similar to those I have used in most of the anthropology I have done. Sometimes the methods of anthropology need to be adapted to fit into the budget and time constraints of evaluation. For example, we may use rapid ethnographic assessment methods for evaluations in which results are needed urgently and quickly. In evaluation we seldom have the means to spend long periods of time in data collection, so our research designs must be focused on specific questions rather than pursuing the more inductive methods of traditional anthropological fieldwork. We don't usually have time to let theory emerge from the data.

By far the most common and useful methods for evaluation anthropology are those used in ethnography. One does ethnography by speaking little and listening a lot. It's amazing how much people will tell you if you ask them the right questions and then be quiet while they answer you.

Interview methods come in a continuum from very highly structured to very open. One common example of a *closed interview* technique are telephone surveys in which the interviewer is careful to ask exactly the same questions, using the same words with all respondents. This is done to minimize bias that might make it difficult to interpret statistical results and to minimize the effect of the error term in statistical analysis.

At the other extreme is *open-ended interviewing,* in which the content of the interview is defined by the interviewee rather than the interviewer. Normally the interviewer uses a list of topics to focus the interview and to keep on topic but is very careful not to bias or "lead" responses. Between these two extremes is a range of semistructured interview techniques that provide more or less guidance to the interviewer and the interviewee in defining the order and content of the information exchanged.

Open-ended interviewing is especially valuable ethnographically. At its best, the outsider provides only a topic and follows up with probes. Participant observation is also an important technique. Because the ethnographer tries to develop description of culture, it requires substantial input from those who live the culture, and, even with shortcut methods, ethnographic evaluation often requires more time than alternative approaches.

Interviews can be done with single individuals or, especially in open designs, with groups of people who have some kind of relationship to a single set of activities. For example, when beginning a field evaluation, it is common to have one or more group interviews with program staff to obtain not only information but also a sense of the group dynamic around the evaluation. Do people communicate well and easily? Or are there palpable tensions in the group? The interviewer can then probe for problems either in the group interview or, later, with individuals. This is the most common way in which organizational dysfunction emerges.

A group interview is not the same thing as a focus group. In a group interview the interviewer is trying to get a sense of group dynamics in some organization. Focus groups seek to get consensus on some issue from a group of individuals chosen based on demographic or social criteria to be representative of some larger group. Focus groups are ideally made up of people who did not know one another before the focus group encounter. The instrumentation guiding the focus group is often closed or semiclosed to ensure focus on the issue in question. Some of my more quantitatively trained clients have asked that I provide them with a count of responses by individuals across one or more focus groups. This is a violation of the method because the individuals might have responded differently in a different focus group or a different context. The intended outcome of focus groups is a group outcome, but you may need to educate your clients (Krueger and Casey 2000).

Participant observation is the learning by doing approach. You participate with staff or clients of the evaluated program in program activities. The evaluator might participate in meetings or program functions. Participant observation requires an instrument, although it is normally quite open. In participant observation you seek in your dress and manner to be inconspicuous. For example, I have done many participant observations in clinical settings, coming in like I was a patient and going through the intake and waiting periods. I was careful not to dress differently from the clients and, above all, not to bring a computer or be seen taking notes. To do participant observation you need to observe, memorize, and go out of the situations to write down notes. Classically participant observation involves living and working with studied people. It is less used in evaluation than in anthropology more broadly, but it is potentially quite useful in getting the ethnographic perspective.

Even if there is not a specific kind of participation observation, it pays to keep one's eyes open in the data collection part of the evaluation. Not all data comes from talking and listening. Unobtrusive observation is an important part of data collection. I once did an evaluation of the effectiveness of steps to reduce smoking among teenagers. On one field trip I interviewed the assistant principal—normally the school law enforcement person—in a high school in a southern state. He explained to me the school policy that prohibited smoking within five hundred feet of school property. "Does this policy work?" I asked. "Absolutely!" He replied. As I was leaving the building I noticed that there were hundreds of cigarette butts on both sides of the door (Webb et al. 2000).

There is considerable misunderstanding about the nature of qualitative data and its "truth value." It can be difficult for those not accustomed to using qualitative methods to appreciate the kind of rigor that goes into analyzing qualitative data. Sometimes they equate qualitative data with anecdote.

The misperception of the linkage of qualitative data to research places great responsibility on the evaluator to plan ways to record and manage data, analyze them, and link evaluation findings to evaluation questions in such a way that they constitute evidence for action. Both evaluators and anthropologists make the best possible use of technologies that we now rely on for most everything. Digital tape recorders are used to record interview data and enter sound files directly onto computers. Few of us ever go anywhere without laptops these days. They are essential to data entry and data management. Text analysis software makes systematic analysis and synthesis of findings possible in such a way that the user of the evaluation can later track the chain of evidence behind findings. More discussion on how to do this is presented in Chapter 5.

CHOOSING THE RIGHT METHOD

No method is automatically the right method for all questions. An ethnographic evaluation will not do what a quasi-experiment does. If you need to know about the outcome or impact of an intervention on a population, use a survey, especially if the usefulness of the evaluation depends on being able to show your own superiors statistical or quantitative evidence.

Most of all, avoid choosing a method before you have evaluation questions and data sources. Sometimes clients lead with method in asking for evaluations. They may specify focus groups or ask you to do a survey. They may or may not be correct in this choice. You can't learn the same thing from a survey as you can from focus groups. This kind of situation calls for some finesse. I always try to get them to tell me what they want to find out and how they plan to use the information. Then—and only then—are we ready to begin choosing methods. It is important to point out that the right choice may not be an anthropological approach at all. If that's the case, so be it.

Clients or partners may approach you and ask for a case study or a survey or focus groups. Make them tell you what they want to know and what they need to be informed about. Make them answer questions like these before you settle on a method. Use ethnographic methods if:

- you need to assess process or outcome in a contextualized way, or
- the criterion for goodness of fit of your explanation is the agreement of stakeholders.

Use another method if:

- you need to know about the outcome of a program based on individuals in a population, or
- the criterion for goodness of fit is based on an est_mate of a population parameter using a statistical or quantitative method.

CHAPTER FOUR

PUTTING THEM TOGETHER: EVALUATION ANTHROPOLOGY

This chapter describes how evaluation and anthropology can be combined into an approach that builds on the strengths of each. I have
asked myself often why anyone would want to bother with the concept
of evaluation anthropology. Don't we already have enough special fields that
have been cobbled together to make something new, only not really? If I want
to claim something new, there needs to be a good reason. I even debated
dropping the whole thing and just call this something like *Anthropology and
Evaluation* or maybe *Evaluation and Anthropology*.

I decided to build out the concept of evaluation anthropology because
I believe that evaluation anthropology is not isomorphic with either evaluation or anthropology. Not all evaluation is anthropological and not all
anthropology is appropriate for evaluation. To be combined into evaluation
anthropology, they must be theoretically and methodologically integrated
and the scope of the combined approach defined. To be consistent with good
anthropology and good evaluation, we need to honor the rules of both fields
and constantly adjust what we are doing to the theories and methods that
both of these fields incorporate as part of their own tool kit.

In the sections that follow I will elaborate a synthesis of evaluation and
anthropology that takes advantage of the strengths of both disciplines in such
a way that evaluations can be embedded in the anthropological understanding
of culture and society. I will explore the position of evaluation anthropology
relative to dominant paradigms and theories in the social sciences and map
out the methodological terrain of evaluation anthropology. In the final section I will have a few words on what evaluation anthropology is and is not.

THE CORE OF EVALUATION ANTHROPOLOGY

Evaluation anthropology is grounded in an overlap between the field of
evaluation and the field of anthropology. Evaluation is the study of the value

of things—programs, projects, products—any human effort in which value is a consideration in success of the activity or choice of alternative approaches to social and cultural problems. Anthropology at its broadest is the study of culture and its role in articulating what humans do as members of societies. Evaluation anthropology concerns itself with the relationship of values to the cultural matrix that influences the perceptions and activities of humans. Everything that humans do as members of societies, including the entities being evaluated, is lived in a complex and multilayered cultural milieu. Exploring how culture intersects with programs, policies, projects—whatever can be evaluated—operates in culture. The manifestation of evaluands in cultural context is the area in which evaluation anthropology unfolds. The contributions of evaluation and anthropology to evaluation anthropology is mapped in Figure 4.1.

Evaluation brings to the mix an operational way of determining and measuring the value of human projects along with theory and methods to define, identify, and investigate the value of these in social context. Evaluators are expert in grounding their work in natural settings where evaluands function. Anthropology brings its depth of understanding of culture and the ways that the value of the things evaluated fits into cultural context. Together they bring to evaluations a vision that can place programs and the social values they seek to serve in a context that reflects the complexity of culture in which they act.

Note that there are vast areas of anthropology and of evaluation that do not overlap. Not all evaluations take culture into consideration, at least not

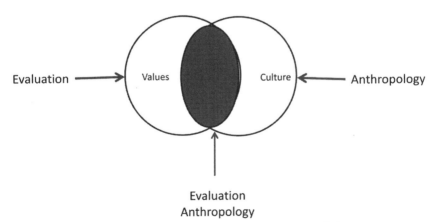

Evaluation
Anthropology

Figure 4.1   Evaluation Anthropology Bridges Values and Culture

explicitly, or else they consider it part of the error term in their measurement. And there is a large body of anthropological literature and activity that has nothing to do with evaluation—in fact is unaware of its existence as a strategy of investigation. Experts may disagree about where these boundaries lie, but evaluation anthropologists from time to time encounter them. For example, as discussed below, there are kinds of evaluation for which anthropology is not appropriate, and many anthropologists are not comfortable with the study of values. Like culture itself, what is or is not part of evaluation may vary in different contexts and around different problems.

The field of evaluation anthropology includes:

- A paradigmatic position that can vary among practitioners but considers various points of view of other evaluators and does not dismiss competing paradigms as invalid prior to investigation.
- A theory of culture that incorporates all aspects of human thought and behavior in the context in which it emerges.
- A commitment to investigating value as a cultural phenomenon that may vary from one community to another or even from one stakeholder to another.
- A methodology that incorporates ethnography but embraces other methods that can provide insight into the situation investigated.
- An analytic strategy that is comparative in the sense that it seeks patterns across multiple cases rather than striving for generalization to all possible instances.

This is not to say that both evaluators and anthropologists do not extend their practice beyond evaluation anthropology. Generally speaking the combined approach covers some of anthropology and some of evaluation. Normally evaluation approaches are negotiated among evaluators and clients coming from a variety of occupational and educational positions. Evaluation anthropology is not coterminous with either field; it defines a territory in which elements of both are combined in a useful way.

Evaluation brings to the mix a theoretical orientation to feasibility, acceptability, and value of human activities established relative to a diverse group of people who are affected by the evaluand—the stakeholders. They provide the theoretical and methodological framework within which to build evaluations that are credible, methodologically sound, and useful to those who commission evaluations. Methodologically they bring scientific rigor and an eye for evidence. They are accustomed to working in interdisciplinary teams. Evaluation methods and theories are the basis of credibility in evaluation anthropology.

Evaluation anthropology can bridge values and the ways in which people act in response to them by making the value orientation of projects explicit. Determining value is the definition of evaluation. Values are incorporated in evaluation design and guide the questions evaluators explore. Consider, for example, an evaluation of an educational program in which the desired outcome is that teenagers will see it as cool *not* to smoke cigarettes. If you do open-ended interviews with students and teachers without probing for the presence or absence of their values around cigarette smoking, the success or failure of this campaign in changing attitudes may be obscured if, for example, your interviewees consider it cool *to* smoke. They are unlikely to reveal this politically incorrect value to an outside investigator unless he or she probes to uncover it. In some parts of the United States a campaign that simply motivates people to devalue smoking may be a success as indicated by who receives the message while not achieving the goal of casting smoking itself as undesirable.

Anthropologists can learn this value orientation from evaluators. Historically anthropology has tended to bind values up in culture, considering it something that will emerge as the investigation proceeds. This may or may not happen or it may not produce the value statements that are necessary for evaluation. It may be counterintuitive for anthropologists to probe for values—you don't want to lead the respondent or offend in some way. To be evaluation anthropologists, we must learn to do it anyway if the evaluation is value oriented, even though this may conflict with some of our training as anthropologists.[1]

Anthropology could benefit from a better appreciation of evaluation as a means of understanding contemporary society. Working with evaluation makes better anthropologists. As anthropologist-evaluators we develop a comprehensive knowledge of culture and how people experience it in contemporary societies. We learn about the complexity of efforts to address social problems in postindustrial situations. By applying our knowledge of values and the relationship between expressed and lived values, we learn about the variation in values within sociocultural systems and how people work out differences to arrive at functional solutions to social problems. We learn about the cost of poor communication in lost opportunities and human suffering, but we also acquire knowledge of how to address these issues and which approaches to doing this are effective. Most anthropologists know little about evaluation because evaluation anthropologists are slow to share their understanding of evaluation with their anthropological colleagues. This represents a loss to anthropology, especially to those who teach it, and those who are new to anthropology.

The anthropological side contributes the perspective of humans who are participating in some activity related to the evaluand. Anthropologists bring a deep familiarity with culture and its effects on everything that people do alone or in groups. Anthropology deals with dynamic systems and can accommodate situations in which things won't stop long enough to be described *in situ*. They seek to detect and describe value conflicts. In the practice of ethnography anthropologists have learned to listen openly and say little in order to capture the perspectives of those living inside a cultural system. They bring this orientation to the evaluations they conduct.

Anthropologists bring to the mix a sensitivity to the complexity of cultural context. This is critical in a world that is more interconnected every day. For example, immigrant populations are key for many social service and training programs. But the Internet has made it possible for immigrants to maintain close daily connection with their families back home. They can closely monitor current events in their communities or origin, even following local soccer teams. This is a far cry from immigrants' experience a hundred years ago who left their home communities with an understanding that they were possibly leaving home for the rest of their lives.[2] Evaluation anthropology grounds the evaluation in both what is known of this real-world context and the effects of culture on life in that context. They see the world as a dynamic system that is constantly adapting to local and more distant influences. Human life today is embedded in a multilayered matrix of politics, economics, ecology, and local priorities (Lansing 2003).

The importance of subcultural differences in attitudes can be demonstrated by an example. I once participated in an evaluation of a national youth smoking-prevention program in a number of different locations throughout the United States. There were marked differences among cities in the effectiveness of the program. In working-class neighborhoods many parents smoked, and children got cigarettes off the coffee table at home. Messages disseminated at school had small effect in the face of this stronger message coming from parents. Although teen smoking is not widely approved in the context of health in the United States, it is tacitly approved in many of the local subcultures in which people make decisions about whether to smoke.

This kind of sensitivity both in and of itself and as a tool of evaluation teams is very useful, but often the evaluation anthropologists must try to disseminate it both to other evaluators and to clients.

Of course, it is necessary at some point to draw a line around what you will study—no one can study everything. But evaluation anthropologists do this on the basis of what they know about the most important contexts in which their work is embedded. What specific situations need to be part of our evaluation? What dimensions of context must the evaluation include in order to get a complete representation of important dimensions of variability? What questions must be asked to tease out the effects of context on implementation and effectiveness of the evaluand? For this reason the development of evaluation planning requires preliminary work, often ethnographic in nature, on what is important to diverse stakeholders.

I am aware that it takes considerable hubris to attempt to define a new approach to anything. I do so with humility, taking into account the many things I don't yet know and the complexity of both fields. But my experience with the integration of evaluation and anthropology has dominated my own professional life. Throughout my career I have told people that I landed on my feet as an anthropologist when I became an evaluator. Over the years I have tried to fill out what I meant by that in concrete terms, mostly in the interest of mentoring new anthropologists into a field that is a good one for us. At an emotional and intuitive level I have been able to build on intellectual habits acquired as an anthropologist and become an effective evaluator in doing so. After all, what is evaluation if not listening closely to informants to discover what they value and whether they perceive that these values are being served? Conceptually—and equally intuitively—I knew that the values people told me about were pointers to complex sociocultural phenomena that generate modes of human life even if the ways in which they do this are obscure to the actors. As anthropologists, we know that what people tell us is the tip of a cultural iceberg; it is in observation, analysis, and comparison that our truth lies. I did what anthropologists do, and by doing this, I learned what clients needed to know in order to serve their constituencies well.

TREADING AROUND PARADIGMS

In previous chapters we have talked about the nature of paradigms in both evaluation and anthropology. In this section I would like to describe paradigmatic decisions as they relate to evaluation anthropology. I will not come up with a recommendation for what paradigm to use. Prescribing paradigms to a diverse group of professionals is a kind of intellectual arrogance I am not willing to engage.

Nonetheless, we need to take some kind of stand on paradigms for evaluation anthropology if for no other reason than the ethical responsibility of being clear about where we stand when our work will affect the lives of others. Also, the choice of paradigm is an important issue given that much of evaluation and much of anthropology come from diametrically opposed paradigms. An empiricist approach supported by a scientific process to generate interpretation is central to most evaluation. A more subjective approach grounded in participants' perceptions is more common to anthropology. There are, of course, evaluators who consider themselves to be pure constructivists. And there are anthropologists who operate from empiricist positions. But training and experience have located most of us in particular discipline-specific paradigms.

Figure 4.2 summarizes the dimensions along which paradigms can range. These ranges will be the structure of the discussion that follows. This is not to imply that the choice of paradigms is a linear one—it certainly is not. Professionals may combine ontology, epistemology, ideology, and preferred methodology in many different ways. But all paradigms must implicitly or explicitly take some kind of position on these four domains of thinking about how to comprehend the world.

Ontology describes positions on where the locus of causation lies—independently outside of the observer or within the social agreements of human groups. The assumption on the empiricist end is that there is one reality "out

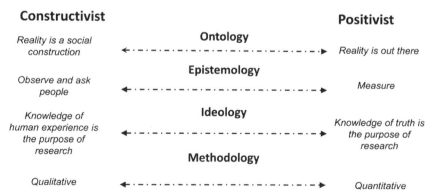

Figure 4.2 The Dimensions of our Paradigms

there" that produces what we see. Although that reality may or may not be knowable to the observer, ever-closer approximations to it are the goal of research. Anyone who observes reality correctly will perceive the same thing. Differences among different observers are due to measurement error and bias.

On the constructivist end, reality is constructed by the observer and/or by negotiation between the observer and the observed. Differences in perception are due to differences in the view of the observer and/or the person who is explaining the situation to the observer. Some researchers suspend judgment on the locus of reality because what reality is doesn't matter from the point of view of the investigator. However, if you examine other parts of their assumptions, you will find at least a default position on ontology in their epistemology, ideology, or methodological choices. This question of the locus of causation—an external reality versus human perceptions — matters to the practice of evaluation anthropology because our ontological position influences how we define the focus of our research, our decision of what is context and what is a research problem, and our interpretation of both. One investigator's research finding may be another's noise.

Epistemology is the grounds on which the world can be known. How do you discover what is happening? The constructivist will argue that you must ask humans for their descriptions and interpretations of what is going on. The empiricist will say that you must have some kind of metric to measure what you see. Lacking a metric for an object or a process, it either isn't there or doesn't matter. There are, of course, many positions between these extremes.

Many approaches—probably most in studies of society—combine observation and measurement. This includes most evaluation anthropology, as few anthropologists or evaluators would take a stand based on nothing other than observation or measurement. At the same time, if anthropology is to be applied to addressing problems, we must find ways to make our findings convincing to the broader society. Thus, we measure what we can.

The issue of emic and etic perspectives discussed in Chapter 3 is an important aspect of epistemological choices. As you will recall, emic perspective tries to get the view of the participant in a social situation while the etic perspective aims for the view of the person outside of the situation—the client, the evaluator, the community from which these people come. These are all perspectives, of course, and neither is empiricist. But it applies to evaluation anthropology. Evaluators usually focus on making sense to their clients and to the world outside of the observed. This is part of the job description. Anthropologists, at least traditionally, seem to be most concerned with making sense to other anthropologists. As evaluation anthropologists, we need to do both. We must communicate what we do to our colleagues to succeed as anthropologists and to the broader society to succeed as evaluators.

Ideology captures the assumptions we carry about why we are doing what we are doing, relative to research or, for that matter, to everything. In the sense of research paradigms, *ideology* relates to the purpose of inquiry. Why are we doing research at all? The question regarding the ideology that we bring to our work is usually the most hidden of paradigmatic assumptions and the one most likely to cause trouble in combining approaches to evaluation. Ideology refers to why the researcher undertakes investigations. On the constructivist side, the reason for a study is to throw light on how humans experience something (a program, product, project, etc.). The empiricists are searching for what is true—or at least arrive at a good approximation to truth—relative to some reality outside of the research situation.

There are many evaluators coming from the empiricist position who are—at least implicitly—searching for truth that will stand up to scrutiny by users. This may be the case, even if the users themselves are not believers in—or don't care about—abstract truth.[3] The constructivist evaluator wants to understand how humans live in the world, even if they seek to do so in an empiricist framework. Because the implications of ideology for the con-ceptualization of studies is so deeply buried, people at opposite ideological positions may confuse each other when they serve together on evaluation teams. Most especially, they will differ on their expectations of standards for data quality and when data collection may be considered complete.

A central task that evaluation anthropologists undertake is to define and translate what we mean by culture to our own teams and to other stakehold-ers. Many evaluators have a sophisticated sense of the culture concept. Others may hold the layman's definition of customs or even of sensibilities to art and literature. Or they may confuse it with society. Or they may be foggy on how culture can simultaneously be similar across populations or communities and display differences in subgroups. They may perceive culture as static at least for the moment of observation. Clients may have similar misunderstandings. One of the first things I do in the start-up phase of an evaluation is to interview all of the stakeholders to try to ascertain their own definitions of culture and of the evaluand. It's best to never assume that others see the cultural situation the same way you do or that the culture concept looks the same across all stakeholders.[4]

In working in the United States or any other stratified society, culture becomes subtle and complex. There are "subcultures," cultural patterns that are shared only by some part of a society and that may or may not be acceptable to others sharing a general culture. Sometimes it helps to distinguish "big-C culture" and "little-c culture." The former is the entire complex structure of shared ideas and behaviors that govern sociocultural interactions in a population of people—for example, the culture of the United States. The latter is the assemblage of rules and behaviors that are manifest in the daily lives of groups of people. For example, in the United States, ethnic groups, social and economic classes, and geographic location are important dimensions of cultural difference.

Finally, methodology is how you find out what you want to know. Methodology goes beyond methods to make judgments about the best way to apply methods rather than simply using methods themselves. Methodology is a theory of methods. The application of methods is fairly simple. Figuring out how methods tell you what they tell you—and the interpretations and limitations of what they tell you—is more difficult. This is why the quantitative-qualitative debate has had such enduring life in the study of societies. Many scientists on either end of the continuum use mixed methods. But if you interrogate them closely, there will be one that they consider primary and the other will be used to support, triangulate, or clarify the other.

The constructivist evaluator seeks truth by compiling, integrating, and comparing the perceptions of different kinds of people living with the program and affected by it. They build a description that depicts the particularity of a specific program implementation embedded in its time and place. Their results are "thick" in the Geertzian sense, providing detailed information on one or more program scenarios (Geertz 1973). The criterion for goodness of fit of explanation to data is stakeholders' agreement that this explanation makes sense to them, that it is "correct" from the inside. These evaluations can be very convincing to stakeholders for the obvious reason that they are designed to be so. They can also produce effective means to intervene, facilitate, and promote programs. Program managers often like these; policy makers are less certain, preferring the support of quantitative indicators of success.

Evaluators on the empiricist side produce rigorous evaluations that seek to achieve objectivity so that at least similar results would be obtained in any similar setting by any evaluator using the same methods. Their evaluations use the scientific method as closely as possible and demonstrate statistically the validity of their findings. The level of significance can be very reassuring to those who must make important decisions about programs because these kinds of results feel "true." And clients can rest assured that, subject to measurement error and bias, any other qualified social scientist will reach approximately the same result because the result is being generated by an underlying reality that is uniform. Reality is like an armature on which we pile the clay of observation. These scientists see the statements of individual human beings (even in focus groups) to be noise, error. They seek to "control" this "bias."

Paradigmatic and theoretical orientations are not straightforward for evaluation anthropologists. We can become very confused by the range of paradigmatic positions available in both evaluation and anthropology. And it matters because our work is undertaken in the interests of clients and very often conducted in interdisciplinary teams. Unquestioned or unknown paradigmatic assumptions can be a source of big problems. For example, I found early on that it is a really bad thing to get an evaluation in the field and discover that you, your client, and members of your team have very different ideas about what kind of data are acceptable and how they should be compiled. Someone who thinks that the reality of the program is producing interview results will probe very differently from someone who is trying to get to the interviewee's understanding of the program. In one case the evaluator is trying to establish the framework on which the program is built; in the other we are seeking to establish the boundaries of understanding that govern how people act within it.

In evaluation anthropology we must articulate a concept of what we are looking for before we start looking. Conscientious data collection and triangulation across as many data sources as possible brings us to a point at which we can say, "This is what I think is happening here, and I have some guesses as to why." We need to be able to articulate why we are doing the research we are doing. Ethnographic work—qualitative work—demands more than the traditional anthropological practice of being dropped into a situation and keeping our eyes and ears open; it demands respect for method and for the linking of method, findings, and results in the ways produced by evaluators. Otherwise our work has little value beyond being interesting. The combination of the anthropologist's sensibility to culture and the evaluators' desire to document what culture does results in what I hope is the best version of the truth we can find, based largely on consistency with a body of information from multiple sources.

But must we decide on a paradigm? What is the right way to think about fundamental assumptions that we bring to the study of humans? The answer to this, of course: there is no right way. First of all, these fundamental paradigm choices lie far below what we consider when we build ways of knowing. This is not to say they are not important. Paradigms affect everything we do because they extend from such a deep, psychic level. They influence what we believe we can know, how we go about knowing what we can know, and how we lead our research to its conclusions. For this reason we need to know where we are coming from paradigmatically. And we need to be able to recognize our colleagues' and clients' paradigmatic frameworks. Evaluation teams can usually work around paradigmatic differences but not unless they know that the issue may be there. Good discussions of "what we are trying to do here" are very helpful at early team meetings.

For many years I treated the question of paradigms as unimportant. They might be grist for graduate seminar discussions, but they didn't matter much in practice. Can't we just resign from this debate and conduct our evaluations in light of what is useful to our clients and ourselves? What difference does paradigm make?

In recent years I have begun to understand that, in spite of the utility criterion for good evaluation, we need to go beyond crude utilitarianism to examine the forces that generate what we see and how we interpret it. A conscious awareness of our perspective on these matters is important because it influences how we treat our data and the people who give it to us. Down deep inside of us we have a map that tells us what we see and what it means. We need to listen as freely as we can, given our own background and our own experience. When I teach evaluation anthropology, I ask students to try to find and describe the things they consider to be inarguably true—their paradigmatic assumptions—in order to see the impact of these beliefs on what they consider to be the nature of the world. It is a difficult exercise precisely because these are baseline assumptions that are seldom brought to the surface and examined. But we all carry them. Try this exercise for yourself. You may find it both unsurprising and revealing.

I feel that I owe you something about where I stand vis-à-vis paradigms. I suppose that I am an unrepentant scientist, maybe even some kind of postpositivist. This has been a difficult position to take in anthropology specifically and in social studies more broadly. Scientific thinking has not been fashionable in large sectors of anthropology over the past several decades. But paradigmatically speaking, this way of looking at the world is so deeply rooted in me that I couldn't expunge it even if I wanted to. Also working as I do in public health, I could not leave the scientific paradigm behind. My clients were epidemiologists and medical personnel. They were are not disinterested in the nature of reality or what can be known from various paradigmatic positions; they enjoy talking about it, even speculating about it as much as anyone does. But for all practical purposes, it doesn't matter. They have a job to do, and my work was part of their job. I am comfortable with this.

The fact that I still consider myself a scientist does not imply what critics often believe it implies. I do not think that it is possible to be truly "objective" in social research. People cannot be forced into a set of categories and analyzed as if they were all alike. But I do believe that some kind of generalization is a useful thing in social research. The utility of measurement in generating new understandings of human beings is limited. I tip my hat to those who do this kind of work. It has just been my experience that, on the practice front in both evaluation and anthropology, we always need to do ethnographic work to understand what is working and why it works in partnership with or in addition to quantitative work. People's perception is very important if what you are trying to understand is people.

I don't know whether there is a reality out there independent of our observation of it. My reading in quantum theory tells me there probably is not (Hawking 1988). But I do believe that there are patterns in what humans do in societies that can be demonstrated. All of anthropological theory depends on the idea that there are regularities to be discovered about human life. I do believe that all social research takes place in a context that is part of what we are trying to understand. Both anthropologists and evaluators have an understanding of multiple perspectives around any issue, reflected in a concern with stakeholders in evaluation and at the core of the ethnographic method in anthropology. Even the most empiricist evaluator knows that what is documented, measured, and explained must pass the believability test with people coming from many different perspectives vis-à-vis the program and its evaluation. It must have face validity. On this front anthropology and evaluation have no disagreement.[5]

I do not know the answer to how you pick a paradigm. I guess in most cases we develop these over careers. However, to help you see what I'm talking about, I will give you the paradigmatic assumptions that I bring to evaluation. I have come to adopt a pragmatic approach to the theoretical basis of what I do. In evaluation the core elements of theory for me are:

- Regardless of the nature of reality, there are patterns and consistencies to be found by directed observation. We can go beyond individual cases with ethnography, but we need to be clear and transparent in how we organize and report our findings.

- People will do the best they can to tell you what you want to know, but they cannot see things from anything other than their own perspective. It's not that some people won't try to mislead the investigator, either deliberately or because they want to protect themselves or others, but usually this is not the case. Often my respondents in evaluation are trying to figure it out themselves.
- The lives of people should be investigated broadly; that is, the categories we use to understand human life must be comprehensive enough to accommodate the variety of human responses to any situation. As a field of inquiry, human life must be understood from boundaries to the inside rather than from central tendencies to the boundaries. We must move from the "typical" to the range of variation in how people live.

I do not have a theory of human motivation, mostly because this is beyond the scope of my professional competence. I cannot infer why people do what they do. All I can know is what they tell me about why they do what they do.

THE METHODOLOGICAL LANDSCAPE

What are the methodological dimensions of evaluation anthropology? By methodology I mean the professional constructs from which we design our approaches to evaluation. There are many choices we must make in choosing methods, and our choice of methods profoundly affects what we can find out. It shapes how the evaluation comes out. You will not learn about the distributions of innovations, the attitudes people have about them, or the frequency with which new products or programs are adopted and used if you restrict your investigation to ethnographic interviewing. You will never suspect the human causes underlying the success and failure of products or programs from the limited responses available in a survey. Experimental designs cannot tell you what influences impinged from uncontrolled contextual barriers. The proper choice and use of methods is part of methodology, but methodology also includes the assumptions supporting the design, use, and analysis of methods.

The evaluation anthropologist must be well versed in qualitative methods and the associated methodological assumptions yet must be familiar with and respect alternative evaluation methodologies. Clearly there is a significant qualitative component to evaluation anthropology, especially in terms of data collection and analysis. But this should never be the governing decision in accepting, designing, or undertaking an evaluation.

You should never lead with method. If you do, there will be some questions that you not only will miss but will also be unaware that they were there for you to miss. Always lead with the question(s) the evaluation will ask. What are you trying to find out, and what do you plan to do with the results? This is a simple set of principles, at least conceptually, yet is it one of the most difficult things for the evaluation anthropologist to do. Anthropologists at least are often overwhelmed with the complexity of the lives of the people they study. I think this confusion is common among most of us who use qualitative methods in the field of social investigation. We have a hard time seeing trees for the density of the forest. Everyone can see the forest, at least somewhat. They brought the evaluation anthropologist in to help them find the trees embedded in this particular forest.

Evaluation anthropologists must be comfortable working with professionals from other disciplines and must have respect for alternative ways of doing research. Only the smallest and simplest evaluations are completely qualitative, and they are often precursors to a larger evaluation effort. Evaluation anthropology usually incorporates the views of many—the client, the evaluators, the people affected by the evaluation results. In fact, anthropology derives its value in evaluation from the combination of anthropological theories and methods with alternative ways of clarifying an evaluation issue.

Evaluation anthropology is a transdisciplinary study more than an arithmetic combination of several ways of doing things. For there to be an integration of the capabilities of members of an evaluation team, one that includes other professionals but also incorporates the stakeholders, the evaluation anthropologist must seek and respect the others' perspectives and contributions to the evaluation enterprise. The power of transdisciplinary work consists in bringing multiple ways of doing science together for complementarity and triangulation. We can see our research from several points of view, and we can compare our findings by building up knowledge from multiple perspectives. It is this integrative character that adds value to evaluation and brings the conclusions closer to whatever version of "truth" we can achieve.[6]

Ethnography is one of the most important tools that anthropology brings to evaluation anthropology. However, there are ways in which ethnography must be adapted to use in evaluation. Often we have neither the time nor the funding to do ethnography the way anthropologists have traditionally thought of it. When I was a graduate student, I absorbed an idea of ethnography that included total immersion in a single group or society for at least a year in the language of the people studied. Inductive methods were favored. Franz Boas, the "father" of American anthropology, taught that "we have to study each ethnological specimen in its history and in its medium" (Boas 1925). Abstraction of meaning outside of specific contexts was to be avoided. We also understood that remoteness was an important part of fieldwork, and many students chose their field sites with that in mind. One of my professors was dropped by parachute into a village in highland New Guinea with only a backpack and a one-hundred-word vocabulary list in the local language obtained from a US missionary. We all envied this, but even as early as the 1970s this kind of experience was difficult to get funded. Today many beginning anthropologists undertake work closer to home or in collaboration with established institutions and development agencies.

In evaluation anthropology, ethnography needs to be more directed in the sense of being aimed at a fairly specific set of questions. And time schedules and budget will seldom be available to do long observations based on an inductive orientation. You need much more sense of question than anthropologists have traditionally had. Many evaluators of all kinds do their work either as part of federal, state, and local agencies or under contract to them. Seldom does the opportunity to do ethnography, in the traditional sense of letting the research problem emerge from fieldwork, come along. Most evaluators need to accept direction from clients in defining problems rather than independently deciding on the problems that interest them. The period of fieldwork for evaluation anthropologists working outside of the academy usually runs from two days to two weeks, often at multiple sites. It is normally much too costly and time consuming to place an ethnographer in the field for a long time.

The tighter focus on client needs and the cost and time limitations mean that ethnography as we learn it in school or in our student fieldwork is not always possible. To do ethnography under the conditions of practice, we must operate from some kind of study plan that contains, to a greater or lesser level of detail, the kinds of data to be collected, instruments for collecting the data, and a data-analysis plan. And usually the evaluation must be completed in a timely fashion (as defined by the client) and within a budget that seldom takes into account the amount of time it takes to analyze ethnographic data. To do evaluation anthropology in an efficient way, consistent with the demands of our contracts, we must plan ahead without putting ourselves into a methodological straightjacket that threatens the flexibility of our inquiry. This means we must think through to the end of the evaluation, anticipating as much as possible the amount of work involved, the likely problems that will arise, and the points in the project when we can adjust our trajectory in view of events.

I once did a project on teen pregnancy prevention curricula in high schools in three states. We prepared a protocol with the study purpose, the method, an analysis plan, and a budget as part of our proposal to do the project. The work began, as usual, with a process to meet with the client and then networking out to find stakeholders. We identified some people who were recommended by the client, and from them we networked out to a few others, but there was a budgetary constraint on how much of this we could do. We developed the study design and instruments and went to one of the states to pilot the study in a designated community. When we arrived, we discovered that we had missed an essential racial/ethnic divide between the African American population and the Latino population cooperating to implement the program. This problem appeared in a coalition meeting in which an undercurrent of hostility on both sides was covered by surface politeness and an inability to focus on anything substantive. The coalition leaders were genuinely confused about this. They would not come out and blame the other ethnic group for the problems of the coalition, but both sides tended (very politely) to attribute it to intransigence on the part of the other group. It became clear that, in this site at least, much of the data collection would need to be conducted separately in both groups in order to get at how the program was supposed to operate in the minds of both groups, how they each used the program, and how they actually behaved. This redesign (and the additional data collection) had to be completed within the budget the client had agreed to when they accepted our proposal. We managed it by sending two rather than three people on site visits and by lengthening the site visit by a day to allow time for separate work with each group.

Ethnography is often emergent from context and situations, and complexity may not appear in the early encounters. The best evaluations I have done using ethnography were the few studies that permitted repeat visits to sites. As most anthropologists have discovered when they return to field sites after a time away, second visits are much more productive than first ones because the rapport and trust needed to produce an ethnographic account are much stronger the second time around. However, seldom do we have this luxury, given a client's need to act and our own contractual obligations.

There is some debate about whether we can really do ethnography under these circumstances. This, of course, depends on how you define ethnography. I have defined it as investigation based on regular contact with relevant people around a problem. The evaluation investigates this problem in its own context by compiling the varied viewpoints of those who operate in the situation being investigated. It is the view from the inside out as seen by participants in a cultural encounter that characterizes ethnographic work. To be ethnography, there must be an iterative exchange between description and interpretation of description and then following up to gauge the adequacy of the interpretation. To arise above simple description, the evaluation anthropologist must be able to establish some kind of connection to stakeholders so that tentative conclusions can be reflected back to them and finalized in the light of their feedback. Without this kind of demonstrable link of findings to informants, we are subject to the frequent criticism that ethnography is "just stories." The stories are sometimes the most convincing part of the results. It is good for them to be there, but to meet the requirements of evaluation, they must be linked to the perspective of stakeholders, on the one hand, and the needs of clients, on the other. It is a tricky balance between the poetry of ethnography and the needs of science.

It has been my experience over my own career as an anthropologist and an evaluator that if one maintains the integrity of the design focus in an open fashion, if one allows for accommodating the unexpected, then one can do ethnography in a short time. One cannot, for example, restrict interviews so much that you are discovering a better or worse interpretation by the interviewee of the question you asked rather than getting at the information you are trying to elicit. Whether it is done in two weeks or two years, ethnography is a dynamic process. One must keep it oriented to the evaluation but provide the widest possible field from which people can respond to questions. For example, informants can be asked, "Can you tell me a little about how you came to be in this job?" rather than "How long have you had this job?

I know that there are both evaluators and anthropologists who would beg to differ with me on many of these points. We have already discussed the contentious issues in which evaluation is embedded. There are many evaluators who feel that qualitative work has no place in scientifically valid evaluation. There are evaluators and anthropologists who argue adamantly that scientific thinking has no place in studying human life. There are anthropologists—and many others as well—who believe that the use of ethnography to assign value to human activities, is a violation of an anthropological version of *Star Trek*'s "prime directive"—do not interfere in the society or culture in which you do your work. The idea of "usefulness" as a purpose of investigation is full of ethical perils for almost everyone who seeks to understand how and why people do the things that they do. However, I have learned that both as an anthropologist and an evaluator you cannot do research in practice conditions without a certain amount of pragmatism in how you build your approach. People don't live in controlled environments. That's just the way it is.

HOW I DO IT

There are, of course, as many ways to do evaluation anthropology as there are to do any other kind of research. If you are already practicing evaluation anthropology, I'm sure your experience has led you in directions dictated partly by your work environment, partly by your methodological preferences, and partly by your own disposition to discovery. If you are contemplating or just starting to do evaluation from the position of an anthropologist, what you learn in your career will contribute much to what evaluation anthropology—or whatever it is called in thirty years—will be like in the future. I am one of many people who have worked to introduce and refine anthropological approaches to evaluation. We are pioneers. Much of what we have learned comes from trial and error. So I would like to summarize the ways I have approached this activity.

I believe that evaluation must be scientific. I know that there is a lot of discussion in anthropology about the relevance of science to human problems, but for the purposes of evaluation, we need to resign from this debate. No one is going to pay a lot of money to support a decision about programs, funding, or staffing based on how people think about things. This does not mean that ethnography is not important—it is a powerful evaluation tool. But it does mean that it needs to be embedded in a scientific approach that combines ethnographic data with other material to reach conclusions on how people *act* in program settings.

So what are the necessary conditions for application of scientific theories to social problems? I think there are three:

- Respect for the rules. Honor you evidence; don't throw any out to make it come out right. Be diligent in your search for your own bias.
- Skepticism. Be a little doubtful about what you believe to be true. If you don't maintain a little doubt, you won't question your own perceptions when you should.

- Flexibility. Be open to alternative hypotheses, new evidence, and new questions. Be alert and willing to incorporate new insights into you work. Thus do we sneak up on reality.

Often, in doing science, we do what we do from instinct, but it is instinct based on training, experience, and respect for evidence. It is also intrinsically dependent on transparency and scrutiny of our work by clients, peers, and the people we study. You need to go out into left field to keep yourself honest.

I tend to approach evaluation anthropology using some version of case-study evaluation and/or utilization-focused evaluation (Patton 2008; Stake 2006; Yin 2006). However, the focus on the usefulness of an ethnographic project is not intuitive to anthropologists unless they are doing a rapid assessment or some procedure in which this is a clear goal. Usefulness, in fact, may be considered questionable in anthropology because the idea of ethnography for a purpose has a bad history in anthropology (see Chapter 5). The way around this is, of course, to ask yourself: "Usefulness for what"? If, as an anthropologist, you are satisfied with your answer, go forward with your evaluation.

Interviews, participant observation, focus groups, and surveys have formed the tool kits of both disciplines. This tends to make us comfortable working together but may mask differences in how we define scientific problems and the theories behind our methods. I am inclined toward mixed methods. Multiple data sources are needed for triangulation of results, an important part of analyzing qualitative data. Although evaluation anthropologists are expert at qualitative methods of data collection and analysis, they are conversant with quantitative methods and use them when appropriate. The methodology of evaluation anthropology emphasizes using as many sources as you can within the constraints of data availability, time, and cost.

Evaluation anthropologists do not collect contextual data to "control out" variability that may affect the main effects they are trying to measure. Others—and most anthropologists—are more likely to make context a part of the observation that is expected to drive variability, deriving context as a product of grounded observation of the situation. But all of them are likely to collect contextual data using similar methods.

The evaluation anthropologist must address the issue of data quality. In empiricist science, validity, reliability, and generalization are the indicators that the data are of good quality and that they, in fact, say what we say they say. These data-quality indicators are critical in evaluation, whether it be qualitative or quantitative. How do we demonstrate that what we assert is true? What can be replicated about ethnographic work, and what cannot, and how do we assess the truth of repeated studies? How do we know whether what we find can be extended to other circumstances in which we did not collect data?

Validity and reliability are critical in any evaluation—indeed, in any piece of science. Validity is best ensured by building clear and comprehensible data-collection plans, teaching them to research teams, and tracking accumulating data on a regular basis for quality and adequacy. Validity is also supported by triangulation across data sources. Do interviewees agree on important points? What are the differences among interviewees in different job categories, relationships to the agency, and sites? Are interview data, observational data, and quantitative data consistent with each other? Where they are not, have we followed up to explore the reasons for these differences? Finally, have we reported the validity checks in our report? No data or data analysis can demonstrate the "truth" of anything. Even parametric statistics give you only a likelihood that you are wrong. Like any researcher, we do everything we can to protect the quality of our data and to present its limitations as fully as possible.

WHAT EVALUATION ANTHROPOLOGY IS NOT

On the principle that you don't really understand what something is unless you have also considered the limit of your definition, I briefly discuss when you should refer the evaluation to another kind of evaluator. Evaluation anthropology is not necessarily the best way to explore any specific problem. It is wise not to choose a method until you have developed an evaluation question because the question you ask will often dictate the approach to it that you take. Whether you are an anthropologist or something else, it is very bad practice in social science to choose a method before you understand the problem you plan to investigate. When method becomes the driving force in evaluation, there is a good chance you will get to the end of the project without the information needed to support decision making.

There are some things that are clearly out of the scope of evaluation anthropology. Evaluation anthropology is not experimental or quasi-experimental in approach. By this I mean randomization and a design that requires tight control of the uniformity of implementation of both the evaluand and the evaluation. This is simply not what we are about here. Occasionally people will try to use ethnographic methods in controlled comparisons, but they are usually lacking in the implementation control needed for an experimental evaluation to be credible. This is not to say that one cannot or should not compare multiple sites in ethnographic studies, but these are descriptive comparisons. They do not have the degree of control, the rigor, needed for an outcome that is intelligible in quantitative terms. If you must have a quantitative result based on a rigorous set of hypotheses, use an experimental evaluator who is experienced in managing this kind of study.

Evaluation anthropology is not naturalist evaluation as defined by Lincoln and Guba (1985) and others. Naturalistic evaluations are grounded in the belief that evaluation—and all social science in fact—must be free of any scientific or comparative end. When you've seen one case, you've seen one case. There are many anthropologists who are quite comfortable in this methodological reality, and it can produce interesting and credible results. However, I have had few evaluation clients who would be satisfied with making a potentially politically salient and costly decision based on this kind of evaluation. In my experience, to be acceptable as evaluation, studies must be grounded in a concept of a reality within which its findings will hold, regardless whether that reality exists in some ontological sense.

Evaluation anthropology is not a strictly "emic" in approach. As you will recall, the emic perspective is that of the participant in a cultural scenario. The etic approach is set in a way that will be comprehensible to the investigator and his community (e.g., evaluators). Evaluation anthropology is methodologically focused on compiling the perspectives of multiple stakeholders, but it is directed to a specific problem rather than one or more kinds of informants. Evaluation and much of applied anthropology is an act of translation of the emic to the etic. Clients, funders, politicians, and other "outsiders" need to know what is going on in the contexts in which they function and make decisions. When we build our findings, it is very helpful to incorporate the framework of those who will use our findings.

Evaluation anthropology does not seek generalizability in the experimental or statistical sense; rather, it tries to discern patterns of activity that are repeated across multiple instances of the evaluand. Patterns are established by comparison, and they are open enough to allow for variability among cases, not by seeking to control them out but by examining them as part of "thick description" (Geertz 1973; Lincoln and Guba 1985). They are not seeking a reality that lies below their observations but instead are concerned with the boundaries of variability within which evaluands operate.

You can use an anthropological approach to your evaluation if you need to assess a program process or outcome in a contextualized, systematic way and if the criterion for goodness of fit of your explanation is stakeholders' agreement that your interpretations are accurate.

If you need to know about the outcome or impact of an intervention on a population, use a survey or another appropriate quantitative method, especially if the usefulness of the evaluation depends on you being able to show statistical evidence to your clients or your own supervisors. Experimental and quasi-experimental evaluations are very effective at doing this. An ethnographic evaluation will not do what a survey or an epidemiological study does. Don't send an anthropologist out to ask a lot of people about the range of opinion around something or the distribution of something in a population. Sometimes ethnographies may be used prior to or in conjunction with experimental and quasi-experimental evaluations. This is fine as long at the ethnography is allowed to remain open in design.

Often the needs of the evaluation require you to refer your client to another kind of evaluator. It is part of your job as a professional evaluator to do whatever is necessary to conduct the evaluation in the best possible way. It is not ethical as an evaluator or as an anthropologist to promise something beyond your professional competence. We will have more to say about this in Chapter 5.

A key issue in both evaluation and applied anthropology is linking method, theory, and practice so that they reinforce each other. For me, the practice of social science has always been a world in which certainty is not possible and truth is context dependent. We combine method and theory to focus in on what is important, given the circumstances. This is much less comfortable than the world of the .05 significance level, but it is also less comfortable than the theoretical certainties of which anthropologists are fond. We all have them, and often we must unlearn them to be effective as practitioners.

These things are indispensable to the "nuts and bolts" of doing evaluation. However, there are also uses of anthropological theory, though we may not recognize it as such. For example, the theory of natural selection as I learned it in graduate school and taught it in Introductory Anthropology has continued to form a framework for me to think through social problems. Things—biological or cultural—are not alike, even if they are related or part of a common pattern; that is, there is variation. Some variants are in some way "better" in a *specific* context. The biological criterion is adaptation. In culture there is, of course, an analogous relationship between variants of—say, agriculture—and the environment in which they are used. Finally, the variants that achieve the greatest success in the specified environment will tend to be selected over those that are less effective. There is selection such that some traits increase in frequency while others decrease, leading over time to a change in the characteristic of the population. Good, simple anthropology and a principal theoretical orientation of mine as an academic and a student works for evaluation and is how I always unconsciously structure my thinking when I define evaluation questions and come up with designs.

CHAPTER FIVE

ETHICS, CLEARANCES, AND ETHICAL DECISIONS

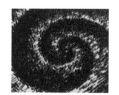

My goal in this chapter is to bring the reader to an understanding of how important ethical principles are in the practice of evaluation, anthropology, and, indeed, any kind of social science with implications for the lives and welfare of people who provide the data to us. We have a special responsibility to consider, understand, and honor our responsibility to individuals, groups, and populations who may be affected by what we do. Poor ethical practice diminishes the value of our studies as well as the validity and reliability of data. News about ethics violations raise the anxiety of people around participating in and supporting research projects in natural settings. And it damages scientists' reputations and their ability to obtain funding for their research.

In the first part of this chapter I will define and describe challenges of ethics in evaluation anthropology. The second part will deal with clearances that may be required to pursue projects, especially projects in which the evaluator works under contract to the government—that is, as an agent of the government. In the last section of the chapter I will summarize as best I can the principles that are key to our practice of evaluation anthropology and will provide practical guidelines for us to think about in approaching ethical decision making in evaluation practice.

There are vast tomes written on the definition of ethics. This is one of the things that sometimes intimidates people who are trying to identify and use ethical principles. At its simplest, ethics is a set of culturally defined principles that serve as guidance to satisfactory practice in the pursuit of some professional or personal responsibility. Important parts of this definition are "culturally defined" in the sense of being part of the shared understanding of members of specific kinds of professions. They are principles that embody values in that they define acceptable practice of a profession in terms of doing good and doing no harm. Finally, they reinforce the responsibility of professionals to serve and protect the people they work with and study.

ETHICS

Ethical responsibility has special importance in both evaluation and anthropology because of the nature of the work we do. The open nature of ethnographic research challenges us to inform people and protect their confidentiality. In evaluation the same privacy concerns arise. Moreover, evaluation is designed to assign values to programs, the performance of their staff, and the welfare their recipients, and it is meant to be critical to scrutiny. Wittingly or unwittingly, evaluation poses risks to the jobs, careers, and livelihoods of those who cooperate with us. It affects the way in which needs of population subgroups, especially those who are vulnerable to failure of social services, public health, and education, are addressed. To those who design, fund, and implement programs, there are political risks that are not always obvious to external evaluators.

Talking about ethics makes many social researchers uncomfortable (Trimble et al. 2012). Partly this has to do with the link of ethics to our accountability for ethical decisions we must make as we pursue our research. As competent research scientists, we are compelled to subject our work to critical scrutiny—our own and that of others. This is unnerving and raises the possibility that we might not get to do the study the way we want to do it or, in fact, any way at all. And most social scientists are not deeply knowledgeable about ethics. True, we encounter it in our graduate work, but it is usually a few class discussions, hardly enough to support the complexity of issues implied in human research. There is a scarcity of graduate courses in ethics in any discipline. Finally, there are many programs and many evaluations that are guided by political concerns and are scoped out in such a way that the "right" questions will be asked and the "right" answers will be obtained (Chelimsky 2012). These things are subtle, not easily spotted by an evaluator with only modest experience.

WHY ARE ETHICS SO IMPORTANT?

Ethics are central to the practice of anything because of the awful things that happen without it. Horror stories abound in evaluation, anthropology, medicine, and many other contexts. We read about them daily in the media. It is significant that they come to our attention as much as they do. This was not always the case. We have learned the hard way to be vigilant about ethics in any research that involves intervention in people's lives.

The concern for justice in human research is well illustrated by the conditions surrounding the Tuskegee Syphilis Study conducted by the US Public Health Service between 1932 and 1972 in Macon County, Georgia. The researchers recruited six hundred impoverished African American men into the study to document the natural course of syphilis, telling them they were in a study of the effects of "bad blood," a folk category that included syphilis, anemia, and fatigue. The study provided the men with free medical exams, meals during exam days, and free burial insurance. Infected men were never told they had syphilis, never treated for syphilis when penicillin became the standard of treatment for the disease in 1947, nor told that such treatment was available. The research study kept participants away from syphilis treatment programs that were available to others in the area, presumably to avoid contamination of the study design.

The study finally became public when a whistle-blower alerted the press to the situation. The study was immediately terminated, but by that time many men had died of syphilis, transmitted it to their wives, and had children born with congenital syphilis, a disease that is completely preventable with penicillin. The Tuskegee Study was widely publicized after it appeared in the *Washington Star* in July 1972. It became a foundation of distrust of the public health system specifically and government more generally.[1] In 1993 I was part of a project to investigate the causes of a spike in syphilis cases in the US South in the early 1990s. Our team discovered that, twenty-one years after the suspension of the study, African Americans in three southern states still gave the Tuskegee Study as their most prominent reason for not seeking treatment for a sexually transmitted disease (CDC 1994). The Tuskegee study exacted and continues to exact a high cost to the health of a population that extends far beyond Macon County, Alabama.

ETHICAL STANDARDS FOR HUMAN RESEARCH

The basis of most ethics statements in the social sciences dates to the publication of the Belmont Report in 1979 by the National Commission for the Protection of Human Subjects of Biomedical and Behavioral Research, hereafter called the Commission. The Commission, made up of scientists, medical professionals, ethicists, and legal experts, was charged to "identify the basic ethical principles that should underlie the conduct of biomedical and behavioral research involving human subjects and to develop guidelines which should be followed to assure that such research is conducted in accordance with those principles" (National Commission 1978: 1).[2]

The Commission focused on biomedical and behavioral research partly because they were motivated by the abuses of medical research in Nazi Germany during World War II and revealed in the Nuremberg War Crimes Trials. The Nuremberg Code, drafted in connection with the trials, was specifically a set of standards for judging physicians and scientists who had conducted biomedical experiments on concentration camp prisoners. The Nuremberg Code became a prototype for ethical behavior for medical research and was extended to research involving human beings more generally. The Commission came up with three standards for ethical research with human subjects: respect for persons, beneficence, and justice.

Respect for persons specifies that ethical research must respect the autonomy of persons as the decision makers in their own lives and requires that subjects participate in research voluntarily after having been informed of the purpose of the research, what their participation will be, any benefits that will accrue to them, and adequate information about potential risks of their participation so that they can make an informed decision about whether to participate. It also calls for protection of persons who, for one reason or another, are vulnerable because they are unable to act autonomously at the time the research is conducted—children, the mentally ill, and prisoners.

Beneficence refers to extending good to people, but it goes beyond this common usage of the term to define beneficence as an obligation to do no harm to research participants, to maximize possible benefits, and minimize potential harm to them in the course of research. The consideration of beneficence in human research imposes on the researcher the responsibility of deciding when it is justifiable to seek certain benefits despite the risks involved and when the benefits should be foregone because of the risks. Even in this case the investigator can never collect any data without informed consent of study participants.

Justice means that the benefits of research should accrue to those who bear its burdens, even if there is also a benefit to the larger society. An injustice occurs when some benefit to which a person is entitled is denied without good reason or when some burden is imposed unduly. Realistically it is difficult to tell a priori what the benefits should be and who is likely to receive them. The Belmont Report proposes five formulations for the distribution of burden and benefits: (1) to each person an equal share, (2) to each person according to individual need, (3) to each person according to individual effort, (4) to each person according to societal contribution, and (5) to each person according to merit.

STORY OF ETHICS IN EVALUATION

Ethics in evaluation is concerned with confidentiality and privacy of all parties involved in an evaluation, including clients, colleagues, and people who participate in the research. It requires that participants in research give informed consent to participate in all ways that their participation will be sought—interviews, observation, and providing documents or things like blood samples. By informed consent we mean that the participants have been made aware of the reason for the research, how the data will be used and by whom, and any risks or benefits of their participation. We must seek to maintain the quality of the data so we can fairly represent our studies. We should get as close to the "truth" as possible, however we have defined that. We should never purposely misrepresent someone. And we have an ethical responsibility to those who commission our work to provide the highest quality research we are able to do.

For evaluations to be feasible at all, evaluators must build trust between themselves and stakeholders of various kinds. Evaluations depend on trust. At the level of evaluation design critical questions to be asked about stakeholders are:

- How do we know which stakeholders have been left out or are not well understood. Omitting stakeholders may lead to results in which an injustice is committed to groups of unrepresented people.
- Are there role conflicts between those participating in the study in any capacity (researcher, client, respondents, or audiences)? For example, evaluators are respected because they do good science, yet most of them are also administrators or employees of contracting firms interested in future awards (Sieber 1980).
- Whose values are served? Whose interests are served? Evaluators are stakeholders in evaluations as much as anyone else. So are the people who fund evaluations. How do we maintain scrutiny for evaluations becoming more responsive to some stakeholders than to others (Morris 2011)?
- What are the ethical risks of long-standing client-contractor relationships in government evaluation? Clients often rely on a small subset of available contractors over time. This makes technical sense, as contractors build knowledge of the client and the issues with which the client must deal. But this can be problematic if client-contractor comfort diminishes the role of other stakeholders with differing perspectives (House 1997).

The emphasis of evaluation on bringing in stakeholders of all kinds raises concern with differences in the perception of the evaluators, public officials, and populations that are to receive programs. Cultural competence is, of course, always a concern. It is an ethical as well as a technical responsibility to build and maintain the capacity to understand and encompass multicultural perspectives in evaluation (Trimble et al. 2012). But strengthening cultural competence may not tell us when we are failing to understand individual or group differences in perception.[3]

Cultural competence is not optional in evaluation. It is a requirement if we are to approach various kinds of stakeholders in a way that builds their trust. Cultural competence refers to all of the kinds of differences in the population of respondents—not only race and ethnicity but also gender, age, and residence (region, urban, rural, homeless). Ascertaining the relevant categories before developing study instruments is part of cultural competence. Finally, both evaluators and anthropologists must be sensitive to themselves as research instruments. The researcher in the field is a screen through which all data must pass. Examine your own feelings, opinions, prejudices, and anxieties about the evaluation, with an eye to identifying things that may bias your ability to hear accurately what others are saying to you.

A great deal of program evaluation is done under the auspices of the federal government. Most agencies are sincere in their desire to obtain unbiased evaluation results they can use to support program decision making. However, political positions are a key consideration when working with officials at any level of government. Programs are embedded in a matrix of past and present policies that reflect the objectives of the government structure in which they are supported, function, and are evaluated. Political positions determine what gets evaluated, how well evaluations are funded, and whether they are used or rest on someone's shelf. To evaluate programs in an even-handed way, we must develop a consciousness of the politics underlying our work. Even then, evaluations can fail explosively because of political misunderstandings (Bechar and Mero-Jaffe 2013).[4]

Finally, we must ask ourselves when we really have informed consent. Informed consent goes far beyond asking a participant for verbal consent or a signed form. The biggest issue is with the definition of informed. Do people really understand what they are being asked to do? What are the true costs, benefits, and risks of participation in the evaluation for various kinds of respondents? The evaluator tries to the best of his or her ability to understand clearly the potential barriers to truly informed consent.

Evaluation quality is also an ethical issue. What happens if you do a poor evaluation? Either a good program is shut down or a bad program is retained without being improved? Or programs that could be better miss out on feedback, even programs that are working well. Clients, staff, program recipients, and the community at large invest in our evaluations. Ethically we owe them a return on this investment. This is especially important for our immediate clients—officials in the organization or agency that has commissioned the evaluation. The people who commission and supervise evaluations very often have their job satisfaction, careers, and reputations on the line. They are dependent on evaluators. Their own supervisors are waiting—not always patiently—for results.

Advocacy in evaluation is a big question, especially in community-based evaluation. Anthropologists learn in their professional preparation to be wary of the point in field research when they are tempted to convert from an observer to a member of the society being studied. One evaluator calls advocacy, acting on the interests of stakeholders other than clients, "roughly the evaluator's equivalent of an ethnographer's 'going native'" (Mabry 2010).

As we saw in Chapter 2, there is a large group of evaluators who favor empowerment evaluation that sets out to conduct evaluation in such a way that the process improves the lives of participants in the project. There are many questions in the evaluation community about whether empowerment evaluation can be considered evaluation, as it deviates from the traditional definition of evaluation as a study of quality of some intervention. From an ethical perspective empowering one group often disempowers others. The choice of whose values to support and for whom to advocate is not clear in any absolute sense but instead relies on the judgment of the evaluator. All of these issues revolve around the justice and propriety of doing evaluations that take strong social positions.[5]

Finally, we should note that there can be no guidance for building specific ethics for specific evaluations, especially those that are ethnographic in nature. Even in the presence of established codes of ethics or ethical guidelines, the evaluator must interpret ethical codes in the light of each case, especially in ethnographic or case-study work, where issues of protecting participants may be difficult to anticipate. In the end ethical vigilance must be grounded in the context of single cases. Ethical decision making involves ethical sensitivity and judgments that go beyond individual codes to incorporate actions that are appropriate given the context of the case in question. This is one reason why it is so critical that both evaluators and anthropologists receive training in ethics that helps them build the relevant judgment.[6]

Like many things in the past decade or so, the evaluations that are undertaken often serve political agendas. To a certain extent this has always been true of evaluation, as there are always stakeholders with an interest in how the evaluation comes out. In recent years there have been more intensive political agendas than in the past among government agencies requesting evaluations. Eleanor Chelimsky, a leading evaluator and former leader of the federal Office of Management and Budget's Program Evaluation and Methodology Division, warns against the "single narrative" in evaluation. Increasingly government programs and policies embody a single idea or a simple cause-effect relationship between programs and their results that may suppress evidence or otherwise prescribe evaluations that come up with a politically acceptable answer. Choices of method may also have political consequences. Different things are likely to come out in a case-study evaluation from a quasi-experimental one (Chelimsky 2008, 2012; House 2008).

So what happens if you've completed your evaluation, and your client says thank you very much and buries it in her lowest file drawer? Or what happens if your client disavows inconvenient results, such as a finding that the program doesn't do anything? What happens if you submit your report, and five weeks later you read an article in the *New York Times* that emphasizes a minor positive finding while totally ignoring the central finding that the program needs serious redesign? Misuse of evaluation happens all the time because evaluations are conducted to support decisions about programs. However, few people are free to make decisions based solely on evaluation findings. There are always political factors in the wings. Informing decisions by considering multiple factors is not necessarily a misuse of evaluation as long as evaluation results aren't suppressed. However, misreporting, exerting pressure on the evaluation process, attempting to massage the results, and using the results in ways they were not designed to be used are misuse and in conflict with the AEA ethical standards (Stevens and Dial 1994).[7]

What can you do? Some kinds of misuses of evaluation by clients or other organizations you can't do much about. Once you turn in the report, that's it. But in your own practice you can be vigilant for pressure to adjust the evaluation process to make specific outcomes more likely, to report results in particular ways, or to skew dissemination of results in some way. There can be subtle pressures from clients to investigate particular kinds of evidence. This is legitimate if they are simply trying to improve coverage in the data collection, but ask them why they want this, what they expect it to tell them. If they can't tell you, look for political motives.

THE STORY OF ETHICS IN ANTHROPOLOGY

For any kind of research undertaken by anthropologists—or anyone else doing research with humans—protecting the interests of respondents and partners is our first obligation. This is why we are so focused on confidentiality, informed consent, and clearance. However, anthropologists are very sensitive about this because the discipline has a somewhat problematic past working as agents of various governments. In the early days of anthropology in the late 1800s and early 1900s anthropologists were often supported by governments to help them manage colonial populations, such as British anthropologists in Africa and American anthropologists for the Bureau of Indian Affairs in the United States.

Applied anthropology was invented during World War II when some of the better-known American anthropologists came out of academia to work for federal agencies as consultants to the war effort, providing guidance to the military in dealing with indigenous populations in war zones, especially in the Pacific (Eddy and Partridge 1978).[8] As part of the war effort, this work was spared the kind of ethical scrutiny it would face today. After the war these anthropologists returned to the academy. However, they left behind a concept of the role of anthropology in government work that was to have darker consequences in the decades following the War.[9]

During the early 1950s AAA cooperated clandestinely with the CIA to provide the agency with lists of anthropologists and what parts of the world they worked in without the consent of their members (Fluehr-Lobban 2003). In reading the correspondence within AAA at the time, it is striking how naïve people were around intelligence work (Price 2003). When the newly formed CIA approached AAA in 1951 with a proposal that AAA work with them to compile a roster of anthropologists and their expertise, there was very little concern within AAA about the propriety of complying with such a request. Things got even more complicated in later years as wars became more complex and politically uncertain. One of the better-known scandals in this direction was Project Camelot, a collaboration between a number of anthropologists and the CIA to compile clandestine data on counterinsurgency movements in Latin America (Fluehr-Lobban 2003). It was the reaction to Project Camelot and to projects during the Vietnam

War that motivated AAA to begin drafting stronger statements of ethics in research.

In the post 9/11 years the United States has once again become engaged in wars with peoples whose cultures they don't understand well. The military has become aware of the value of anthropologists in translating and negotiating with the native populations of war zones. In 2008 the issue of anthropologists in the military was given new impetus when the US military proposed the Human Terrain Systems (HTS) Project in Iraq and Afghanistan. The basic plan proposed that HTS teams made up of degreed social scientists who would be embedded in military units would produce cultural information on local peoples in the war areas. In 2007 a defense contractor responsible for recruiting social scientists into the HTS program circulated an advertisement for social scientists to participate in HTS teams. The circular described the role of HTS as providing "soldiers direct social science support in the form of ethnographic and social research." Needless to say, this roused considerable concern in the anthropological community, especially in light of the history of the discipline in related areas. Within days many professional associations publicly disavowed the HTS project. In 2008 AAA appointed a Commission on the Engagement of Anthropology with the US Security and Intelligence Communities (CEAUSSIC) to compile and review the HTS program and make recommendations to the association (AAA 2009). The final report of CEAUSSIC was released in December 2008 and concluded that due to its intelligence function and the lack of external review, HTS "could not be considered a legitimate professional exercise of anthropology" and was "incompatible with disciplinary ethics and practice."[10]

The HTS incident raised an issue with the proper management of research disclosure to the public that set up a collision course between ethically conservative anthropologists and the growing influence of anthropological practice within the profession. The question was one of whether all data collected by anthropologists must be made available to the public, thereby facilitating a "watch dog" policy for government research on the part of AAA. This position is an impossible one for practitioners to observe because much of the work we do is either proprietary or confidential for other reasons. The lines were drawn between those who wanted a strict ban on failure to disclose data or a more flexible process of decision making on the basis of individual situations. Part of the heat generated around this issue comes from a failure to consistently distinguish between secret, or clandestine, research and proprietary research. The purpose and results of clandestine research are hidden from everyone. Research participants—respondents but also research partners—may not know what kind of work they are doing or what will happen to it.

Clandestine research is a danger to the respect of persons required of any human research, and it runs counter to the spirit of science and scholarship that seeks to make information available to others. Clandestine data collection is not acceptable for anthropologists no matter what. However, proprietary data compiled by practitioners for clients must be kept undisclosed for commercial purposes or because revealing the data publicly would cause harm to some sectors of the population. For example, data on HIV/AIDS patients must be treated with great care because of discriminatory policies against HIV-positive individuals. Proprietary or confidential data, subjected to all of the precautions stated in ethics codes and clearances, must be accepted or else anthropologists can no longer practice within AAA. Such a rigid stand by AAA on proprietary research seems unlikely at the present time. However, it remains a tension within AAA and within anthropology more generally.

ETHICS STANDARDS AND GUIDES

Most professionals are guided by some kind of ethics code normally created and monitored by professional organizations. Ethics standards range on a continuum from strictly enforced codes to guidance that leaves the actual application of ethical principles to the professional who is using them. Professions that have licensure requirements of some kind (health professionals, social workers, lawyers) tend to have ethics codes that are binding on all licensed to practice that profession and may take action, either on their own or through governments, to interdict ethics violations.

For social sciences and humanities, disciplines with a significant academic component, professional ethics statements focus on helping professionals make informed decisions about ethical issues. However, the decisions themselves are made by professionals and rely on professional judgment. They are usually called guidelines in recognition that ethical behavior always involves some judgment about what is acceptable in social research.

In evaluation and in anthropology the conditions that affect research are difficult to identify in advance. There is no way that all contingencies that affect our work can be anticipated. Some events that we think may be substantial problems never appear. More commonly, things we didn't think about appear and need to be addressed during the course of research. All of this means that the protection of the interests of people in evaluation depends heavily on researchers' vigilance and judgment. Ethics codes are designed to help us identify likely issues and to plan ahead of time so as to avoid violations of people's rights, their privacy, and their short- and long-range interests. We are obliged to become knowledgeable about ethics codes that guide our own professions and related ones in which we work. For those of us who evaluate, this includes the ethics codes governing evaluation as well as those that are promulgated in our own professional organizations.

For social sciences the following issues seem to be addressed by all ethics statements in some way.

- Technical adequacy—It is not ethical to attempt to practice a profession (or to do science) without an acceptable level of technical rigor. Do the best professional job you can. Stay current in your profession and grow in competence.
- Honesty and integrity—Don't falsify anything—ever. Disclose information about your research as appropriate. Insofar as possible, try to guard against misuse of research.
- Respect the people you study and/or evaluate. Be a conscientious protector of their rights and interests. Keep promises to them about confidentiality and data protection. Obtain all necessary human subjects' clearances.
- The common good—Insofar as is possible, use the tools and practice of your discipline to improve the amount of good in the world and diminish the amount of bad. Be conscious of the social and political implications of what you do, and act especially to minimize harm.
- Teach conscientiously and inculcate professional ethics and standards into students and others who rely on you for guidance, and don't steal the labor or ideas of your students or colleagues. Give credit where credit is due.

Table 5.1 summarizes the relevant parts of ethics statements: the Guiding Principles from the American Evaluation Association, the Code of Ethics of the American Anthropological Association, and the statement of Ethical and Professional Responsibilities of the Society for Applied Anthropology. Each of them cover the same basic ideas, but they differ in their emphasis because of the different issues in their professions. Evaluators work in areas

Table 5.1 Common Themes in Ethical Codes for Evaluation and Anthropology

	American Evaluation Association	American Anthropological Association	Society for Applied Anthropology
Technical adequacy	Emphasized. Deliver technical quality; communicate evaluations accurately; practice within your competence.	Implied but vague; be responsible for accuracy of reported work; maintain integrity in research.	Accurate reporting of our competencies; report research accurately; attempt to avoid misuse of our work.
Honesty and Integrity	Honesty to clients; reveal conflicts of interest; present results honestly.	Honor the moral rules of scientific and scholarly conduct; don't cheat, falsify results, etc.	Implied throughout but not explicitly discussed.
Respect for People	Emphasized. Includes all persons involved in evaluation, defined as stakeholders.	Emphasized. Do no harm; respect well-being; consult to establish a working partnership with research community. Determine in advance whether groups or individuals want anonymity or recognition. Honor their request. Informed consent depends on nature or project.	Full disclosure of research. Only voluntary participation; maintain confidentiality; advise people of likely limits of confidentiality. No specific mention of informed consent.
The Common Good	Serve diversity of public interest; disseminate results; maintain a balance between client and other needs.	Disseminate research whenever possible; be candid about biases; explicitly endorses advocacy.	Do not recommend action harmful to interests of community studied; very vague on society as a whole.
Teach Responsibly	Not explicitly mentioned	Teach well and sensitively; teach ethics; give students acknowledgment for their work.	Teach well; orient to needs of larger society; teach ethics; acknowledge student work.

that affect decision making and the welfare of populations of people. Thus, AEA focuses on technical adequacy and honesty of evaluation as well as on the interests of stakeholders. Only stakeholders are mentioned in the AEA section on Respect for Persons. The AAA code of ethics reflects the academic nature of the association and emphasizes the highly variable application of anthropological methods in field situations around the world and on the quality of academic endeavors. SfAA serves applied anthropologists and is phrased in terms of the responsibilities of practitioners to the wide communities of people who may be affected by their actions. All of them are phrased as guidance or principles. None of these associations assumes responsibility to arbitrate ethical problems or impose sanctions on ethical violations.

Ethics are dynamic and changing constantly as modes of human research change. Ethics codes—and revisions of ethics codes—uncover emergent issues that develop as the conditions of research change. New kinds of research in multimedia and social media brings forward unprecedented ethical challenges on a continuing basis.[11]

DILEMMAS IN ETHICAL DISCUSSION

There is a much debate on where the line lies between ethics and morals and how each of these concepts is defined and used. Some people think ethics are group standards of behavior. Others consider them to be an internal guide to behavior. And there is abundant discussion of the implications of personal ethics on a wide variety of social problems. I have chosen to leave this discussion to the philosophers. Personal ethics is an individual matter and, although it influences our professional activity, is beyond the scope of this discussion. In this chapter we are not talking about personal ethics but rather professional ethics.

Personal ethics are important to the living of our lives. And they support professional ethics. But professional ethics are *not* common sense. It requires training, experience, and judgment to make ethical decisions about what we will do and not do in designing a scientific study that depends on people to reveal things about their professional activities, jobs, welfare, and lives. Some argue that ethical responsibility extends beyond doing no harm to doing as much good as we can. But what is good and to whom can be quite complex.

After a while in any profession people develop a sense of ethics so that obviously unethical things are readily detected. This is a reasonable expectation as one acquires experience in ethical review and ethical decisions. However, one can develop more ethical certainty than is justified. Most unethical things are not things people chose to do; they are mistakes that occur because the investigator didn't think of something. When it comes to ethics, don't trust your instincts. Always have proposals, research protocols, analysis plans, and reports reviewed by colleagues for ethical soundness . The more eyes, the better.

Responsibility for ethical soundness of social research belongs to all those who participate in one way or another in our research and evaluation projects. The principal investigator obviously has lead responsibility to ensure that ethics are served in all steps of the work. However, all members of the research team, including programmers and data managers, have a role in protecting privacy, confidentiality, and data quality. Research participants, such as program directors or staff, who are responsible for connecting the evaluator with their own colleagues or clients must also be aware of their obligation to be clear about the evaluation, to ensure confidentiality of all participants, and to avoid using even indirect coercion to motivate people to participate.

There has been much discussion over the past decade in both evaluation and anthropology about the obligation to not only to do no harm but to go beyond that to do good. This trend developed with postmodernism with its focus on the loci of power and its effects on the powerless (Foucault 1994). Both evaluators and anthropologists very often deal directly or indirectly with poor and disadvantaged people and the programs and activities that serve them. What does our understanding of ethical principles and behavior tell us about whether and how we should build the welfare of the powerless into our work? In evaluation this dilemma has appeared in connection with empowerment evaluation (Fetterman 2001), responsive evaluation (Stake 1995), and deliberative democratic evaluation (House and Howe 1999). All of these evaluations are designed to bring in program recipients as stakeholders and as participants in designing, implementing, and reporting evaluations that are expected to affect them. These kinds of evaluations confront us with decisions about our own values and our position on advocacy in evaluation.

It is a characteristic of the human being as research instrument to make our interpretations of what is going on an intrinsic part of our thinking about everything, including our research results. There is no way for us even to pretend to conduct "objective" observation. In this sense our emotions and persuasions about research topics are part of how we see and interpret our data. Pretending to be objective has been a scourge to scientific approaches to human activities for a very long time. Anthropologists have known this since the days of Bronislaw Malinowski in the early twentieth century. Evaluators began to question this perspective in the early 1980s with the development of naturalist approaches that seek to ground the evaluation in the perceptions of the evaluated. I agree that inclinations toward particular points of view are present in all of us who have chosen to study people for a living; the best we can do is to be vigilant for our own viewpoints and honest in acknowledging them. There is no problem with personal opinions. We can make our positions around issues explicit, and conduct our work so that we try to find as many kinds of stakeholders as we can and include all of their opinions in our results.

Opinions about the role of advocacy in evaluation range across a continuum, from the traditional view of evaluators as objective observers and reporters to those who believe there is a moral obligation to do what we can do to improve the lives of those with little power in the political system. At the positivist end of the continuum are those who believe that any opinion about the context of the evaluation detracts from its scientific quality and introduces bias into the results. Others hold that advocacy is at least intrinsic to all evaluations in the sense that we always must choose whose perspectives to seek in our implementations and the weight we give to the assertions of various stakeholders. For example, Jennifer Greene (1997) argues for advocacy as an absence of value neutrality—that is, a specific value commitment to an idea or alignment with a group of stakeholders. Evaluators should be aware of and honest about their own value commitments rather than assuming a position of impartiality. Adoption of a value position does not necessarily imply endorsement of programs espousing that value; programs themselves may be good, bad, or indifferent without regard to the values that the program holds.

CLEARANCES

When you conduct research on human beings, there will almost always be clearances of one kind or another from institutions charged with overseeing such research. Clearances are reviews of research plans that are required before the research can be authorized in order to check for conditions that might imperil human protections, regulations, and laws controlling the collection and dissemination of information. The specific clearances you will need depend on the kind of work you are doing and on your clients' requirements. When I first began practicing anthropology as an evaluator, I was unaware of some of these requirements. My education in clearance requirements was a trial-and-error process. I would like it to be easier for you.

However, if you are a principal investigator or a project director, it is your responsibility to discover and comply with clearance requirements. This involves careful review of all agreements to conduct work—grants, contracts, internal funding—so as to ascertain what clearances are required and to investigate the process for obtaining them.

INSTITUTIONAL REVIEW BOARDS (IRBS)

IRBs are a special case of human subjects protection—a subset of ethics. They are standing committees made up of researchers and human rights leaders who review and modify protocols for research involving human subjects in order to protect subjects' basic rights. IRB clearance is required for most social research, including evaluation. IRBs are maintained by large research organizations, hospitals, and universities. There are also private IRBs that can do this review for a fee.

It is the responsibility of IRBs to determine whether the project is research—that is, if it collects data meant to be generalizable. If it is research, the IRB determines whether it meets the above criteria of respect for persons, beneficence, and justice. If not, they require changes to bring the research into compliance. IRBs are required by law for any federally funded study.

IRBs define research as an activity designed primarily to obtain knowledge that will then be used to generalize to other settings or things. It is distinguished from collecting knowledge about how to do anything other than generalize. IRB clearance is applied (1) if data are to be collected directly from humans in any way, and (2) if the project falls under the rubric of research (i.e., is intended to generalize).[13] However, you cannot make the decision about whether your project requires IRB clearance; it must be made by an IRB.

IRBs require from researchers:

- A procedure for informed consent that is noncoercive and provides enough information in a clear enough way for the prospective study subject to make a decision on whether or not to participate. No attempt should ever be made to convince or persuade someone to participate.
- A method for ensuring confidentiality of data consistent with the study design. Always collect as little identifying data as absolutely essential for your project. For example, if you need to follow up with the same people, you will need a way to do that. Even here, minimize inclusion of identifying information in the data base.[14]
- A scientific method that is technically sound and rigorous enough to provide data of benefit to someone that is worth at least as much as the risk to respondents.

- Confidentiality protection procedures—these are very important to IRBs. They want to know how the data will be collected, analyzed, and managed to protect the identity of individuals. Disclosure of what you are told, of your informant's identity, even of the fact that someone participated in a project can have consequences for their personal privacy, social position, job, and age, and the disclosure may harm them in ways you didn't think of. The only protection people have from such consequences is scrupulous protection of their confidentiality.

IRBs usually want some kind of justification for the data you plan to collect. It is a good idea to always collect as little personal information as possible—only what is needed for the purpose of your study. Even in this case you need to protect personal information of any kind because sometimes information that you must have to interpret the data may be enough to identify a person if disclosed. For example, in evaluation you almost always need to know the person's occupation or position. In the small world that most businesses and agencies inhabit, this will frequently identify people. So you also need to be really careful about how you report data.

Compliance with IRB is deadly serious for those who do human research. One reason is that most IRBs have a Multiple Project Assurance (MRP), which means that the federal Office of Human Research Protection (OHRP) allows the IRB to review projects free of oversight from OHRP as long as they subject their IRB to periodic review and recertification. If you lose this MPA status, you need to individually clear every single project you do through OHRP. This takes a lot of paperwork and a long time, and it is costly for everyone concerned. Because it is such a hassle, IRBs are very conservative in what they require in terms of review. Many research organizations require IRB sign-off on every single project, even if it has no human subjects. This is extreme, though not uncommon.

Everyone has specific IRB requirements, and you need to check out the requirements for the organization or organizations with which you will be working.[12] Most university IRBs review faculty and staff research, but for student research they require IRB review only for projects limited to reviewing proposed research that will lead to publication. But remember that you cannot decide whether your project requires IRB review and clearance. Regardless whether you are faculty, staff, or student, you must submit your proposed project to the IRB for this determination. I would check with the IRB of your institution if in doubt.

OMB CLEARANCE

We cannot leave this topic without considering clearance of federally funded research by the federal Office of Management and Budget (OMB). The Paperwork Reduction Act of 1982 mandates that all data collection *funded directly or indirectly by the federal government* must go through an OMB clearance process if the same questions will be asked of more than nine people. The definition of "the same questions" is up for debate and is usually decided by the administration of the agency seeking the data collection or by OMB reviewers. The purpose of this law is to ensure that the government does no frivolous, unnecessary, or duplicative data collection from the public. So data collection plans are reviewed for quality and likely value of the data.

The OMB requirement was quite a shock to me when I first began doing evaluations under contract with the federal government. I was familiar with IRB requirements because I had done research in university settings. The reason that this matters to us is that any data collection undertaken under contract with the federal government falls under this regulation. Contractors collect data as agents of the government. You may never need to do a government clearance, but to be an evaluator, you should be aware of them. You don't need to figure out how to do it ahead of time, but at least if it comes across your desk, you will have heard of it.

OMB clearance is a very tedious process. Although it is the agency (government) that bears the responsibility to obtain the clearance, preparation of an OMB clearance package is technically complex, as it must demonstrate the quality of the data. The government normally assigns this work to contractors, who in turn assign it to the most junior technical staff available. So if you get a job with a company that contracts with the federal government, you may become more expert than you ever wanted to be on OMB clearance requirements. Good luck!

CHAPTER SIX

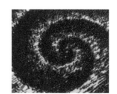

METHOD IN EVALUATION ANTHROPOLOGY

So you've got an evaluation to do. Now what? To become a professional at anything, you need to learn something about the background, vocabulary, and definitions in your field, but there comes a point when you need some concrete guidance on precisely what to do.

In this chapter I will give you some advice on how to build an evaluation. As you should have deduced by now, there are a lot of different ways to evaluate, a lot of different goals and objectives, evaluation purposes and designs. I have given you the way I have done evaluation over the past twenty-five years. It is not the only way to do it. In my experience most program evaluations follow roughly the same process in getting the evaluation up and running and producing results, conclusions, and recommendations, although their objectives, scope, and the methodologies used will, of course, vary. You will undoubtedly develop many of your own ways of doing things, if you haven't already.[1]

Before proceeding with this discussion of method, I would like to point out an important difference between evaluation methodology and that set of methods that drives more open ethnographic approaches. In our training as ethnographers, especially as anthropological ethnographers, we were told that we should look as holistically as possible at our ethnographic inquiries; in fact, this openness is one of the great strengths of ethnography, however it is used. But we must discipline the investigation when it is done as evaluation. Evaluations are done for a reason, to achieve a purpose. They demand focus on a finite set of evaluation questions.

This does not mean that your ethnographic evaluation must be deductive in concept or analysis design. Many evaluators use grounded theory, for example, in which hypotheses are allowed to emerge from the data themselves. It does mean that—inductive or deductive—evaluations must focus on a specific topic. If you are commissioned to evaluate tobacco-use prevention in an American Indian population, you cannot allow yourself to be drawn

Evaluation: A Cultural Systems Approach, by Mary Odell Butler, 115–156. © 2015 Left Coast Press, Inc. All rights reserved.

into a study of religious ritual or kinship unless these affect tobacco use and its prevention. If you do this, you may be doing something interesting, but it is not evaluation.

A FRAMEWORK FOR EVALUATION

Evaluations done under contract are costly both economically and politically. And as you should suspect by now, there are many different ways to think about evaluation. For this reason it is best to have in mind a generic framework that you adapt to specific projects. I have come up with an evaluation framework to structure this chapter. The precise methods, tips, cautions, and approaches to completing an evaluation come largely from my own experience (and my own mistakes!). I have presented a schematic framework for envisioning the steps in an evaluation in Figure 6.1. Please do not accept this as canonical in any way; you will develop your own styles of doing this as you gain experience. This is one way to organize program evaluation in such a way that you include everything that is needed.[2]

The evaluation begins when someone (the "client") has a need for evaluation in order to act on some program, product, or project (the "evaluand").[3] Should this program be initiated? Is this product ready for market as designed,

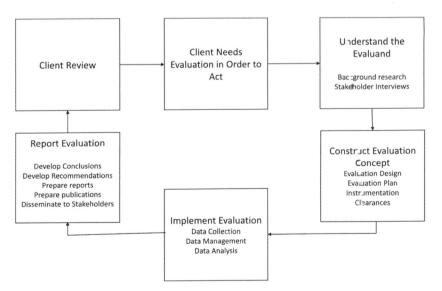

Figure 6.1 A Schematic Evaluation Framework

or does it need to be changed in some way? Are these projects achieving what the donor organization envisions in funding this program? The point is that someone has requested an evaluation to be used for some purpose. The first step when you undertake an evaluation is to describe the evaluand in as much detail as possible from documents and interviews with people who are connected to the evaluand in some way—as funder, operator, recipient group. Based on the information you compile during this step, you can move on to design and plan the evaluation. You then implement the evaluation plan and develop conclusions and recommendations based on the evidence you have compiled. You report the evaluation to the client, who then acts in a way that is informed by what the evaluation has discovered.

There are many specific models that are part of the evaluation literature and used to identify stakeholders and evaluation questions or even to specify the evaluation concept. For example, the RE-AIM model is often used in public health evaluations to determine the degree to which multilevel interventions (system, community, clinic, individual) interact to demonstrate program impact.[4] I have usually found these models redundant in light of what the client and the other stakeholders tell me about the program. However, they do provide an orientation that is sometimes useful and has the indubitable advantage of already being accepted by the client.

There are also guidance documents developed by government agencies and academic evaluators, laying out models they have used to guide evaluations. When you begin an evaluation, you should check with your client about whether there is any model they especially like. You don't necessarily have to use their source, but it is good to know what it is and to see whether there is any significant difference in what you think and what your client thinks an evaluation is. If you are doing the evaluation based on a research proposal that you yourself prepared, the client's idea of what an evaluation should look like is at least implicit in their request for proposals. If you have not responded to a request for proposals, then your first evaluation task is to investigate the issue of evaluation approaches with the client.

UNDERSTAND THE EVALUAND

Many evaluators try to begin with evaluation design. This is seldom the best way. When you start an evaluation, you do not know what the most appropriate design will be, even if you wrote it up in a proposal in great detail. People in government agencies or private organizations are people in need of an evaluation, but they are seldom evaluators themselves. They have a pretty good idea of what they want to have at the end of the evaluation but may not be sure how to get there. The evaluation method they have chosen to request may not be the best one. To help all of you come up with the best way to do the evaluation, you as evaluator need to get as smart as you can about the evaluand (program, policy, product) and the reason why this particular evaluation is being undertaken at this time.

There are two reasons why you should begin with this step and continue working on it throughout the evaluation. First of all, you probably don't understand the evaluand, the kinds of actions and people who are part of it, and the evaluation needs of all parties to the evaluation. You need to be familiar with the design, the goals, and the current state of the evaluand to identify the right evaluation approach. Secondly, in many evaluations this is an opportunity to establish the baseline description of the evaluand before you begin.

ENGAGE STAKEHOLDERS

One of the first activities in your evaluation will be to identify and interview stakeholders. A stakeholder is someone or some organization that has an interest—or "stake"—in the outcome of the evaluation. Stakeholders can make or break an evaluation and its subsequent use if not properly incorporated in the evaluation project.

Normally you will be doing the evaluation for someone else who is funding it. The client is the first stakeholder you will talk to. By definition, they are the primary stakeholder because they initiated the whole process. The first job is to determine what the evaluation must do from the point of view of the client. You interview your client and read any relevant information that the client suggests. You should ask the client questions like:

- Why are you doing this evaluation, and how will you use the results? Why at this time? The answers to these questions will tell you a lot about the stakes in the evaluation in the client organization. And they will tell you if some special problem or some new deadline led to the need for the evaluation.
- What do you expect to learn from it? Clients have unspoken ideas about what they hope to achieve with the evaluation. This has a big effect on evaluation design. Try to engage them in enough of a conversation about expectations so you are likely to uncover unexpressed needs.

- Are there critical timelines that must be met for this evaluation to be most useful to you? Does the client have a reporting requirement, a production schedule, or a national meeting for which they need the evaluation results?
- Do you know of any political problems that may affect the evaluation? What are they? This tells you about the political value of the evaluated activities and the evaluation itself. You need to make sure you include input from those who are resistant to the evaluation or the program. The earlier you find this out, the better.
- What kinds of people do you think will be affected by the evaluation? Can you suggest any people we should talk to before committing to an evaluation design?

You should leave this meeting with a pretty good idea of what you need to know to begin an evaluation design. Sometimes these will be meetings with one or more individuals; sometimes they will be group meetings. If everyone in the client organization shows up for a start-up meeting, the chances are good that the evaluation is politically important in some way.

You can—and sometimes must—do these meetings as teleconferences. However, face-to-face meetings are much better because, for anthropologists at least, a great deal of information can be gained from nonverbal cues. Allow at least an hour for one of these meetings. Two hours is better, especially if it is a group meeting.

After the start up meeting, you may want to talk to a limited number of other stakeholders to figure out what the program is, how it operates, what the client needs to know about it, who important stakeholders are, and special perspectives expected from this stakeholder.

FINDING STAKEHOLDERS

You identify other stakeholders by networking out from the client or other primary contact for the evaluation. Usually you begin with the most central people and network from there. Ask them for contacts; ask their contacts for contacts. In assembling stakeholders you also need to come in from the periphery. Try to find people who are outside of the program but should logically be stakeholders. Or people who used to be involved and no longer are. These people will give you an entirely different point of view than you get from insiders. How far you go in finding stakeholders depends on the complexity of the problem you are examining and the scope of the evaluation. I usually stop looking for stakeholders when I am no longer getting new information. Sometimes this may happen after two people; other times it may take a dozen or more.

If you fail to incorporate all of the right stakeholders, you may get an incomplete and biased view of the program. You can miss large pieces of relevant data because you don't know they are there. There is no perfect way to guarantee against missing stakeholders, although certainly you should incorporate any who appear after the evaluation starts. As the evaluation proceeds you may see gaps in the data indicative of a missing data source. Ask yourself whether there is someone who might be able to tell you something about them. For example, if you find that no one is quite sure how a program is delivered to a part of the recipient population, it might be good to find the person who is supposed to be delivering it to these people.

No matter what you do, sometimes you miss something. If it's something important, it usually shows up in the later stages of your project. For example, you may discover that a community organization delivering a program is supported by the Chamber of Commerce and is eager to deliver to the sponsoring organization what it wants. When that happens, follow it out and at least interview newly discovered stakeholders.

Advisory panels are a special stakeholder encounter, often a very useful one. Some government agencies and some private funders mandate use of advisory panels; other times you might suggest it. Advisory panels bring together a number of stakeholders from different perspectives, program implementers, implementers of similar programs, recipients, or professionals. They can be very helpful, especially if their involvement in the evaluation project is current and ongoing.

An expert panel is a group of subject matter experts gathered for a specific reason. In evaluation they usually serve to refine needs, make concrete solutions, and ensure buy-in from clients. They are costly and usually only meet once, then dissolve. Experts are important if you are doing a project that is technical in some way and/or politically charged. Experts can explain the background problem to you, develop the right questions, and bring buy-in from key policy makers. They add a lot of credibility to evaluations and are often well worth what they cost. Experts should usually be used in a review capacity—helping refine the problem, revising instruments, and helping craft conclusions and recommendations. It's best if they can provide ongoing support to the various stages of the project. If possible, you should identify them at the beginning of the evaluation.

EVALUABILITY ASSESSMENT?

Sometimes, after you complete your stakeholder interviews, you find that it will be difficult to impossible to evaluate the program at this time. An *evaluability assessment* may be done when you find yourself in this situation. I can think of five situations that may show up in preparation for an evaluation and call for an evaluability assessment:

- You find out that the program's goals are unrealistic because there are inadequate resources to do what the program hopes to do.
- Administrators don't know how to achieve the program's goals/objectives.
- Data needed to assess the fit of outcomes to program theory are either unavailable or not feasible to obtain.
- You find that the program has not been sufficiently implemented to have outcomes, and there are no concrete plans to do so in the short run.
- Policy makers cannot—or will not—use evaluation to make changes.

Evaluability assessments seek the information needed to determine whether an evaluation can or should be done. Very often it tries to determine whether the value added by evaluation is likely to be worth the funds spent on it. Evaluability assessment is an evaluation in itself and usually a whole project. Sometimes program staff request one of these after an initial year of a program or when they need to know how to build an evaluation plan for the program. It is common to do an evaluability assessment as the first step in an evaluation agenda (a series of increasingly specific evaluations) for a large program that will end with an outcome evaluation.

For example, an evaluability assessment may be done if a program has been operating for twenty years, and now someone wants to know whether it's working as it should. In government programs "someone" is often Congress. In nongovernment programs it is usually some kind of funder of the board of trustees. In any event, it has important consequences for the program and must be done with the same care as any other evaluation.

Sometimes you may be asked to compare the program activities and achievements to the program theory. *Program theory* is the way program developers thought the program would achieve its objectives, how it would work, and what population it was to reach. In this kind of evaluation your job is to look at the program theory, assess the theory against the actual operation of the program, and make recommendations about what needs to happen to revise the program theory so it can achieve better results, bring the actual operation of the program into better alignment with the theory, or change program operations so that it can be evaluated at a later time. Things you can do to determine whether you can do an evaluation and how you can do it are (1) review a limited amount of research literature to see what works with similar problems, (2) read program documents describing what the program is supposed to do and how, and/or (3) conduct a limited number of individual or group interviews with program staff, clients, or other stakeholders.

Program documents are a good place to look for program theory. Most of the time the program theory is written down at the time the program concept is developed, or it may be incorporated in legislation if there is a legislative mandate. In start-up meetings for evaluations program staff are usually eager to load you down with documents. Review these in light of why they were created. If they are progress reports to funders or attempts to leverage support, for example, they are designed to sell the program. This may give you a biased version of the how well the program is doing. Similarly, if the report shows that the program is breaking down, people may want to know what happened before they take the program back to the drawing board. In this case the program's real achievements can be obscured because people become preoccupied with failures. Accept information from program documents as one source among many.

Look for evaluations of similar programs—programs that are similarly designed to reach similar populations with similar services. For example, successful substance abuse prevention programs directed to minority youth have some characteristics in common. Look for these. You don't need to do an exhaustive literature review for an evaluability assessment; your search should be focused around specific criteria and should cover no more than the past five years.

DESCRIBE THE PROGRAM: LOGIC MODELS

This is a second preliminary step to be completed. It involves developing a program theory or concept that will form the infrastructure on which you will build an evaluation design. It is essential to understand this clearly if the evaluation design is to be properly directed to the critical elements of the program. What you are doing here is developing as full a description as you can of what the program is and how it is intended to work. This may be the original program design as written in the program documents. It may be the information you gain in the initial stakeholder interviews of how they believe the program operates to achieve its goals and objectives. More likely it will be a combination of these and any other information you can glean to help you understand the program concept.

Program theory is a detailed description of the relationship between program resources, services, activities, and outcomes. It is the idea of how the program should operate in the minds of those who developed it. It may be explicit, as, for example, when it has a legislative mandate, or it may be implicit and needs to be reconstructed from the participants in the program.

Program theories are often built on a logic model, a structure or map of how the program is intended to operate to achieve its goals. The program logic model maps the set of cause-and-effect relationships that the program developers and implementers believe links the program activities to anticipated program outcomes. A program logic model is a map that visually depicts the program theory that links the program input to the program results. Here is an example of a generic program logic model.

Other times logic models may be more complex. The following is a logic model that governed a three-year multi-million-dollar evaluation of a CDC program to evaluate compliance with CDC STD screening guidelines by primary care providers of HIV-positive men who have sex with men (MSM). The evaluation was focused on the quality of communication between provider

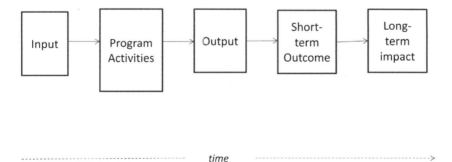

Figure 6.2 **Generic Logic Model**

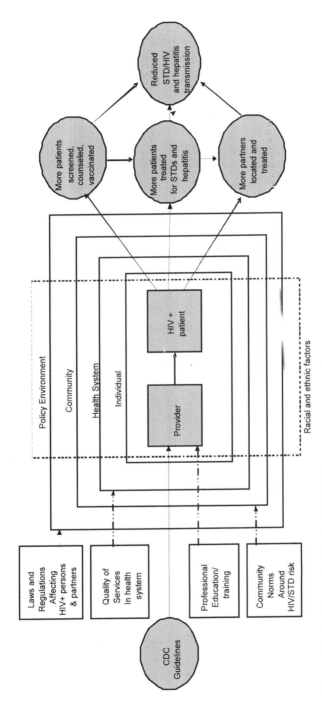

Figure 6.3 An Example of a Logic Model

and patient around risk factors for transmission of sexually transmitted diseases. This example embeds the core interaction the evaluation considers—the transfer of information between provider and patient—in four levels of context considered important to the effectiveness of this program. The outcomes on the right side are the outcomes that the initiative hoped to achieve. (Hoover et al. 2010. Safran et al. 2013)

You do not absolutely need to build a logic model to do an evaluation. It is a useful map to make sure you have everything included, and the verification of logic models by stakeholders is a good test of your understanding of the evaluand. However, some evaluations don't use logic models and test findings against a priori criteria of success, hypotheses about how the evaluand works, or even external models of what attributes a successful evaluand will demonstrate. The RE-AIM model described above is one example of this kind of assessment. However the findings are to be interpreted, it is important to verify that your evaluation design is done in such a way that your findings will be testable against something.

Getting the logic model right is a big job. There needs to be empirical investigation of the program before you do the logic model. And you work with stakeholders to review drafts of the logic model until the stakeholders agree that this is how the program is supposed to work.

The reason that working out a logic model in close consultation with program developers and staff is so important is that stakeholders do not necessarily understand how the program is supposed to work. Flawed program theory is a major cause of program failure. Building a logic model will help you to pick up these kinds of situations.

Another consideration at this stage in the evaluation is to look for breakdowns in program theory. These disconnects are a source of program failure and are often behind situations in which different kinds of stakeholders are working against each other because they are trying to do different things. Places to look for breakdowns in program theory:

- The program logic doesn't hang together. There are disconnects. For example, a program to correct adolescent behavior that doesn't specify how to reach adolescents.
- The assumptions are incorrect. For example, juvenile crime prevention programs based on a curfew assume that the teenagers who are likely to be a problem will comply with the law. The program is likely to reach those teens whose behavior isn't a problem.

- The program's objectives are not feasible given the available time and resources. For example, a program to prevent teen pregnancy with an after-school program for sixteen-year-olds by urging abstinence is likely to require more out-of-class counseling than most schools can afford.
- The program logic model is too nonspecific to assess because you can't get a clear idea what it is trying to do. For example a program to reduce heart disease by encouraging people to exercise and eat healthy may not be evaluable unless measurable outcomes of some kind are specified. To design such a program, you would need more precise information on *how* they plan to do this and what they expect to happen as a result.

FOCUS THE EVALUATION DESIGN

At last you know enough to design your evaluation. The primary requirement in evaluation design is to assure ahead of time that the data you collect with be systematically solicited in such a way that they can be used to build evidence. If your evaluation does not produce credible evidence for your findings, the evaluation itself will not be credible.

Evidence means simply that you have collected data from all sources in an unbiased way, that you have analyzed all of the data into findings, and that conclusions are derived from findings in a way that can be seen by anyone who tries to reconstruct your results. To do this you need to build evidence onto the evaluation design up front. When the analysis begins, it is too late to do this work.

One way to link evaluation features to ensure that evidence can be deduced from the evaluation process is illustrated in Figure 6.4. The logic model lays out the components and processes that are expected to occur if the evaluand is effective. Evaluation questions are derived directly from the logic model by examining each link in the logic model and asking what would need to happen for this linkage to function effectively. These questions are incorporated into the instruments that are to guide data collection and are answered in data analysis to produce findings. The findings are then compared to the logic model to determine which functional linkages appear as expected, what alternative ways have people found to accommodate these functions, which functional linkages don't work at all, and whether the logic model needs to be revised to reflect the evaluand as it is understood postevaluation.

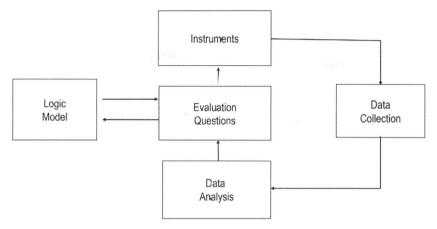

Figure 6.4 Building Evidence in Ethnographic Evaluation

THE EVALUATION QUESTION (S)—
WHAT IT IS AND HOW TO FIND IT

The evaluation question is the crux of evaluation design and one that people for some reason seem to find the most difficult. As an evaluator, you will spend a lot of time struggling with yourself, your team, and your clients to define one clear question that contains what they want to know. It is what the evaluation is about, the topic that will orient everything else.[5]

An evaluation question specifies what it is you need to know at the end of the evaluation. It is best if you can get it down to one question. For example:

> How has the XXX Outreach Program affected the use of ESOL classes by members of the immigrant community?

For more complex evaluations you may need more than one. For the MSM study referred to above, we had three:

- Determine the extent to which the specific recommendations from the national guidelines are being integrated into public and private clinics that provide ongoing care to HIV-positive persons with an MSM risk factor.
- Identify the facilitators and barriers to adhering to specific recommendations in the 2003 national guidelines as part of routine HIV clinical services for MSM at each clinic.

Table 6.1 Evaluation Questions and Sub-Questions

Overall Evaluation Question:	Is the population receiving Program A showing improved knowledge, attitudes and behaviors as envisioned in the design of Program A?

Evaluation Sub-Questions:

Are the people who the program aims to reach aware of and participating in program activities?

Are members of the population defined above aware of Program A? Were their impressions of the program accurate?

Do members of the target population believe in the importance of the health problem that it targets? What is their opinion of how likely the program is to be successful?

Do participants in Program A display the knowledge, attitudes and behaviors that Program A hopes to produce?

Do participants in Program A show different health behaviors than others of their group in the general population?

- Identify systems-level "lessons learned" at each clinic that may help to improve delivery of the recommended services to their patients.

These "big" questions then have subquestions defined for each. The subquestions in turn define what specific topics must be included in instruments.

Table 6.1 shows an evaluation question (with subquestions) that was used to develop instruments for one of the evaluation questions in the MSM study diagrammed above.

THE EVALUATION PLAN

In doing evaluations with multiple players it's very important to have a written evaluation plan to keep everyone on the same page. An evaluation plan is not the same thing as the evaluation design.[6] The evaluation design lays out the logic and the scientific and technical requirements of the evaluation; an evaluation plan is a document specifying what will happen in the evaluation and normally cannot be completed until the technical requirements of the evaluation design are known. It is shared by all members of the evaluation team and with important stakeholders, most especially the person or organization that has commissioned the evaluation. The evaluation plan is the central guide for everyone involved in the project. It should have the following elements:

- A statement of the purpose of the evaluation. Why is it being done, and for whom? If you know, say what the evaluation will be used for.
- A description of the program in as much depth as is needed. You may express this as a narrative or as a program logic model or both. The important thing is to understand what the thing being evaluated is trying to do and how.
- An evaluation question and subquestions. What is the main question or questions the evaluation will address? Subquestions are specific items or inquiries needed to fully address the main question or questions.
- A narrative of evaluation activities (evaluation plan), specifying data collection plans, analysis plans, and any other description of what will be done during the evaluation. How will the evaluation be done? What data collection methods will be used? How will the data be analyzed? How will conclusions be developed?
- Instruments to be developed for each data source—interview guides, surveys, focus group guides, abstraction guides for documents.
- Necessary appendices—management tools (task flow diagrams, project staffing charts, schedules for project activities), informed consent, site-visit procedures, literature reviews.

The first two components of your evaluation plan come from your work in the first two steps of the process. You have talked to stakeholders and built a description of the program. These should be summarized and included in the evaluation plan. You probably will have done a literature review by now. I don't usually put these in the evaluation plan itself; the plan should be limited to things directly relevant to the evaluation. The literature review will reappear in your final report. For now either hold it or put it in an appendix it if you think members of your team will want it for reference.

Build into the evaluation plan measures to support staff during data collection site visits. Do not assume that you yourself will have consistency across time and across multiple site visits unless you take steps to manage it. You can do this with a site-visit plan, a written summary of site-visit procedures that is carried into the field by all researchers and consulted on a daily basis. A site-visit plan is similar to an evaluation plan but focuses exclusively on the site visit. It should include site-visit procedures, procedures for managing deviations and emergencies, and how data should be managed in the field. Appendicize all instruments, informed consents, and so forth. Add other convenient things—contact information for people in each site, maps with interview sites. Compile it so it can be carried in the field.

You will need to train people to use the site visit plan—don't just throw it at them. First of all, you probably haven't anticipated every point. Some things will improve as a result of training. Also, everyone will leave on the same page. I use role playing in doing this kind of training. Usually it is done in a half-day meeting of all members of the evaluation team.

TOOLS FOR EVALUATION PLANNING

When pulling together an evaluation plan, there are some tools that are very useful because they help you visualize everything and assemble a lot of information in one place. By mapping the whole evaluation in your mind (and on paper!) beforehand you can avoid a lot of costly and frustrating missteps.

One of the useful tools to include in the evaluation plan is a picture of a program logic model. Another tool to help you manage ongoing activities is a task structure map. Task structures are a list of steps in doing an evaluation. Figure 6.5 shows a task structure map that defines the basic components of evaluation activities. There are two important things about these. First of all, they show clearly what activities should be completed in what order and which ones are dependent on the completion of prior ones. Secondly, they show which things feed each other and must be—at least partially—done at the same time.

- Task 1: Stakeholder meetings. Meet with people and figure out what the evaluation is going to be about.
- Task 2: Design evaluation. Develop evaluation protocol, including evaluation questions, program description or logic model, data collection, and data analysis plans. Usually there is a draft and final version. Clearances, discussed in Chapter 5, are part of this task.
- Task 3: Data collection. A lot of the work. Schedule and conduct interviews, focus groups, and surveys using the evaluation protocol. Enter data into the computer in the appropriate way.
- Task 4: Data analysis. Statistics, text analysis, integration, and summaries.
- Task 5. Prepare final report. Includes introduction with evaluation questions and problem description, method as actually used, presentation of analyzed data, conclusions, and, if appropriate,

recommendations. This often includes an oral briefing of policy makers. There is a draft and a final version. Reports should include an executive summary of no more than ten pages. This brief document is the most important part of your report because it is all most people will read! More about this later.

Usually you figure out the task structure as part of the proposal process. The reason for this is that you must have a task structure to figure out how much a project will cost. Task structure is often presented as a flow chart similar to the one included as Figure 6.5.

Several important things are clear in this particular task flow diagram. There is an order in which parts of the project will be done. Task 1 must be completed before Task 2 can be done. Also, you will notice that Task 3 and Task 4 will be done simultaneously; that is, data collection and data analysis will feed into each other. Data collection will be done, analyzed, and then fed back into data collection if new information needs emerge during the analysis. This is a good way to do studies that aim to develop a body of knowledge.

You can add the names of staff to the task flow diagram if you wish to designate subgroups or teams to carry out particular tasks. For example, if you are combining interviews and focus groups for data collection, you might want different specialists to work on each of them. It is best to staff the project

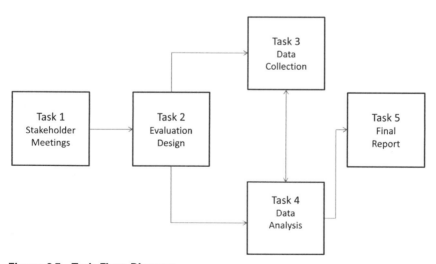

Figure 6.5 Task Flow Diagram

as completely as you can at the beginning. If you can't do this, specify the role of each unnamed person.

A useful management tool is a project organization chart. This is an important aid to decision making and communication. It maps communication and reporting lines. Among other things, it keeps people from skipping around the project director and going straight to the client, a big mistake in contract research. An example of a project organization chart is shown in Figure 6.6.

Finally you need a schedule for how long all of this will take. (See Table 6.2.)

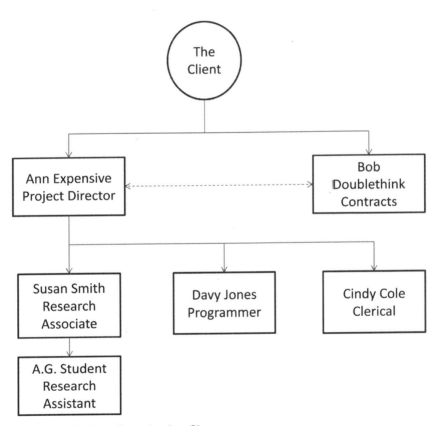

Figure 6.6　Project Organization Chart

Table 6.2 Project Schedule

Schedule of Deliverables and Project Activities			
Project Month	Activity	Deliverables	Due Date
Project Start [Date]			
Month 1	Task 1. Stakeholder Meeting (Client)	Meeting Summary	Two weeks after meeting
Month 2	Task 1. Stakeholder Meeting with national stakeholders	Meeting Summary	Two weeks after meeting
Months 2-3	Task 2. Evaluation Design	Draft Plan Final Plan	15th of Month 3 End of Month 3
Months 4-7	Task 3. Data Collection	Report on status of data collection	End of each month of data collection
Months 7-10	Task 4. Data Analysis	None	N/A
Months 11-12	Task 5. Reporting	Draft Final Report Briefing for client Final Report	End of Month 11 First week of Month 12 End of Month 12
All months	Monthly Reporting	1-page report on project status with financial statement	15th of each month following the end of the reporting month.
Project ends [Date]			

IMPLEMENT THE EVALUATION

This section deals with what an old boss of mine used to call "doing the work"—that is, implementing and managing an evaluation. At the start of this, you have an Evaluation Plan and you are ready to start collecting data. So what do you do now?

CONTROL OF EVALUATION DESIGN—USING AND MANAGING YOUR EVALUATION PLAN

As part of your evaluation plan, you thought through the linkage of activities in your evaluation plan to the implementation of your evaluation. You have developed data collection procedures, data management, and data analysis plans. Now it is incumbent upon you to use it. All staff working on the evaluation must refer to it regularly. Be sure to use you evaluation plan to guide data collection rather than improvising in the field. This doesn't mean you can't innovate or adapt to conditions; you will almost certainly have to do this in a lot of evaluations. But you should try to respect your original evaluation plan as you do so.

A plan in evaluation (and any other science) is a living document. It will evolve. But when you change things, be sure to document them. Write down a full description of the change and link it somehow to the evaluation plan:

- You can keep a journal and note the change there. This is what I do in the field, but it's not the best way. It's too hard to track changes over time.
- You can update the plan itself. If you do this, resave the document as version 2. *Never* overwrite the original version of your plan.
- You can put a box or other formatting set aside in the original and resave it as version X. I do this because it lets me see the changes easily when the time comes to write up the methodology for the final report.

Regularly make sure that everyone is working from the latest version. This is one of the most difficult issues of plan control when you are doing an evaluation with a team of people, especially in projects that require field investigation in multiple sites. It is kind of scary when your team is trying to figure out which version of the plan to use.

This case of version management is very difficult in large, complex projects with a lot of players. It applies to plans, site visit guides, instruments, and informed consent documents. I don't have any special way to handle it except to pay careful attention to version numbering (XXX_v1, XXX_v2,XXX-v3, etc.).

SITE SELECTION AND SITE VISITS

Anthropologists do a lot of site visits because we do a lot of ethnographic evaluations or evaluations with ethnographic components. Evaluators also do this because programs are almost always implemented in communities that vary on characteristics like size, region of the country, socioeconomic status of the population served, etc. Site visits enable you to compile comparable data in different kinds of communities as well as capturing important differences among them.

The choice of sites to participate in the evaluation can be a big problem, especially with clients who are trained in population-based research methods.

You almost always have a limited number of sites you can visit, which is determined by the evaluation budget. Your goal in choosing sites to visit is to get the best possible coverage of site characteristics that are known (or suspected) a priori to represent important differences in the implementation of programs.

You and your client may not agree initially on how to do this. For example, in my work with CDC, I found that the epidemiologists at CDC understand random sampling well, but they are not always in touch with the fact that site selection is a logical partner to sampling. Clients will often initiate an evaluation having already identified what projects they want included, usually based on political factors (they have agreed to participate, they don't have any big political issues right now, they are one of our best [or worst] projects.) There can be a lot of bias in evaluations that proceed in this way. First of all, they often make the well-known error of selecting cases on a dependent variable (how well/poorly the program is operating). Secondly, there is no way to judge the representativeness of the resulting set of sites.

Having said this, the instances of program implementation ("sites") are almost always "purposive" samples—that is, samples selected on some stated set of criteria rather than drawn at random from a "population" of available sites.[3] There are a number of reasons for this. Normally evaluators can only include a limited number of sites and want to get the most representative set of program implementations available. The number is determined by how many sites you can afford within the budget. Secondly, random sampling may incorporate programs that are not well enough implemented or interesting in terms of how the program can operate. Site visits are labor intensive for evaluators and hosts. Random sampling results in a loss of information in sites that have little to teach us about the program.

You select sites by defining ahead of time the characteristics of sites that are likely to affect how the program is implemented. This is usually done based on information from stakeholders and in consultation with clients. Following this, you describe all candidate sites on these criteria. You eliminate sites that are poor candidates for known reasons (won't cooperate, have a brand-new project director, etc.) Finally, you pick the best set of sites you can get based on coverage of the site-selection criteria. At this point you can listen to client requests and include the sites they want as long as they fit into the selection scheme.

Normally you want to get the maximum variation across a set of site-selection criteria that are related to dimensions along which programs are likely to vary. Some examples are size of the community, funding available to the program, size of the group of program recipients, rural-urban settlement pattern, and variability in program design that may affect outcomes. The site-selection criteria are an empirical question depending on the characteristics of the specific program.

I have given you an example of a site-selection matrix in Table 6.3. In this example five Indian tribes must be chosen out of an eligible group of fifteen. Your stakeholder interviews and your document reviews have suggested that rural-urban location, region of the country, and the amount of program funding are likely to affect achieving program objectives. There are a number of possible sets of five sites that will do, but some are better than others. I have left the last column blank. Try this as an exercise.

One final word of caution: it has been my experience that it is a really good idea to avoid instances of programs that are known to be failing. It may be intuitive that you should include some successes and some failures so you can understand the factors contributing to each; however, in any program that is well enough designed to have any successes, the failures are almost always due to idiosyncratic factors—there were many changes in leadership, the population for which the program was designed was unavailable for some reason, the project director embezzled the funds and moved to Venezuela, and so forth. It is distressing to discover this in the field when you have expended the cost of a field trip on a program that can tell you nothing useful about program success or failure.

Table 6.3 Example of a Site Selection Matrix

Tribe	Location	Kind of Organization	Amount of Grant Funding	Decision
Alcadian	Minnesota	Tribe on reservation	$250,000	
Beloit	Wisconsin	Tribe on reservation	$60,000	
Onotoway	North Carolina	Tribe on reservation	$500,000	
Pajarito	Wyoming	Tribe on reservation	$50,000	
Manuit	Tidewater, Virginia	Tribal organization	$35,000	
Federated Tribes of Northern California	Eureka' California	Tribal organization	$300,000	
Santa Nina	Arizona	Tribe on reservation	$250,000	
Far Plains Danaman	South Dakota	Tribe on reservation	$185,000	
Jocoya	Fresno, California	Tribal organization	$23,000	

DATA COLLECTION

Kinds of data collection that are most common in ethnographic components of evaluations are probably familiar to most people trained in the social sciences. They include interviews, focus groups, direct and participant observation, surveys, and analysis of documents. This is the standard tool kit of ethnographers everywhere. You may also use additional or new modalities. GPS analysis may be used where the geographic distribution of something is important. Economic analysis may be used if you need to assess the impact of cost on program effectiveness. Feel free to be innovative in thinking about how you will find out what you need to know. This is only good ethnography. As is almost always the case with ethnography, you will normally use more than one of these methods in some combination. You will often do a mixed-method evaluation in which qualitative and quantitative methods are combined (See Greene and Caricelli 1997).

Choosing people to interview—once again, try to build a framework for selecting interviewees that is linked to the evaluation plan. List kinds of people you need (project directors, local officials, service providers, recipients of the program, etc.), then populate the site visit schedule with people based on stakeholder interviews, job positions, and so forth. Build a list, and a schedule for each site visit that specifies the position of the interviewee and the kind of data collection and interview instruments to be used. Contact information for interviewees and focus group members is a good addition to the schedule.

The first step in any interview or focus group is informed consent. Whether this is written or verbal depends on your IRB clearance. (See Chapter 5.) Even if consent is verbal, give people a copy of it with a telephone number to contact if they have concerns. At the beginning of the interview emphasize that if any question or topic makes them uncomfortable, they can skip it and that they can end the interview (or leave the focus group) at any time.

Interviews—structured, semistructured, or open—are used to get information and people's perspectives on that information. The structured, semistructured, and open dimension is a continuum ranging from structured interviews, where the same questions are asked of all interviewees, to open interviews, in which interviewees are given a topic and asked to talk about it. In the middle are various forms of semistructured instruments in which people are given a set of questions or topics with probes to be used as appropriate. The instruments that are most commonly used in evaluation are semistructured because there is almost always at least some information that is standard across all interviewees. For example, "Tell me a little about how you became involved with the XXX program." These include standard questions with probes and simple lists of topics to be addressed at some time in the interview.

Focus groups bring together a group of people who are similar on some relevant dimension to discuss some specific topic. A focus group is not the same thing as a group interview—that is, a group of people brought together because they are knowledgeable about the program and will respond to a multiple question instrument of some kind. A focus group has—as the name implies—a focus. You will define one single clear question for focus groups to address. Control the process so that people more or less converge on this issue. Classically focus groups are about attitudes or perceptions of something rather than facts. There are better ways to get facts (Kreuger and Casey 2009).[7]

Select focus group participants for their similarity relative to what you want to talk about (e.g., clients, agency personnel, social workers, etc.). Ideally focus group members are not known to each other, are not related, do not all work together, and so forth. The reason for this is that preexisting relationships among participants may bias the results toward dominant clusters of people in the group. However, in program evaluation this is not always possible. Agency staff involved in programs are guaranteed to know one another, and even in other categories of participants, communities around the program and its population comprise a small world. In this case you need to weigh the value of the group process in producing consensus against the potential bias resulting from peer pressure.

Transcribe focus groups verbatim. This is a good idea for any kind of verbal data, but you can take notes on other kinds of interviews. Focus groups are about group perceptions, so you usually can't judge well enough what matters in real time.

Telephone focus groups are very useful for people who are hard to reach and comfortable thinking on the telephone (e.g., health care providers, bureaucrats), and they are sparing of budgets because they require no travel. They are especially useful for physicians and other hard-to-recruit people. Ensuring evenness of responses across all participants is harder in telephone focus groups than it is in face-to-face settings. Don't use telephone focus groups with people who are not accustomed to providing information by telephone; it will make them nervous and bias participation to the more extroverted members of the group.

Observation—participant or other. In evaluation we seldom have resources or time for prolonged participant observations. But look for opportunities to participate. For example, you might work as a receptionist in a clinic for a day, participate in meetings or community events, or observe in a market. If you do this, try to be as unobtrusive as possible. Dress appropriately and don't attract attention to yourself. It may be okay to take notes, but in some settings this will make people suspicious. I once did a project with a lot of observation in sexually transmitted disease clinic waiting rooms. I brought jeans and T-shirts for this; my business gear would have focused suspicion on me as some previously unknown kind of bureaucrat. I didn't tape or take notes either.[5] Whatever you do, never mislead people about who you are and why you are there if they ask you. There is an ethical issue of not misleading people about what they are participating in.

Speaking of equipment, I usually avoid tape recorders in observations, but I would advise you to use what you need. People get used to tape recorders pretty quickly, especially with modern compact ones. It's a good idea to explain what you are doing and what tapes will be used for. For photos or videos , you can save yourself a lot of trouble later if you get a written release to use them at the time you take them.

Surveys are very good for getting information about a set of facts and/ or attitudes and/or perceptions from similar people. The limitation of surveys is that there is less depth of information than there is with more open methods. However, if there is a specific kind of information you want from a lot of people, it's really great.

Never try to make a survey come up with information that is beyond the capability of the design by, for example, adding open-ended questions. It is a data analysis nightmare, and you can't control for bias by probing. I'm not saying never to use an open ended question; however, I try to limit them to matters of fact where I'm not sure of the categories (e.g., occupation, which office you work in, who you report to). It is a real temptation to use these for attitude questions. I've usually found the amount of useful data is not worth the analysis effort. It's better to use interviews or focus groups if you want people's values.

Document abstraction—Always check for relevant documents when you are collecting data in the field. They tell you what was supposed to happen, provide facts in a readily accessible and verifiable format, and may turn up aspects of a program that will show up no other way (i.e., program objectives that everyone had ignored in practice either because they were too hard or irrelevant).

Use a document abstraction format of some kind. If you have a lot of similar documents (e.g., reports of various kinds), you can use a questionnaire format. Or you can just build a list of things you want to know from documents and use it for the documents as a whole. The goal is to know afterward what questions you asked of this data source. Of course, record unanticipated things relevant to your evaluation.

GUARDING AGAINST BIAS IN DATA COLLECTION

You cannot avoid bias in program evaluation; you can only minimize it. Bias in data collection comes from several sources:

- Ignoring a significant source of relevant data—for example, failing to interview program participants, not knowing about documents or relevant stakeholders, and so forth. Always scrutinize your data-collection plan for significant omissions and probe them with stakeholders. Ask stakeholders "Here is my list of interviewees—can you think of anyone important I've missed?" However, be aware that you can't always interview everyone or even all types of people. For example, I did not always interview patients in clinic settings because of the complexity of getting clearance to talk to them.
- Errors in sample selection—for example, using sites recommended by a significant stakeholder without investigating the relationship of this site to others on relevant program characteristics. Is this an especially effective program? Is it a problem program that the client is having trouble with?

Always envision samples—whether of people, documents, or observations—relative to a set of units you could have included. Then look for systematic differences between the people who are in your data and those who are not. For surveys, of course, use an appropriate sampling design. But for qualitative data you must be as rigorous as possible in selecting units to include and the implications of these inclusions for perspective on the program.

Awareness of bias and honest reporting thereof is the most important thing to do about bias. The first step is to cultivate an attitude of alertness to this potential that stays turned on throughout data collection.

Control your data collection plan. You have thought this through in your project design. Protect this thought. Do what the plan says, and document deviations.

Take all steps possible to correct bias—for example, by replacing lost interviewees with an alternative that is as similar as possible.

Call on experts as needed. For example, if you plan to sample, talk to a sampling statistician. It will vastly improve the credibility of your evaluation and keep you from making embarrassing mistakes.

DATA MANAGEMENT

I have called this section data management, but it's really research management. When you interview for a job as an evaluator, one of the ways you can really impress people is to show that you are aware of these management needs for any research project, certainly for evaluation. Very few people are trained in this. Most people learn it by trial and error—very costly in nonacademic settings, where all labor bills by the hour.

It has always been startling to me how much data you accumulate in ethnographic evaluation and how quickly. You plan and plan, and then you finally get to the field, and they inundate you. This is why your evaluation plan should have a data-management plan. When you get to the field, it is too late to think about data management. There is nothing worse than collecting data and then losing it because it wasn't processed correctly.

The data management plan is a roadmap that tells you where data should go and to whom. These are always useful. They are critical if you have multiple players in your evaluation team. You need a written plan about what data will be collected, by whom, and what will happen to it. This is normally done as part of your evaluation plan. I also add a step-by-step guide to the field or site-visit plans that people will take to the field.

Also, there needs to be quality-control procedures to ensure that what you think is going into the database goes there. Review what's in the database on a regular basis before you get to the analysis. It is very distressing not to be able to find the data you need.

DATA MANAGEMENT IN THE FIELD

When data management goes awry, it almost always happens in field data collection. Failure to manage on-site data collection in accord with the evaluation plan is the biggest problem in large studies with multiple field teams.

When you go out to collect data—whether it's in focus groups or street intercepts—there is always a lot going on. You are meeting people, obtaining informed consent, interviewing them, and interacting with them. Things can get so busy that an ethnographer may almost forget to write down the data. This is to be avoided by developing explicit procedures for managing field data.

You need to have a structure of some kind for managing hard-copy and electronic data and specific procedures for getting data into them, especially during site visits. Develop a regular procedures for downloading taped data at the end of each field day. Digital tape recorders can be obtained that will load sound files directly onto your laptop so you can immediately send it to whoever is responsible for processing the data. These are an enormous help. If you don't have access to tools like this, type or fax your notes to clerical staff each evening or morning.[8]

Make sure everyone knows what to do and how to do it. Things to be considered include how to prepare, identify, and mark interview and focus group tapes. Tapes should be physically marked with the location, date, and time of the interview, but not the name of the person or people involved. In addition, the first item on the tape should be the number identifying the data collection event, the date, time, and site, if appropriate. It's best to do this before the interview if you can, like in the car on the way to the meeting. You can always write over it if the interview doesn't work out somehow. But it is really easy to forget this in the rush of meeting the people and starting the data collection.

Keeping good field notes is a core skill for ethnographers. These contain your own version of what happened and marginal notes taken in the interview, if there are any. Carry a journal for notes, especially in the field, but really throughout the development and implementation of your evaluation. I do this because I am an anthropologist and I did this when I did my dissertation research. They don't often teach us things like this. I recommend that you get in the habit of writing ideas, random thoughts, and observations down. When they are gone, they're gone.

Field notes should be written up as soon as possible after the interview, ideally no more than twenty-four hours. I usually try to schedule interviews or focus groups with an hour in between to allow for immediate write-ups. This is a luxury you don't always get, but it's worth considering. If not, we're talking some serious midnight oil!

BUILDING AN EVALUATION DATA BASE

You will want a central location in which to organize data from your evaluation. How elaborate it is depends on the scope of the evaluation and the number of people working on the project. Here's what I usually include in the evaluation database:

- A file drawer and/or a computer file containing all documents for the evaluation—evaluation and site visit protocol, instruments, meeting notes, correspondence, and so forth.
- A computer file subdivided by site, if appropriate, containing electronic copies of all correspondence, field notes, documents, typed up transcripts, and so forth.
- A document file containing all documents provided in hard copy, with a catalog. If there are electronic documents, put them in the same catalog. And keep it in a special document directory.
- A computer file containing quantitative data as appropriate. I usually break this up into subdirectories for raw data, codebooks, programs, and analyses (Excel spreadsheets, Access data bases, or any other way you have of managing numeric data).
- A computer file containing all text analysis work including interview transcripts, codebooks, coded data, coding reports, and so forth.
- A journal file for field and other notes I make as the evaluation proceeds. If there are multiple researchers, a subdirectory for each of them. These kinds of notes are critical for interpretation as you go on.

Keep what data you can on a server if you have multiple people using them. You (or someone) will need to maintain control of what goes into the database, especially in a large multiplayer evaluation. I usually designate a data manager responsible for maintaining the database. Other members of the team submit data to this person, who uploads it to the evaluation database. On a smaller evaluation, especially if you are the only evaluator, you can keep track without this help.

Another good thing about a server is that it is usually backed up automatically. Even if it is, you want to be vigilant about backups. You can probably imagine how awful it is to need to reconstruct one of these. Archive everything at least monthly, more if data collection is proceeding rapidly.

DATA ANALYSIS

One of my clients used to say that we transform data into information; from information, we build knowledge. Raw data is of little use to anyone until and unless it is organized in such a way that an observer can study the analysis results and obtain knowledge from them. The major task in data analysis is to move data from a dispersed raw form into a format in which you can see it all at once. Data display is 90 percent of data analysis—whether your research is qualitative, quantitative, or both (Miles, Huberman, and Saldaña 2014).

I will talk about theories that underlie analysis, then I will go on to look at coding, integrating findings from different data sources, discerning and describing patterns in the data, developing conclusions from findings, maintaining the linkage of evidence to conclusions, and hypothesis testing.

THINKING ABOUT ANALYSIS

There are two ways to think about how you collect and interpret data. Deductive data analysis is an approach in which you decide ahead of time what hypotheses to test and what data to look for so you can do that. You then design your evaluation to get predesignated data. This approach is most often used with positivist "scientific" study designs. At the other end are inductive approaches in which you let knowledge emerge from the data, asking no specific a priori questions. This is the kind of data most often used in qualitative approaches such as ethnography.

This is, of course, a continuum, and most evaluations combine both. Where you stand on this continuum will affect how you do your analysis. Generally speaking, deductive studies rely on mathematical and/or statistical testing of quantitative data against the expectations of hypotheses. Inductive studies rely on qualitative compilation of data into categories that are then reviewed for results. Qualitative analysis is highly iterative, with preliminary data analyses generating new questions that are then tested against the data.

To understand how inductive methods look, let's talk a little about grounded theory. The idea behind grounded theory is to let the data speak for themselves. The challenge is to come to data collection *without a priori hypotheses*. Analysis is an iterative process between coding and summarizing data, examining for tentative hypotheses, and assessing and refining tentative hypotheses by testing against more data. The advantage of this is that you find out a great deal that you didn't know to ask in the beginning. The disadvantage is the chance that you will find nothing (or little) that is really useful to your client. I have never seen this happen, but we have to be open to all possibilities. Grounded theory is a very important social science method, and it is great fun. We don't do a lot of it in evaluation because it is relatively costly to keep going back to the field for more data. However, it sometimes is done when the purpose of an evaluation is exploratory (Strauss and Corbin 1990). With a deductive approach, you develop an idea of what is going on (hypotheses) then go out and test your hypothesis on data. This is what you do when, for example, you have developed a logic model for an evaluation, and you want to test the fit of the model. In this case you develop an hypothesis for each important linkage in the model, design your study to demonstrate these linkages, collect data to test the linkages in the program logic model, and analyze the data to respond to a priori questions about whether the model is a good fit and, usually, what can be changed to make it work better. The advantage of this is that it can be focused on what you need to do, user's needs, and known conditions. The disadvantage is that, strictly speaking, you don't learn anything that you didn't think to ask at the outset. If you are a deductive purist, discoveries not anticipated by the model are back-burnered for later investigation in another study.

Most things are somewhere in the middle. There is an iterative process of preliminary analysis, data collection, and more analysis. Then you proceed to ask the questions you started with. Eventually the evaluation process begins to generate information you didn't anticipate and may seem to have a life of its own.

For our purposes, you need to keep your eye on the ball of stakeholder needs (what have they asked you to investigate), but keep the other eye out for surprises. This is a big part of what makes evaluation fun—there are always surprises.

Sometimes you need to follow up with additional data collection to fill out what is known about new findings or to verify new discoveries in other sites or with other stakeholders. In practice you do as much iteration between data collection and data analysis as you can afford. If something is uncertain, you can go back to stakeholders and clarify what doesn't fit. Never change the data, but try to amplify what you know.

CODING: BUILDING FINDINGS OUT OF DATA

Tons have been written about how to code qualitative data. It's enough to scare you to death. Moreover, mostly people just tell you what software to use but aren't always clear on what to do with it. I am not going to talk about how to code here; it's beyond the scope of this chapter. However, I am going to try to convince you to learn how to do it if you don't already know how.

Coding is simply flagging or marking passages of qualitative data—interview or focus group transcripts or notes, documents, observations, diaries, logs, memos—in such a way that the important parts of the flow of information are drawn out for comparison and the development of findings. Analysis is guided by a codebook that defines the codes to be used and is used by all coders to ensure consistency and replicability of coding. Once the data are coded, you sort them in some way so that passages of text with the same codes are assembled. At this point you can look at them all at once and deduce what you have learned across a group of data-collection events—interviews in a single site or interviews of program directors across sites and all interviews.

There are lots of rules about how to go about doing this. However you do it, it is critical to the credibility of your evaluation that you do it consistently and with quality-control measures built in. Coding is in many ways the soft underbelly of qualitative research. If you can't demonstrate to clients and skeptics how you made and documented coding decisions, you are vulnerable to the accusation, so often confronted by qualitative researchers, that your findings are "anecdotes" or "impressions."

Analysis takes a lot of time and effort. I have almost always underestimated, sometimes drastically, the amount of time it will take to code, sort, and summarize qualitative data. Experts estimate that this analysis task will require two to four times as long as it took to collect the data in the first place. You must bear this in mind when you estimate the cost of your projects. Also I have found this hard to explain to clients. I have sometimes educated them by letting them try to code an interview!

Participant observation, unobtrusive observation, and documents can also be coded using the same codebook. However, I'm not recommending you do it this way. These data sources are better summarized or examined directly for confirming information of findings from qualitative data. Coding them is costly and time consuming and not usually worth the effort. Unless there are a lot of participant data, describe them in a narrative format and use them to support your findings.

You will have a lot of data from different data sources coded in different ways. You want to somehow lay out your data in such a way that you can view it all at once to figure out what it says. In the dark ages, when I did my doctoral work, I wrote everything on three-by-five cards and arranged and rearranged them on the dining room table until they began to make sense. It took forever, and I had to hope that my kids didn't mind eating in front of the TV. (Mine didn't!) Now you can use qualitative text analysis software to answer evaluation questions. This is a tremendous improvement over the old way. The logic of doing it is the same, but computers make it easier or at least less demanding of space.

Data analysis of an evaluation with multiple data sources and/or sites is a matter of matching patterns of relationships in and across sites. It is a process of seeing whether the same or similar relations of data are found across multiple sites. Are the same variables associated with the same values in all sites or in some subgroup of sites?

I use a procedure called pattern matching. There is a lot written on pattern matching strategies (Miles, Huberman, and Saldaña 2014). Basically pattern matching involves classifying bits of analyzed data in some kind of format—often tabular—in which you can see it across all data sources and across all sites. The following steps are one way to do it.

Step 1. Build findings for each data source for each site. Summarize all of the coded data for each question for each site and each data source to figure out what that source tells you. Do it site by site if you have multiple sites. At this stage do the analysis separately for each data collection method.

You can put these data in a matrix, but this can be very laborious. For data coded in qualitative analysis software, the software will produce "reports" listing each entry for each code. I find that reading through these, noting central tendencies and important deviations from central tendencies, is adequate. Once you have reviewed the data, write preliminary findings up in a narrative format.

Step 2. Arrange the summary findings for each data source for each site. Load your findings from Step 1 into a matrix similar to the following one. Summarize findings for each question across all data sources. Enter into the rightmost cell of the matrix. I do these matrices in Excel for ease of manipulation. However, I have on more than one occasion done the whole process with a pencil and a hard-copy form.

Step 3. Arrange and summarize findings across sites. Take the summaries from the rightmost columns of the Step 2 analysis and load them into a cross-site (or cross-informant type) matrix. Summarize cross-site findings in the rightmost column. The two analysis steps of this process are shown in Tables 6.4 and 6.5.

Relational databases will help you do this by computer. Packages like Access will pull together all references to a defined variable across multiple data sources and sites. However, before you go this way, make sure you understand the logic of your analysis. Although these findings are shown as a few words in a cell, they will actually be about a one-paragraph narrative. And the process of developing these is dynamic and iterative. You may redo this several ways to display findings in the best way. When you are done, you will have a table with a summary of findings across each site and across all sites.

From your analysis, go back and develop answers to the evaluation questions noting consistencies, inconsistencies, unexpected findings, disagreements. Look for things that don't fit. These may be the most interesting. Most especially look for discontinuities between what you thought the program looked like and the perceptions of stakeholders about the actual program. These are usually the key points for intervention. Are these the patterns predicted by the logic model? What are important variations in your data? Are the stakeholders implementing the program correctly? Are they trying to achieve something different?

One advantage of this fairly rigorous approach is that the intermediate tables allow a user to trace your reasoning from raw data to findings. This

Table 6.4 Pattern Matching Step 1—Compare Findings across Data Sources in a Single Site

	Summary of findings across data sources for each site SITE = Site A		
	Data source 1 Interviews	Data source 2 Focus Groups	Data source n Documents	Summary of Question X
Question 1: Relation to program	finding	finding	finding	Summary of findings
Question 2: Barriers to program implementation	finding	finding	finding	Summary of findings
. . .	finding	finding	finding	Summary of findings
Variable N: Suggestions to improve program	finding	finding	finding	Summary of findings

Table 6.5 Pattern Matching Step 2—Compare Findings across All Sites

| | Summary of Findings For All Sites | | | |
	Site A	Site B	Site N	Summary
Question 1: Relation to program	Summary from Table 6-3	Summary from Table 6-3	Summary from Table 6-3	Cross site findings
Question 2: Barriers to program implementation	Summary from Table 6-3	Summary from Table 6-3	Summary from Table 6-3	Cross site findings
. . .	Summary from Table 6-3	Summary from Table 6-3	Summary from Table 6-3	Cross site findings
Variable N: Suggestions to improve program	Summary from Table 6-3	Summary from Table 6-3	Summary from Table 6-3	Cross site findings

is very important with qualitative data because it allows you to counter any later criticism that your results are "impressionistic" or "anecdotal."

I have presented this analysis procedure as though it were for an evaluation in which the primary interest is variation among and across implementation sites. However, it is really just a technique for classification. You can, for example, use the same procedure across types of interviews (federal staff, state staff, nonprofit organization staff), types of programs (public schools, private schools, middle schools, secondary schools). This approach can accommodate data analysis whether it is arrived at deductively or inductively or anywhere in between.

However, you may not need to use this fairly laborious approach as long as you develop a way to:

- include all of the data,
- devise a way to link the findings to the data, and
- maintain a paper trail that will allow others to substantiate the basis of your findings.

ASSESSING THE WEIGHT OF THE DATA

A difficult issue in qualitative studies is determining what can be concluded from the data and figuring out how much the data support a point of view. In quantitative analyses there are statistics and levels of significance. In qualitative studies the implications of the analyzed data are more a matter of interpretation. This is strength of qualitative work, but it makes some people uneasy.

Sooner or later a client will pressure you to "quantify" your qualitative data, to count the number of times something came up in interviews, the number of a particular response, the number of interviews in which something came up. The worst thing is trying to get you to say how many people in a focus group said something. This is a violation of the focus group method. Focus groups are seeking integrated group findings rather than a concatenation or count of individual opinions.

It is natural that quantitatively trained scientists want to quantify things. They need to understand the stability or robustness of findings; that is, would the same findings appear in a different set of sites or a different set of interviewees? This is easier in quantitative work because you can use the numbers, and there are lots of indicators of the relative "weight" of findings within and across sites. So people can specify what conclusions are strongly supported and which ones have weaker support.

There are schemes for weighting qualitative data, but most are risky. First of all, they impart a false sense of quantity to something that isn't quantitative. Secondly, they may mislead because mechanical interpretation of qualitative data is almost always incomplete in terms of the effects of context. For example, a finding that "technical capacity makes program X work" may have a different meaning in a context where technical capacity is abundant from one in which it has to be assembled from volunteers with great difficulty. The arbitrary assignment of a "weight" to this finding may thus overemphasize this factor in high-tech sites with greater access to resources.

Qualitative data require inference about how strong support is for a particular position. Some estimate of this is critical for establishing the credibility of your evaluation.

Here are some things you can do:

- Use all of your data; present all your data. Appendicize if you must, but people need to be able to reconstruct your reasoning. I present the whole matrix (usually cleaned up for grammar and language, but be careful not to change the meaning). This has the beneficial side effect of getting across to your client how much work this is!

- Do not go beyond your evidence. Clearly mark what belongs to the data and what belongs to you. Speculation is legitimate—you have expertise. But say when you are doing this; for example, "One would infer from this that . . ." or "This suggests that . . ."
- When you are coming straight from the data, say that "the data demonstrate or show that . . ." so the reader can track the reasoning.

BUT WHAT ABOUT GENERALIZATION?

A question people may ask about your evaluation goes something like this: "How do I know my evaluation results can be applied to other programs you didn't look at?"

Strictly speaking, you can't. Generalization is not usually part of the deep ethnography that characterizes qualitative methodologies. Certainly you cannot specify that your findings will apply with a specified probability. Theoretically you can't do that with statistical methods either, but you can guess how likely you are to be wrong. This is comforting. It has been my experience that if evaluations are done in a technically sound way, the findings will apply more broadly. In fact this is why program evaluations are done. But you cannot demonstrate generalizability. Be honest with your clients and colleagues about this. If they must have statistical support for generalizability, they must do an experimental, quasi-experimental, or other quantitative evaluation.

What you can do is to suggest that logically your results are likely to apply broadly given certain conditions:

- That you have built a model with adequate construct validity—that is, that it adequately describes what happens, all things being equal.
- That you have selected cases and observations without bias.
- That you have conducted the inquiry faithfully according to the protocol.
- That you have analyzed all of the data.

Given that you have done a methodologically rigorous evaluation, it is likely you have a fair idea of what new instances will look like, all things being equal.

Which, of course, they never are, whether using statistical or logical generalization.

Such is science.

THE ESOTERIC ART OF THE RECOMMENDATION

Recommendations are evidence-based suggestions for future action. These were a big problem for me when I first started doing this. Who am I to tell the CDC (or any other client) what to do?

However, recommendations aren't what you personally think should be done, and they don't depend on your expertise. They depend on the evidence. Evidence must support recommendations that are attributed to the evaluation. The value of the recommendations depends on this.

Recommendations should never be based on a priori decisions, politics, or some other factor. If you plan to support recommendations with the evaluation, the recommendations must be derived from the evaluation's evidence.

Match recommendations closely to stakeholder needs and capacities. Recommendations should be grounded in stakeholder perceptions as brought forth throughout the evaluation. If they are not, the political will to implement them—especially if they are difficult ones—is largely absent.

Recommendations must be feasible, practical, and acceptable. Don't recommend things that can't be done. Although it would certainly improve TB morbidity to improve housing along the border, this is not likely to happen. Also, don't recommend things over which the program implementers have no power—for example, localities should assign more nurses to TB therapy. Finally, unacceptable recommendations are to be avoided, things like mandatory TB testing of everyone applying for a job.

You can do a good, productive evaluation without recommendations. There are a lot of situations in which this is fine. For example, sometimes evaluation conclusions are passed up the administrative hierarchy, and policy makers come up with recommendations. Sometimes you evaluate just to determine whether the program is working or whether it is addressing needs.

DISSEMINATING THE EVALUATION

The final step is to disseminate the results of your evaluation in such a way that they can be used to inform program design, modify the program to be more effective, or replicate the program somewhere else. The worst fate an evaluation can have is to "sit on the shelf"—that is, be archived without being used to improve or develop new programs. This is, after all, the purpose of evaluation. To facilitate use, you must get your evaluation in front of those who can use it, and you need to sell it to them. They will want to know it's accurate before acting on it or recommending that someone else do so.

FINAL REPORTS

Final reports provide documentation of the evaluation that is especially useful in replicating your evaluation in another context or program or at a later time. The most important elements are:

- Purpose and background: Why the evaluation was undertaken and for whom. What the evaluation question(s) were, background of the program, or problem investigated.
- Description of the thing you evaluated, with the logic model if appropriate.
- Methodology: How you did it—the real way, not the plan. There are almost always deviations from the plan or protocol. These belong in the report. Depending on how complex the methodology is, you may want to append a detailed method section.
- Findings for each evaluation question, sometimes in a single chapter, sometimes a chapter for each evaluation question.
- Conclusions: What do you think about the findings? What do you conclude across cases evaluated?
- Recommendations: Explicitly link them to evidence.

Describe the program *as it was evaluated*. Don't assume that it will be the same as it was at the beginning of the evaluation when you come back to review it. It won't be if you implement the evaluation. Also, with staff turnover, no one may remember the good—or bad—old days: write it down.

Describe stakeholders who helped you with the evaluation. Also include any stakeholders who weren't involved in evaluation design but were discovered in the course of the evaluation. Once again, this information is critical for subsequent evaluation design in the evaluated program or elsewhere.

Always do an executive summary. Very few people are willing to read an entire report unless there is a good reason for them to do so. Most people will read an executive summary to decide whether they should read the rest. Sometimes and for some people, a need to know can be met simply by reading the executive summary.

Final reports themselves should be no longer than they must be.

Append things generously, sometimes in a separate volume. Informed consent, instruments, literature reviews, analysis tables, or detail (especially for qualitative analyses) are all important support for the evaluation. These are your chain of evidence. They should contain everything people will need to interpret your evaluation and support the recommendations. A congressional staffer once told me: "I almost never read the whole thing. But I need to know that the proof is there." This became my rule for completing and documenting evaluations.

Remember, the purpose of the final report is to support your client in taking some action. The most important thing is that it be both accessible and all be there somewhere.

BRIEFINGS

A common way of getting your report to stakeholders is to prepare and present a summary of the project in an oral briefing. This is often a requirement of evaluations. It is normally done between the draft and final versions of the final report so that listeners can provide feedback to the final report.

A major purpose of evaluation briefings is to obtain input from stakeholders about the evaluation results and/or the recommendations. This information is then input to the final report.

Briefings are like any other research presentation. It has two components, both important: a summary of the evaluation and summary of its results and recommendations. It is often but not always accompanied by PowerPoint (or some equivalent) presentation of the evaluation and its results. The art of the PowerPoint presentation is an important part of doing an evaluation. Most especially, it is critical not to make these presentations too long. The average briefing lasts an hour. For most people, this is fifteen to twenty PowerPoint slides. Beyond this, it is likely to become what experienced bureaucrats call "Death by PowerPoint."

The content of your briefing should cover the most important points in your final report but much more succinctly. I usually prepare PowerPoint presentations from the executive summary. This is also a way to ensure you have the right stuff in the executive summary.

USE MANY WAYS TO GET YOUR EVALUATION OUT THERE

A written evaluation report is only one means of getting the evaluation out to users. In fact, reports often go straight onto the shelves of busy people who are intimidated by their weight. They intend to read them but seldom have the time. Use as many means of dissemination as you can reasonably do within your own resources. Different people have different styles of acquiring information. Cover the bases as much as you can. Consider alternatives instead of or in addition to a written final report.

- Use the blogosphere but only with authorization from your client. They are usually eager to get results out, but the whole social media thing is still the Wild West. Exercise judgment and caution.
- Slide shows at professional meetings are great. You get a lot of key stakeholders in one place, and it focuses attention. For example, when I was doing public health evaluations, an important venue for getting results out was presentations at national meetings of state and regional public health professionals.
- Newsletters—regional and national, paper and e-mail—are an especially good way to access people who work directly with programs.
- Make summaries available on as many relevant websites as possible. Always ask your client, however; this almost always has some kind of political implications.
- E-mail dissemination to lists of key stakeholders works well as long as the presentation is succinct.

WHAT CAN I SHARE WITH STAKEHOLDERS?

Your stakeholders have done a lot to support your evaluation, and they want to know how it came out. In fact, they may ask you whether they will get a report from the evaluation. Very often nonclient stakeholders who have worked with you throughout the evaluation never hear anything about its fate, making them skeptical of evaluation or its usefulness. But a question that often comes up is: How much can you share with your stakeholders and in what level of detail?

First of all, before making any promises or sharing any data or documents with stakeholders, get buy-in from your clients. Even though you just finished the evaluation, you still may not be fully aware of the political sensitivities surrounding the evaluation and/or the program. If you can get agreement from the client, it is a good idea to disseminate a summary of results in some way. I have worked with public health clients who are usually willing to share as much as possible with stakeholders. You may not be as fortunate. In any event, check your dissemination plans with the client.

Best of all is a discussion of the evaluation findings in a face-to-face meeting with stakeholders. But this is costly. You may be able to do it if it can be made to coincide with a professional meeting of some kind, but even then, you need to deal with busy meeting schedules. Alternatively you can send stakeholders a summary by mail or e-mail and solicit their feedback in a systematic way—for example, a Delphi or other written nominal group process in which they are allowed to comment on each other's comments. Or you can develop a form for responses.[9] If you disseminate the evaluation this way, always have a deadline for comments and be prepared to follow up to get responses. Partial response is a big source of bias. You will get more of the people who loved it or hated it than the people in the middle who may have constructive input.

You may ask for a review of your findings from stakeholders you worked with when you developed your evaluation plan. In this case you will probably have a pretty good idea of what their interest in the outcome of the evaluation is. They call them stakeholders because they have a stake—that is, an interest in the outcome. Their comments can be expected to reflect this.

I never send raw data to stakeholders. Stakeholders are not working full time as evaluators. They need a summary of findings based on your interpretation of the evidence. One page is best; two pages max. Use bullet points!

Be scrupulous about protecting confidentiality when you share results with stakeholders. Most program stakeholders are living in a really small world. In specialized program areas people tend to know each other professionally. You must not just protect identities but should also be careful about releasing information that might be attributed—correctly or incorrectly—to an individual. I am very hesitant about using quotes that might identify someone because of speech patterns. They are interesting, but people have often been in multiple conferences with your interviewees. This is why bullets are good; they make you think it through to the point at which you can present the data clearly without identifying sources.

Do not treat postevaluation comments from stakeholders the same way you treat data that were collected using your evaluation plan. You must contextualize what you hear in terms of the respondents' interest in the outcome of the evaluation (their "stake"). It is your job to compile the positions of all stakeholders, pull the main positions out of them, and interpret their implications for the evaluation.

When I first began doing evaluations, I let stakeholders review and comment on the data that they themselves had given me in interviews. I found that I lost all the interesting stuff because, on second thought, they didn't want it in the record. This is another reason why you need summaries for them to review.

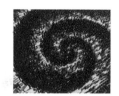

CHAPTER SEVEN

JOBS AND CAREER PLANNING

In this chapter I will pull together some of the lessons learned about building careers in evaluation anthropology from my own experience and from that of many colleagues and students I have worked with over the years. Some of this may apply to you, and some may not. It is also worth noting that my career extended over forty years. The context in which I did things has changed dramatically over time. I was just walking along trying to survive, and I fell into evaluation. It's not that simple nowadays (Butler 2005).

But I have hired a lot of evaluators and anthropologists and done job recommendations for a lot more. And in the past two decades I have taught evaluation to many people both in professional workshops and at two universities. I have an idea of what works in my own domain and possibly in some others.

MY EXPERIENCE

I am a practicing anthropologist specializing in program evaluation of public health programs. For the past twenty-five years I have loved my job. There have been tough moments, of course. But by and large I have gone to work in the morning bemused that someone was paying me to do this and paying me pretty well. I have done ethnography in all of the states except North Dakota—and I almost made it there—and five foreign countries. I have grown professionally as an anthropologist, a scientist, and a human being in ways that I would not have dreamed of at the beginning. I tell people that I never could have planned my career to turn out as well as it did. I knew too little of the choices available to me at the time I worked all of this out (Butler 2006).

For me, the development of my career was a random walk. I did what I was doing until the next thing showed up, then I did that. I built a PhD in anthropology on the base of a premed major, something that served me well as I moved into thinking about health and illness. I built a career in evaluation when an academic career failed. In recent years I have gone back to the academy, bringing with me my knowledge of evaluation. When I look back, all roads are straight, leading to where I am now. But it sure didn't look that way at the time.

By a series of fortunate circumstances I got an academic job one and a half years before I completed my doctorate. I was teaching cultural and biological anthropology in a joint sociology-anthropology department. The training I got from my sociology colleagues as I finished my dissertation gave me a tool that was of great value in my later thinking through of social and health programs. I was denied tenure, possibly the worst moment of my life. After a couple of strange starter jobs, I eventually landed on my feet when the Battelle Memorial Institute hired me to do program evaluations, largely for the Centers for Disease Control and Prevention.

The trouble with a career assembled by the winds of fortune is that it's hard to tell others what to do to replicate your own experience. This is probably fine. I'm not sure anyone truly replicates anyone else's experience. Still, there are lessons learned, and better and worse ways to pursue a career. Knowing what I know now, I think I could have spared myself a lot of discomfort if I had planned a little better than I did.

SO HOW DO I GET A JOB?

People ask me this a lot. It is our major concern when we are students and after we enter the work force. For anthropology students as well as for many others entering the social sciences at this particular time, we are asked by well-meaning friends and relatives what we plan to do with these (impractical) degrees. It seems like most people are training for careers in international business or computer science or medicine—a course of study in which a fairly specific kind of job is the expected outcome. We're not like that. And it's a little embarrassing not to know what you will do at the end of your academic career.

This is an especially difficult dilemma for those engaged in graduate training in the more traditional scholarly disciplines, those who have depended historically on academic teaching and research for careers. With decreasing academic budgets and a smaller number of students due to the high cost of university education, academic jobs are fewer than they once were. Getting one of the few university tenure-track jobs has become more a matter of being in the right place at the right time than on systematic working of the job market. For new graduates and midcareer scholars, the prospect of finding an academic job is daunting. Many recent graduates make do with several adjunct teaching jobs that pay little and have no benefits. There are better alternatives in the nonacademic sector, whether your degree is a bachelor's degree, a master's degree, or a doctorate. But most people coming out of academic settings don't know how to find them.

There are a few guiding principles for going about this:

Principle #1. You almost always have to do the scariest thing. There is no easy way to do this. I have tried sending my résumé to people. I have tried searching advertisements. I have tried in some desultory ways to ask my friends and my own professors whether they knew of any jobs. In the end I discovered that the only way to do this is to approach people and risk rejection. Jobs emerge from networks and personal connections. Personnel departments usually do the paperwork for the people who can actually hire you. I have always found it terrifying to approach people I don't know to ask them for something. I have had to get over it. So do you.

Principle #2. Be systematic, and keep track of what you are doing. Nothing is as distressing as not being able to find a potential employer's office after you step off the Metro or forgetting who you talked to about the research job on environments and the social marketing job on educational interventions. Your job hunt is like any research project; get yourself organized before you start, and stay organized as you go. Avoid embarrassment.

Principle #3. Be open to everything. As you will see below, a job hunt is exactly that—a hunt. Your understanding of jobs will improve as you go. Don't prematurely reject leads because they aren't in the middle of your plan. In the interim between my academic and my practicing years I had a job as an economic analyst and as an SAS programmer. These were never things I especially wanted to pursue, but they were interesting jobs, paid me when I was hungry, and taught me things that were useful in many ways later on. This doesn't mean you should never say no, but listen carefully before you do.

In the sections that follow, we will get to specific ways you go about doing this.

THE DIMENSIONS OF EVALUATION CAREERS

First of all, we need to distinguish between a job and a career. A career is a trajectory that plays itself out over time as you build skills, expertise, and interests. Careers tend to cluster around areas of expertise and topic areas, but these may be quite broad. And the path of you career will emerge over time, sometimes providing you with surprises. Career changes, of course, are part of our working vocabulary. I have done this several times. The important thing to know about career change is that it's always an option. You are never truly saddled with any particular path; you can always change if you have the will to do so.

Jobs are parts of careers and make up the steps in the development of your professional life. Of course, not all jobs are career jobs. My job as a computer programmer, for example, was not really a career job even though I loved it and learned useful things from it. I did this job to feed my family. It's okay to do this. Sometimes we have no choice. But career jobs are progressive in the sense that they build on each other to strengthen your expertise and your résumé. It is to be expected that you will hold several jobs over a career. The single job from graduation to retirement is a rarity nowadays.

The medium in which careers exist, however, is jobs. So in this chapter I focus on jobs. There are many ways you can hold a job as an evaluator. Some of the important considerations are:

- Academic or nonacademic? A lot of evaluations are done out of academic departments or research institutes associated with universities. If you dream of an academic career, there is room for evaluation in combination with disciplinary training and with training in evaluation.
- A full-time evaluator or a part-time evaluator who does this as part of some other job? Your evaluation can be done in a context in which you have another title, and evaluation can be all or a part of your work. Examples of positions in which evaluation is important are government administrator, educator, and health organization staff. You can work for a large government, business, or nonprofit organization in which evaluation is part or all of what you do.
- A builder/doer of evaluation or a consumer—that is, a program person who uses evaluation?

Any of these positions relies on a knowledge of evaluation method and theory. You can't use an evaluation if you don't understand its purpose as a tool for improvement. If you are looking for a job in which you will evaluate as part of some other function—for example, you are a program administrator who must report annually on how programs are going—an understanding of evaluation will be a big help and, possibly, a big selling point to a potential employer.

You may be an internal or external evaluator. You can be part of the staff in an organization in which you are responsible for internal management of the quality of programs or activities, or you can be an outside evaluator working for a consulting firm or as an independent consultant to provide an outsider perspective on how programs are doing.

You can do evaluation successfully with either a master's or a doctoral degree. Outside of academia there is little discrimination by degree unless you are working for an agency that considers degrees important for its own reasons. For example, NIH and CDC may require doctorates not because you need these skills but because they consider it a necessary condition for being a scientist. However, it has been my experience that once you begin evaluating, experience is more important than education.[1] Of course, you may change your position on any of these as you move through your career.

WHAT WILL YOUR JOB LOOK LIKE?

A good place to start mapping out what evaluation jobs might look like is to see the ways that ethnographers have put together evaluation jobs. Evaluation anthropologists are found in many different settings and combine anthropology with evaluation in many different ways. There are a number of roles that anthropologists (and other social scientists) assume as they conduct these evaluations. The following array of evaluator roles attempts to capture some of this variety. These roles are not necessarily mutually exclusive; many of us have seen ourselves in several of them at different stages in our careers. These are ideal types. You will probably come up with new ones. However, it is likely that over time you will work with most of these types of evaluators, depending, of course, on your work setting.

The Professional Evaluator. There are now people who study evaluation in graduate schools and have advanced degrees in evaluation. These people may be either academics or may work for businesses or agencies outside of universities. Many of these people conduct evaluation research to test the effectiveness and scientific quality of evaluation methods. They are often—but certainly not always—experimental, quasi-experimental, or survey experts. However, more and more professional evaluators are pioneers in developing naturalistic and qualitative approaches to evaluation.

The Academic Consultant. This is an academic-based evaluator, often with a full schedule of academic responsibilities, who provides advice to evaluations on a short-term basis. The results of the evaluation are not necessarily directed solely toward the project or agency personnel but may be more widely disseminated in journal articles. Although not specializing in the work of a single agency, consultants usually specialize in a single issue area (e.g., the cross-cultural application of mental health service delivery to refugees).

The Evaluation Anthropologist, Sociologist, Psychologist, Educator, and so forth. These are normally nonacademic-based evaluators who have learned skills in graduate school and/or the practice of evaluation. Historically, until in the twentieth century, most program evaluators, especially those doing ethnographic and case-study work, came from this group. Normally formal academic training in program evaluation was not completed, nor did the career begin in a program evaluation post. Applied research skills originally honed in the practice of anthropology (and other disciplines) are brought to bear on public-, private-, or not-for-profit-sector evaluation projects. I count myself in this group.

The Internal Evaluator. This is an academic- or nonacademic-based evaluator who is embedded in an organization devoted to program development and specializes in facilitating an environment conducive to the evaluation process. This can be a sensitive position, as the internal evaluator often has conflicting loyalties to the organization that employs him/her and the quality of the evaluation inquiry. Often these evaluators are responsible for developing and directing internal monitoring and audit processes. It is essential that rapport be developed over time with key administrators and peers for this approach to work. The facilitator works at a relatively high level within the hierarchy and is adept at empowering others.

The Educator. This is an academic-based evaluator who specializes in the formal training of others. This person conducts occasional evaluations. Although concerned with the empowerment of others, the educator is particularly interested in the transfer of knowledge, the enhancement of technical skills, and the mentoring of evaluators, most of whom are graduate students. Journal articles and other publications are seen as the primary way of disseminating this knowledge.

The Technical Expert: This is a nonacademic-based evaluator who is expert in applying particular evaluation tools. For example, the mixed methods coming under the rubric of outcome-based evaluation might well be in the tool kit of such a person. Quantitative and qualitative methods usually are well balanced in this person's arsenal, often to be applied in domestic or overseas contexts under challenging political conditions.

The Meta-Analyst: This is an academic- or nonacademic-based evaluator who is especially adept at analyzing the strengths and weaknesses of others' program evaluations. Among the more daring—and at times reviled—of the program evaluators, the analyst is capable of instilling either joy or fear in others' lives through professional presentations and publications (Butler, Copeland-Carson, and Van Arsdale 2005).

You can probably spot a number of dimensions in these approaches to evaluation. There are many characteristics that influence what you do. In fact, you may not be an evaluator at all; you may become a consumer or a user of evaluations.

WHERE WILL YOU WORK?

Evaluators are found everywhere, but here are some common kinds of organizations that hire evaluators in some capacity or another. The kind of organization you work for to a large extent determines the content of what you evaluate.

Businesses need to understand the relationship between people and products either before products go on the market or afterward. Product evaluations assess how people interact with products and what is likely to make them successful or unsuccessful given specific conditions. Businesses hire anthropologists directly. These jobs tend to pay quite well.

Technology Development/Technology Transfer. As the kinds of technology available expand and as new applications of technology are developed, evaluators are called on to clarify the human factors that may determine whether technology becomes a part of people's lives or fails because it doesn't fit with the ways people are willing to do things. This is an excellent role for anthropologists.

Community Development. Evaluation anthropologists often work as evaluators conducting needs and resource assessment and evaluating outcomes of community-based programs in the United States or elsewhere. Empowerment and participatory evaluations most often occur in this context. These evaluations are very often initiated by universities or community-based organizations (CBOs). Sometimes schools or health departments do community development projects.

International Development. This is anthropology's most traditional focus. The US Agency for International Development, many private international nongovernment organizations, and government agencies commission evaluations to demonstrate to funders the effectiveness and productivity of international development operations. Many of these evaluations are conducted under contract with companies specialized in doing these kinds of evaluations.

Foundations, international nongovernment organizations (NGOs), and charitable organizations of all sizes have these jobs. Few nonprofits, except for very large ones, can hire staff evaluators. Other staff positions in the nonprofit sector—for example, program administrators and analysts—have some evaluation components and may be a vehicle for crafting an evaluation-related career. Be prepared to multitask across many functions in these jobs. If you like diverse tasks, these are good jobs.

Education. Evaluation first developed within education as a means for assessing the efficacy and effectiveness of educational programs and was closely linked to measurement of achievement. School systems or educational institutions often hire internal evaluators. These used to be almost entirely experimental or quasi-experimental. They are still inclined in that direction, but educational evaluations have become more varied and flexible than they once were. School systems now do evaluations of community organizations linked to or supporting schools. These are often qualitative.

Environment. Assessments of the impact of humans on environments, ways in which people utilize environments, and processes of change in human-environment interactions are important areas for evaluators. Most of the people I know who are doing environmental evaluations are parts of federal agencies, university research centers, state or local governments, or private voluntary organizations.

Government. Government is a major consumer of evaluations. Government agencies at the federal, state, and local levels use evaluators—either internal or external through contracts—to assess whether they are meeting their own performance objectives and whether programs they operate are achieving their intended results. A lot of anthropologists work in government agencies and are often project officers for evaluations. These jobs are labeled "policy analyst" or, simply, "analyst." You need to talk to someone in the agency to see what the job is really about. Topics considered in these evaluations obviously depend on the agency. Surf the web to find out more.

Health Services. Public and private organizations that deliver health services in the United States and elsewhere do evaluations to assess health care needs in populations, determine how people choose and utilize health services, and identify barriers to health care delivery. Studies of cultural competency of health care organizations and service delivery are especially important areas for evaluation in which the anthropological perspective is needed.

Managed care organizations, clinics, and hospitals hire either external or internal evaluators to assess how they are doing in serving the populations in their catchment area. This interface between organizations and communities is a great place for anthropologists, especially if you have done research either in communities or health care settings.

Public Health. Evaluations of public health programs are done for federal and state agencies and for foundations and other nonprofits. They seek to know whether public health programs are reaching target populations, what barriers to prevention and control exist, and what factors govern the acceptability of public health services. These are done both internally and externally. Many of them are done under contract with companies with demonstrated expertise and experience in public health evaluation. Local health departments often have their own evaluators to assess their own programs.

Social Services. Evaluators often assess state or local programs designed to serve populations that need social support programs to help them cope with special barriers they may encounter in maintaining daily life. Some examples are evaluations of social welfare programs for the poor, programs designed to assist immigrant and refugee populations as they adjust to life in this country, or programs to assist physically or mentally disabled people in accessing and using services available to help them maintain a normal life.

Research. Evaluation anthropology careers can be applied or primarily oriented toward basic research. Evaluation research is a largely academic pursuit focusing on the development of method and theory for evaluation. At the present time there is a blossoming of innovative qualitative methods and inference in evaluation. Anthropologists have a natural niche in advancing this research agenda. Evaluation research can also inform anthropological scholarship. To cite just one of multiple possible examples, community development evaluation can inform political anthropology.

Independent Consulting. You may be able to build your own business in evaluation by promoting your research skills to evaluation clients. Independent consulting is a common way to start in evaluation for those who already have some skills and experience in either evaluation and/or the subject matter programs. Getting started can be an anxious process, and it can be slow. You must identify clients and sell yourself to them on an ongoing basis. But you can start with one client. You should do careful research before embarking in this direction unless you are an experienced evaluator. Can you find clients, and can you deliver what you promise? One way to start is to combine independent consulting with an academic job or other part-time endeavor. You will need to become adept at developing proposals and managing project budgets to be a successful consultant.

WHAT WILL YOUR JOB BE CALLED?

I used to joke with my family during one of my long periods of unemployment that "Yes, I looked for a job today. I looked in the *Washington Post,* and there weren't any jobs for anthropologists." This attitude characterized much of my first job search. I never saw a job ad for an anthropologist, although I did see some for archaeologists. This exercise with the want ads was often an excuse to knock off the job search until tomorrow. I didn't know where to look, and I didn't know what to look for.

Of course, you will not find a job listed for an "evaluation anthropologist" in nonprofessional sources. And your job may be advertised as almost anything. You need to read the job description to know what they are. Here are just a few that I pulled off the American Evaluation Association website that were advertised for master's-level candidates:

- program evaluator
- evaluation technical associate/assistant
- researcher
- research associate
- qualitative team manager
- study coordinator
- external evaluator

And a whole bunch of others. If you would like to repeat this experiment yourself, go to www.eval.org, "Career," then "Search jobs."

WHAT ELSE SHOULD I LEARN?

I think that one of the reasons that anthropologists and social scientists of all types do well as evaluators is that we are really good learners. The traditional field experience teaches us a lot about how to learn quickly. However, there were things that have been especially useful tools. These, of course, are different for different people. Mine are:

Statistics. I took a doctoral exam in statistics in lieu of taking an exam in German. This was one of the best things I ever did. Even if you don't go far into doing statistics, it's really good to be able to understand statisticians.

Programming. I learned SPSS when I was doing my dissertation because my adviser forced it on me. I was not thrilled, and I complained a lot. But when

I was an unemployed assistant professor of anthropology, I got a job as an SAS programmer. The understanding of the logic of quantitative analysis acquired on this job was a big help later when I began building mixed-method evaluation designs. If you enjoy computers, get good at some useful software. I especially recommend data-management and text-analysis software. This is very empowering.

Languages. Spanish. I have lots of other languages at some level. But Spanish I consistently use in my work. That's because the United States is the way it is. If you work elsewhere, you will need other languages. It's very hard to do either ethnography or evaluation if you don't speak the language. Also, whenever a project came up in a Spanish-speaking population, I got to do it!

Project Management. Any opportunity you have to manage research in any capacity, grab it. Management at some level is a key element of almost all professional jobs. You will eventually be called on to manage a project. Management skills involve the ability to make and execute a plan, share the plan with other people on the project, and monitor how the plan is being implemented.

Financial Management. Learn how to estimate and manage a budget. This was the hardest thing for me to figure out. Usually I was supported by a budget office that fed me information, but it was my job to monitor the fit between activity on the project and resources available. If you can find a workshop—face-to-face or online—familiarize yourself with cost management. It will bring abundant benefits. Cost overruns are bad for your career![2]

These kinds of skills set you apart from other applicants for a job. Employers assume that there will be a training period for project cost management and that mistakes will be made. This can be embarrassing and costly. They feel really good when a candidate demonstrates an awareness of the importance of these management skills. Make sure that these assets are listed on your résumé and come up in job interviews.

HOW TO FIND A JOB

Job hunts require planning and ongoing attention. Finding a job is a project, just like an evaluation or painting your house or anything else that has multiple activities n an interrelated chain of events. Like any project, you build a plan with the flexibility to change in the face of changing conditions or unanticipated events. Additionally, the steps proposed here may overlap. Step 1, Getting Smart, will probably continue through your job hunt. Others will be more typical of stages of your job hunt. Once you make a plan, don't ignore it. Revisit it about once a month to revise and expand it.

A job hunt is like a research project, so you will find that many of the skills you use in the job hunt are also what you will do on the job. You will collect data, talk to people, define what you want, and go for it. There is nothing here that you haven't done before. It's just that you are doing it with a job in mind.

STEP 1: GET SMART

Decide what you want to do and where you would like to do it. This doesn't need to be precise, but it's hard to look at the whole world at once. You can change and modify later, but you need to start somewhere. Think about what an ideal job might be and write it down. No limits. This is purely for you. And don't forget to consider geography. If you want to live in New Mexico, put this in your plan. Most of us live where our jobs landed us and never really thought about this. You can at least consider where you want to be before you commit.

Read up on evaluation as a discipline and be prepared to talk about it in job interviews. You have begun that process here. If you are in a job search, keep current. You never know when you can score points in an interview by being aware of the latest controversy. Skim blogs and websites on a regular basis, and investigate evaluation in your own area(s) of topical interest. What evaluations have been done in protecting tribal rights, preventing kids from smoking, marketing widgets—whatever you care about. If you don't have this kind of specialty yet, look for fields that excite you.

This process begins early in your education and will probably continue through your career. But for this process you want to focus on the content and context in which you might like to work, at least for a while. You can change your mind later; many of us have. But the longer you wait to do this, the harder it becomes. People will seek you out for expertise that you have acquired in your first couple of jobs.

STEP 2: NETWORK, NETWORK, NETWORK

It isn't possible to overstate the importance of networks in finding a job and managing a professional career. Most professionals get jobs from personal interaction with potential employers or people who know employers. This doesn't mean you shouldn't do other things to get a job, but you should try to stay connected with people working in places you would like to work in. Also, network building is an important tool you will nurture and use throughout your entire career. I have found that mine gets more important every year.

Your network is the most important asset you have, and you will go back to it over and over throughout your professional life. It is also, of course, invaluable in researching the job market, interviewing for information, and seeking reassurance if it gets hard. Make sure the right people in your network know that you are looking for a job. Like many people who have been around for a while, I am often asked whether I know someone who might be good for such and such a job.

Start building a professional network now if you haven't already. Everyone you know, certainly anyone you have ever worked with, is a potential contact. This includes present and former employers, people you know from professional organizations, people you have collaborated with on projects, and relatives who are knowledgeable about what you are doing.

Get business cards made with your own contact information and anything you consider important about you. You will get them from your company when you get a job. When I retired, I designed my own online and reorder when I run out. Cards cement your name in the minds of those you meet and makes it possible for them to find you.

Manage your contacts. Write down their name, contact information, area of specialization, and relationship to you or to other institutions. Try to keep track of everyone you meet who has any connection to what you want to do. I keep my network on my iPhone and back up frequently. I like this because I always have all the information I need at hand. Or you can devise some method for filing business cards.

STEP 3: INVESTIGATING YOUR JOB MARKET

Do your ethnography. Very little can be learned from the written page. This is the point at which you must begin to talk to people about jobs. You are not yet looking for a job; you're now trying to define the market for you skills in an area in which you would like to work. If you've gotten this far in this book, you probably understand how to do ethnography. Now you will do ethnography in the job market.

Interview for information. This is a trick I learned on my second job hunt, and it is very effective. Many of you may have done this as part of graduate practicums. You identify professionals, contact them, and ask them whether you can talk to them for a brief time (fifteen minutes is the norm) about what their job is like. You can tell them you're doing a job hunt, but emphasize that this conversation is not about a job; you want to talk to them about their jobs. Respect promises that you make to your interviewees. It is very uncomfortable to have someone pressing you for a job you don't have. And honor the fifteen-minute time limit: arrive on time, and leave when you promised you would.

You are doing ethnography in the job market to ascertain what jobs are like as they are experienced by people who hold them. What are the tasks, problems, and issues that come up? You can do this by networking in your network. Investigating the job market itself will build your network if you ask contacts whether there is anyone else you should talk to. Be honest about what you are doing, that you want information. Assure people that you are not asking them for a job, that this is part of your preparation for a search.

Most professionals are willing to do this if you come to them and if it is a limited amount of time. As ethnographers know, people love to talk about themselves and their own lives. And many professionals are committed to mentoring each other. Admittedly it can be daunting to contact people. When I did this, I had to cold-call people or write them letters. E-mail has made contacting people easier, but sometimes you have to follow up with a call. If someone declines to meet with you, just go on to the next person. Learning to deal with rejection is part of looking for a job. It is also part of being a professional.

STEP 4: PREPARING FOR THE JOB MARKET

You will start the actual job hunt by preparing a short résumé.[3] A résumé is a sales document. Its purpose is not to get you a job but to get you a job *interview*. You are trying to get the attention of people who can hire you. It is different from, for example, a curriculum vitae, which catalogs everything you have done as a professional. Use a curriculum vitae if you are looking for an academic job. Nonacademics usually don't have the time to wade through a fifteen-page CV.

Because this résumé will be widely circulated, it needs to be somewhat generic in that it will be read by many different people. At the same time, it must be specific enough to get the attention of organizations that have jobs in your target area.

You need to think about the job of the employer in selecting interviewees for specific jobs. In my own experience hiring evaluators and researchers, I would often get as many as a hundred résumés from candidates from my company's personnel department. When I reviewed them, I made three piles:

Yes, No, and Think About It. After I had scanned all of them (maybe thirty seconds each), I put the Nos (about 60 percent) and the Yeses (maybe 10 percent) aside. The remaining 30 percent in the Think About It pile I read carefully and assigned them to the Yes pile or the No pile. Then I went back to the Yes pile (maybe ten to fifteen résumés) and prioritized them, and the top three got called for interviews. If none of them worked out, we went to the next person on the list until we filled the job. Normally we interviewed at least three people before we made a decision on who to hire. Once the person was called for an interview, the priorities no longer counted. A good or bad interview guides hiring decisions. However, if your résumé doesn't make it through this stage, you are no longer a candidate for this job.

At the point of these first reviews I have only your résumé (and maybe a cover letter) to judge you. I consider your résumé to be a sample of your standards in producing written material. You want your résumé to get you into the top three or at least close to that. The following things govern my review decisions:

- The résumé is clear. I can understand what you are trying to say. There aren't too many words or words that are mysterious or inappropriate. Evaluation jobs, no matter who they are for, require this kind of clarity. People need to be able to understand what you are saying.
- Important features are relevant to the job and easy to find. This is one reason why you have done all of the research in Steps 1 and 3. You need to distill the information you have into a job that you would like to have. Highlight any skills and experience you may have that are important to the job you are seeking. Sometimes these things are bonuses that set you apart—computer skills, research skills, and any experience you have had that relates to what you want to do. You may think that telemarketing job was a bust, but it tells me that you can do telephone interviews and are not timid about contacting people.
- The résumé is attractive and well produced. Remember you have thirty seconds to sell me. If the résumé is too wordy, poorly produced, or messy in any way, it goes into the No pile immediately.
- There are no grammatical and spelling errors. This leads to immediate rejection of your résumé. You need to do more than spell-check it; you need some other person to read it and look for errors. Also, I am turned off by words that don't really mean what they are trying to convey. This usually happens when people are trying to use long words because

they think they are impressive. Beware long words and words that are seldom used in normal conversation. You are trying to communicate in a clear and pleasant way. Full sentences are not always necessary, as long as a partial statement conveys the information you want to get across.

- The résumé is one page long, maybe two at the outside. This is the thing that people most often have trouble with. It takes clear thought, precision, and efficiency of communication. Remember you are trying to sell. The full list of your accomplishments can come later.

What should be in your short résumé?

It depends, of course, on what you want to get across. At a minimum it should have:

- Your contact information at the top—your name, address, phone number, e-mail. If you have a website, put it here.
- Your education—degrees, universities, and year—can be simply listed. They speak for themselves. Feel free to omit your high school unless that's the only diploma you have.
- Your work experience, especially that which is relevant to the job you're looking for. What you do with this and how can vary. If you have had twenty jobs in the past five years, list only those that relate to your search. If you have space, include a sentence on what about this job is relevant. For example, if you had an administrative job while you were in school, highlight things like maintained computer files, used Access, helped students solve administrative problems.
- Any special accomplishments like publications, awards—whatever you think might make you stand out.

Do not include references in this résumé, but you can put in a statement that references are available on request at the bottom. You don't want people calling your references before you get a job interview.

There are some things I don't especially like to see in résumés, although opinions differ on what these are. You will need to use your own judgment when deciding how to handle these.

I am turned off by résumés that are structured around your career goals or what kind of job you want. You need to think this out carefully before you can do a résumé at all. But I have specific kinds of jobs. I am far more interested in what I want than what you want. And I find it boring. I know your career goals aren't stable unless you are at least forty years old. And what if you want the wrong kind of job?

Do not include personal details like hobbies, interests, or travel experience. I don't need to know right now that you like spelunking. These are all interesting things about you, but I will find all this out later.

Other materials you might want to bring to a job interview are a list of references and a list of projects you have done or publications. Although these don't fit into the short résumé, they are good to hand out at job interviews.

Finally, let me reiterate the importance of having at least one other person review your résumé before you use it. There will be mistakes that spell-check misses, and you are too close to the content to see all errors.

STEP 5: APPLYING FOR JOBS

Now that you have your résumé, you are ready to start looking for jobs. The first step is to circulate this résumé widely to organizations that are advertising for jobs you might want, anyone you interviewed for information, and people in your network who may know of jobs that might fit you. You will also carry copies of this résumé with you when you go to information interviews and job interviews. You will take it to professional encounters of all kinds (meetings, social events, projects). Use your judgment to decide when it is appropriate to give out a résumé. You might not want to do this at your father's retirement party, for example. You can always tell people you are looking for a job and, if they seem interested, send them a résumé later.

Next, you need to get your résumé into the hands of the person who can hire you. This will almost always be a professional who is supervising technical work. Personnel departments get you nothing; their job is to advertise the job, circulate résumés, and do the paperwork required by the employer. You will, of course, have to deal with them. For example, most employers now want you to apply for the job online. Do what they require, but don't expect results. Often I have explained to a person who has had a successful interview how to apply online for the job. At this point the job is filled, although the interviewee may not know it yet.

Apply for a *lot* of jobs. Research jobs on the web, and circulate your résumé to key people in your network and those you have met in your background research. Don't make the mistake of falling in love with a job in an interview and stopping your job search while you wait to see whether it pans out. If you get a second job offer, you can call the first interviewer and ask how close they are to making a decision. Then make your decision in light of what they tell you. There is no reason not to do it. Employers expect it.

Don't be afraid to take a job that falls short of your dreams. Hey, it's only a first job. You have probably heard you need to have a job to find a job. If you do your job well, offers will begin to come across your desk. But first you need a foot in the door. Don't take a job you loathe, but don't be too picky either.[4]

STEP 6: THE JOB INTERVIEW

A job interview is different from an information interview. It is a dress rehearsal for the job. Can you articulate your understanding of the job and your qualifications? Can you work well with existing staff? How will you work with clients? Will you be a credible professional?

Try to project confidence in your qualifications for the job. You have learned a lot in the early part of your job search. Of course, there are a lot of qualified people for any job, but you are probably as qualified as anyone else. So lay that worry aside. In all of the interviews I've been in on the hiring side, people get hired because the interviewers like them, feel comfortable with them. In my interviews on the applicant side I finally came to understand that interviewing me was their job. My job was to interview them to see whether I could be happy working here. It helped a lot to focus me on the specific job, and in at least one case, it kept me from making a mistake in switching jobs. See Box 7.1 for what the whole process looks like to the people who are interviewing you.

Before the interview find out as much as you can about the organization and the part of it you would work in. Read any ads for the job carefully. The problem with professional job ads is that employers often don't know exactly what they want, so they ask for everything they might conceivably want. You should focus on the skills part of the ad and not get discouraged by the scale of their expectations.

Think about salary *before* you get into the interview. If you are a serious contender for the job, someone will ask you for your salary expectations. They must know this to take your application to the next step. So make this information part of your research. Ask people with similar jobs what they make. Look online for comparable jobs. The Bureau of Labor Statistics has information on the pay ranges for specific jobs.[5] Even if you have to guess, it's better to guess than to look surprised when an interviewer asks you about

---

Box 7.1 Rapport in the Job Interview: What the Employer Sees

I have interviewed many people for many different kinds of jobs. Here's what it was like for me:

First of all, I have a problem. There is too much work, not enough people and the current staff are getting surly. I desperately want to put someone in the job! But it has to be someone who is competent or I get yet more surliness and may have to go through the enormous hassle of firing a bad hire. Oh yes, and I have fifteen minutes to do this interview before I have a client meeting.

So here comes the applicant.

The first thing I notice is your appearance. Will you freak the client out or do you look professional. This is not the time to make a fashion statement. Attractive but sort of conservative. Does your attitude show competence and confidence? Are you knowledgeable about the employer and the job? Do you ask good questions? Can you articulate your positions well? Have you thought about the job?

All of this happens in the first minute of the interview.

If you fail on these criteria, you may get the job, but now I'm worried about whether you are personally capable of working here. You now have fourteen minutes to convince me.

If you look like a good prospect, we have a pleasant discussion of the job and how you might fit into what we do. When you walk out, we both feel good.

---

your salary requirement. Also check out fringe benefits—health benefits, vacation time, and incentive pay.

You probably learned this in third grade. Send an e-mail to follow up and thank people. It makes them feel warm and fuzzy. I prefer e-mails to personal notes, just because it makes you look up to date; almost no one sends handwritten notes anymore.

STEP 7: PASS IT ON

Now that you have a job, you yourself have gotten pretty savvy about how to do this. Don't retire from your professional networks. And consider carefully opportunities to pass your experience on to others. I have given you my experience here. Yours will be different. Our understanding of the role of anthropologist evaluators and those of social scientists in the job market is in its infancy. But it has grown in recent years because of the contributions of people who have been out there in the field. Publish articles and contribute to blogs, seek out local groups that mentor unemployed people in your discipline, tell your story over and over—you never know what will motivate and encourage someone else.

So this looks like a *long* process. Will it take the rest of my life? Of course not. But how long it does take is a hard question to answer with any response other than *it depends*. I would guess it will take anywhere from three months to a year from Step 1, depending on the demand in the job market and luck. If you need a job to keep your household afloat while you hunt, I would recommend a job that is easy to find and has flexible hours so you can be available to meet with people during the work day. This may sound like a hassle—it is. But this is your *life!* Time invested now will pay dividends later.

RESOURCES

How do I find the things I need to get smart and find potential employers? The web, of course! This is not the only way, but it's a good place to start. AAA, SfAA, and the American Evaluation Association all have websites that post jobs. Also, if you have a specialty—education, environment, public health, international development—search the websites of their professional organizations. The American Evaluation Association website is especially good for evaluators because this is where a lot of people go if they know that an evaluator is what they need. Many large cities have local evaluation societies. The one in Washington, DC, for example, is called Washington Evaluators. Their meetings are rich sources of evaluation exposure and job resources. And you get to meet people who hire. There may be other local professional networks for practitioners in your discipline. For example, in Washington, the Washington Association for Professional Anthropologists (WAPA) is a very important resource for anthropologists seeking jobs. These kinds of associations are great because their meetings and activities will bring you together with people in your profession and your community who are doing evaluation and can give you advice based on their knowledge of these specifics. They also help you to get known.

CHAPTER EIGHT

FUTURE PATHWAYS

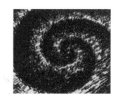

W hen I was a kid, I ran across an aunt's copy of the 1939 New York World's Fair Program. It was fascinating. The participants in that event envisioned a world in which the houses would all be molded of plastic (tried without success at the Montreal World's Fair many years later) and we would all commute in our own private airplanes (can you imagine the traffic and the fatalities!). There were even pictures of this new world. By the time I got ahold of this in the early 1950s, this world wasn't going to happen in my lifetime and maybe never. Prognosticating about the future is a free exercise. Even if you're wrong, nobody is likely to remember. So here goes.

WHEREFORE EVALUATION?

In 2011 I went to the annual meeting of the American Evaluation Association, something I don't always do. But I was part of a panel (on evaluation anthropology actually) and I had never been to Anaheim so I went. While I was there, I ran into an old friend of mine, a well-known evaluator who specializes in quasi-experimental evaluations of prevention programs in communities. "I feel strange here," he said. "Everything is about qualitative evaluation of some kind of another." A scan of the program supported his contention. There was an abundance of sessions dealing with new uses, new directions, and new approaches to qualitative methods in evaluation. Also, there were plenty of anthropologists there and presenting in sessions. It was very gratifying and very reassuring.

There are a number of trends in evaluation that will increase the value of anthropologists and other social scientists working in the qualitative domain as evaluators over the next few decades. There are changes leading to more use of qualitative methodologies, participatory approaches, and a focus on making inferences from the study of localities. Evaluation is globalizing and moving into other parts of the world. There is pressure to identify and correct ethnocentrism and power differences as evaluators approach communities.

These are all things anthropologists do well. In the future there will be important jobs, interesting jobs, and fun jobs for us as evaluators if we learn to apply our skills in the field of evaluation.

The dominance of the evaluator as an agent of government using experimental methods to evaluate the outcome of government programs is attenuating for a number of reasons. First, experimental and even quasi-experimental studies are costly and may fail to produce findings that are useful and practical in managing programs. Second, there is a lessening legitimacy of and trust in government on the part of program developers and implementers, forcing agencies to incorporate more participatory evaluation methods in their portfolios. This is not to say that experimental designs are no longer important; these kinds of evaluations are still the best funded and, to some, are still the only way to achieve truly valid results. But the use of experimental designs is less dominant in evaluation than it once was.

The distrust of experimental evaluations also comes from a more scientific direction. Because experimental evaluations imply administering a standardized test or "treatment" to a large number of people across a large geographic region, they obtain results that were easily interpretable. However, the standard experimental approach seeks to iron out differences among individual cases. This is intrinsic to the design that assumes an underlying reality that governs programs and can be demonstrated if you "control out" differences. The experimental method tends to be short on the kind of detail that distinguishes one implementation from another. Some of these differences may be linked to program effectiveness and cost effectiveness. But these may be folded into the error term in an experiment.

The past decade or so has seen the development, elaboration, and use of qualitative and mixed-method approaches. In fact, qualitative approaches have become so effective that, as House points out (2001b), the dispute over which methods are best is effectively over. I am less sure of this than he is, but still, as qualitative approaches to evaluation become more widely used—and qualitative analysis becomes more systematic—they also became more precise and more credible. People began to trust their results as they became more familiar with things like ethnographic methods. And policy makers and program staff can use the detailed and actionable results they produced directly in program change.

At one time government at the federal, state, or local levels was the primary—indeed, almost exclusive—users of evaluation. Now independent evaluations are being conducted at all levels of governments and by private foundations, businesses, and other organizations. This increasing visibility of evaluation as an effective way to understand what you are doing and its effects on the community has been good news for us all. It is good for us because as evaluation becomes more "local," it also becomes more participatory. Community evaluations are almost always directed by a coalition or consortium of community members who are vigilant to make sure evaluators know everything that may support evaluation findings.

Other changes in evaluation have followed on this shift to more local and more qualitative approaches. Cross-disciplinary approaches have become more important because a wide range of professional competencies is usually needed to understand the diverse perspectives of communities, social groups, and organizations. In participatory approaches evaluators are partners of the community in making evaluation happen. House discusses a shift from "value-free" evaluations, in which only "facts" are considered, to evaluations that treat social facts and values as the same kind of thing, describable and analyzable in the same ways as "hard facts" (House 2001a). This is a shift away from the positivist position that facts stand on their own and judgments about those facts are irrelevant. To many evaluators nowadays, values *are* social facts and can be treated as such.

Evaluation as a profession and as a valued activity is going global. Globalization and the emergence of an international evaluation community as well as collaborative projects between US evaluators and those in other countries has created a whole new field that is just beginning to emerge. To participate in this new and exciting kind of evaluation, we need to learn to be good partners to evaluators in host countries where we work. An evaluation conducted internationally cannot correctly penetrate the local situation without help from those who live and work in the society that incorporates the matter being evaluated. Evaluation across national borders is scrutinized and critiqued for ethnocentrism on the part of foreign evaluators and a failure to understand and accommodate to power relations in the host society. Anthropology has dealt with this problem—effectively or ineffectively—over its entire history. Of all people, we should be able to help address this problem as we move into our careers.

Chelimsky (2012) points out the critical nature of educating ourselves in a political environment. The political context is not something we can "control out" of studies. Even when I started evaluating things in the early nineties, evaluators were anxious to remain politically neutral in considering their role as evaluators so as to avoid biasing their evaluation. We have learned in the past couple of decades that this is almost impossible because everything we touch as evaluators is political. Evaluations are usually requested to resolve political positions, to support someone's idea of what should be done. Evaluation in the hands of users is political power. Evaluators are at least dimly aware of the political implications of their work. They worry about hegemony and the power of evaluators as experts to blind them to the perspectives of the powerless or even to understand how political power works to privilege some and disenfranchise others.

WHEREFORE ANTHROPOLOGY?

I got into practicing anthropology after I failed as an academic. I was denied tenure in my eighth year of undergraduate teaching, really through no fault of my own. And it no longer matters why. I was on the street, an unemployed assistant professor of anthropology. As everyone always used to ask me, what was I going to do with *that*? I couldn't imagine what to do or what would become of me. Was I still an anthropologist? Did I have to recareer, maybe go back to biology? Where would I look for jobs, and what could I possibly tell people I could do? I had no knowledge or skills to handle these questions and no place in the anthropology of the 1980s where I could look for help.

After a few false starts, I stumbled into evaluation by a series of happenstances. I had never heard of evaluation, didn't know what it is or who did it, but alas, I had a job doing it. Surely I would be able to figure this out the same way I had figured out how to do ethnography. I landed on my feet as an anthropologist doing evaluations of public health programs on the ground in communities, state and local health departments, and other countries. It was an incredible piece of luck. The CDC at that time didn't realize that an anthropologist was what they needed in order to understand what was going on out there. I was one of many people who taught them that they did.

It's not this way anymore. In working with students over the past decade or so, I see things changing. Increasingly student anthropologists choose careers in anthropological practice from the start, some because they are realistic about their chances for a rewarding academic career. Others, however, have found professors, role models, and mentors who turned them on to the achievements and sense of personal efficacy that come from pushing on the state of the world around them and seeing it respond, something that happens often in the practice of anthropology.

The world has changed too. Employers come looking for anthropologists to help them develop products and programs, estimate the impact of what they do, and communicate with diverse audiences. A few years ago the US Department of Labor approached the National Association for the Practice of Anthropology (NAPA) for assistance in developing a Standard Occupational Code and title for anthropologists. This is a real advance in the visibility of anthropology out there beyond our own enclave.

We live in a moment when anthropology as a discipline is beginning to move to the center screen of people who are trying to understand how to run the world under conditions of diversity, globalization, rapid culture change, economic dependency, and seemingly endless tribal wars. Working with others to understand these things is a real opportunity for anthropologists everywhere. For us to leverage these opportunities into employment, we need to move beyond the controversies within anthropology about what we are trying to do and what constitutes a real anthropologist. Most especially we need to move beyond the academic-practice divide—if for no other reason—for our students. It is our job—all of our jobs—to create for the next generation an anthropology that effectively integrates the teaching of anthropology in the broadest sense with the dynamic stage on which anthropological practice occurs.

Of course, people have been saying this for years. There has been some movement in the American Anthropological Association (AAA) toward better integrating practice into the discipline with the Committee on Practicing, Applied and Public Interest Anthropology (CoPAPIA), now established as a standing committee of the association. But the big changes need to come—among other places—in academic departments of anthropology, some of which are still telling students that a practitioner is a failed academic.

If you are an anthropologist, I encourage you to stay in anthropology. When you go into practice, this requires a deliberate effort. Many of us don't do it and will argue that you shouldn't either. It can be discouraging to work with anthropological associations as a practitioner. For example, AAA is still strongly biased toward academic interests; every gain for practitioners is hard won. But it would probably be easier to win battles if so many excellent practitioners hadn't simply retired from the field. Either the role of practitioners grows stronger in the professional anthropological associations or practitioners will get discouraged and leave. When this happens, anthropological associations will turn into learned societies where esoteric things are debated. Any public vision that we have been able to create of anthropology as a dynamic part of the world will attenuate and eventually disappear.

Finally, I think we're living in a time of great uncertainty. At one time Americans were comfortable that science would provide the answer to everything, that all you needed to do with a program was to determine as carefully as you could whether it "worked." The last decades of the twentieth century and, so far, all of the twenty-first have taught us that certainties aren't certain! Many of us have learned that it's usually best to suspend judgment and see how it turns out.

And for now that is where I'll leave the future.

APPENDIX A

GLOSSARY OF TERMS

action anthropology—Anthropological position that says ethnographers must move beyond static description of culture to provide studied peoples with information and technical assistance needed to improve their lives.

Advisory Panel—A short- or long-term committee of evaluation stakeholders from different perspectives brought together to guide an evaluation at any or all stages of its development. Their purpose is to ensure that the evaluation is well-articulated with the program.

anonymity—No personal identifiers are ever collected as part of research data.

anthropology—Discipline defined by a central concern with culture and with the broad conditions of being human.

applied anthropology—That branch of anthropology that uses anthropology to address real-world, contemporary problems. Found both inside and outside of the academy.

attribution—Establishing that an observed program outcome was a result of a program intervention rather than unrelated or spurious events.

Belmont Report—Findings of the National Commission for the Protection of Human Subjects of Biomedical and Behavioral Research in 1979; forms the basis for IRB guidance.

bias—Distortion of perspective in a study that comes from the investigator's or the respondents' preconceived ideas of how the world works; may be conscious or unconscious.

briefing—Oral presentation of an evaluation conducted for clients upon its completion; includes all aspects of the evaluation; PowerPoint often used.

case—A single instance of some program or organization described in depth.

case study—Research in which some unit of analysis (the case) is studied in depth with the objective of obtaining as complete a description as possible relative to some topic.

client—Person or organization that requests an evaluation; usually pays for it and plans to use it for some purpose.

closed interview—Interview that is guided by an instrument with specific questions and answer choices. The items must be administered in the specified order; probes are specified. There is usually no interviewee-initiated input.

community—A group of people linked by social ties into an organization that serves some purpose; may be based on geography but also can be established on the basis of shared interest, political commitment, profession, or affinity. As the name implies, communities imply some kind of regular communication.

confidentiality—Protection of subject identity in such a way that personal identifiers are not linked to data records but may be kept in a list under lock and key.

constructivist—Philosophical stance that holds that reality is assembled by each observer and will differ from person to person.

context—The physical, social, political, and ideological surroundings in which some human activity occurs. Context is a critical part of qualitative study.

cost-benefit study—Estimates both direct (monetary) and indirect (non-monetary) benefits of a program per unit cost.

cost-effectiveness study—Estimates of the direct cost per client served or per unit outcome.

credibility—An evaluation is of sufficient quality for decision makers to use it to guide decisions; requires quality, validity, reliability.

culture—The learned, shared ideas and behaviors that people have because they live within a particular group of human beings.

cultural competence—Programs are designed and implemented in a way that is sensitive to and responsive to the cultural context in which they are presented.

deduction—Pattern of observation that seeks to test ideas against reality. The idea, or hypothesis, is prior.

Deliberate demographic evaluation—An evaluation approach in which the stakeholders are brought in in an inclusive way and invited to surface and discuss counterclaims around the evaluation issue. Full and open discussion of all claims is used to reach evaluation findings.

double-blind study—An experimental approach in which neither the investigator nor the subject knows whether the subject is in the treatment or control group; controls for bias in random assignment and in administration of the treatment.

efficacy—A study or measure of how well a program can do in achieving what it seeks to achieve under optimal conditions. Pilot studies in which an idea is tested under optimal conditions is an example of an efficacy study.

effectiveness—A study or measure of the ability of a program to achieve results under natural conditions of implementation.

emic—Observation of an activity or structure from the perspective of insiders in a cultural system.

empiricist—Use of a scientific approach to generate evidence for some interpretation of reality.

empowerment evaluation—Evaluation is a tool that supports participants in a program in achieving their own goals to improve their lives.

epistemology—Concern with the nature of knowledge and how we acquire it: Do you observe people or do you measure what you see?

ethics—Responsibility of human researchers to protect the rights and interests of subjects who participate in their research.

etic—Observation of an activity or structure from the perspective of an outside observer (like an anthropologist or an evaluator).

ethnography—An approach to investigating some kind of human community by seeking to understand cultural events as they are experienced by the insider.

evaluability assessment—Study to determine whether a program is sufficiently implemented and coherent to support an evaluation at the current time; done prior to a more extensive evaluation.

evaluand—The entity that is being evaluated. It can be a program, a process, a project, or anything else that can be described well enough to be evaluated.

evaluation—A scientific endeavor conducted for the purpose of describing the worth, value, and/or effectiveness of some activity directed to serving a human need or solving a human problem.

evaluation anthropology—Synthesis of evaluation and anthropology theories and methods to develop and implement evaluations that take advantage of both disciplines; explicitly does *not* include all of the evaluations that anthropologists do, only those that integrate both disciplines into something synergistic.

executive summary—A summary of an evaluation containing a problem statement, method, results, and recommendations; about ten pages long; important part of final report.

Expert Panel—a group of subject matter experts gathered to refine needs, make concrete solutions, and ensure buy-in from clients in an evaluation. They usually only meet once to review and revise specific products such as evaluation plans or reports. Experts are important for projects that are technically complex or politically charged.

experimental evaluation—An evaluation that seeks to assess program effects by comparing a group of individuals receiving some program exposure (treatment) with a group receiving either no program exposure or an alternative program. Respondents are randomly assigned to program (treatment) and nonprogram (control) groups before the program begins.

external evaluator—An evaluator who does not work for the organization running the program to be evaluated; may work for a university, a consulting firm, or as an independent evaluator.

external validity—The data that are collected apply to other similar situations; that is, they are generalizable to units that were not part of the study.

face validity—A set of results is plausible, i.e. it makes sense to an intelligent observer.

feasibility—The degree to which something can be put into effect within realistic limitations.

focus group—A data-collection technique in which a group of people selected on some set of criteria are asked to respond to a research question in open discussion.

formative evaluation—Evaluation that seeks to detect changes that will improve a program prior to full implementation.

generalization—Extending findings from a research entity to other similar ones that were not studied.

Government Performance and Results Act of 1993 (updated 2010)—Popularly known as GPRA (Gip-ruh); legislation designed to make government agencies responsible for the results of its programs according to measurable criteria; funding based on results.

goal-free evaluation—An evaluation that asks whether the program achieved a desirable outcome; not concerned with what the program intends to do but with what it actually accomplishes.

grounded method—A very inductive approach that lets research questions arise from the population being studied; resists a priori notions of what is happening in the research context.

group interview—Convene participants in a program or project for an informal discussion of the program; goal of group interviews is usually an understanding of the group dynamic; not question directed like a focus group.

Hawthorne effect—The idea that the fact of observation alters human behavior.

ideology—System of beliefs that governs how we live our lives; cultural and often invisible to those who hold it.

impact evaluation—Evaluation of the effects or a program on the population reached or intended.

implementation fidelity—the degree to which a program is implemented according to the program plan.

induction—Pattern of observation that seeks to determine general principles by systematic observation. The observation is prior.

internal evaluator—An evaluator who works for the organization managing the program or project to be evaluated; usually a full-time employee who does routine evaluations and audits.

internal validity—The data that are collected are accurate; that is, they provide a correct version of what is observed or measured.

institutional review board (IRB)—Appointed group of experts who review research for compliance with standards to protect the interests of human research respondents. IRBs are assembled by universities, research foundations and organizations, and private businesses. They must be certified by the federal Office for the Protection of Human Subjects (OPHS)

Informational interview—A brief interview with a professional to discuss their job, their employment and their professional activities. It is different from a job interview.

logic model—A map of program theory or rationale; diagrams what conditions govern whether a program achieves the objectives it sets out to achieve.

methodology—Theory underlying how we use methods; goes beyond methods to the rationale for them.

mixed method—An approach to investigation that relies on combinations of both descriptions (qualitative) and measurement (quantitative) methods to generate answers to a shared research question or questions.

multidisciplinary—A research project or an evaluation that operates across many different disciplines and combines them in such a way as to utilize the strengths of each.

needs assessment—a study done to determine the needs of a population and/or their priorities for meeting needs.

nongovernment organizations (NGOs)—Private or public programs that seek to address human needs independently of any single government; very important in international work.

Office of Management and Budget (OMB)—Federal agency charged with budgetary oversight activities.

OMB clearance—Review and evaluation of research funded by the federal government on the basis of benefits, costs, and necessity of the research for the taxpayers. Required for all studies in which the researcher is a government official or is acting as an agent of the government in which more than nine respondents will be asked the same set of questions.

ontology—Concern with the nature or being or reality: in this context, is reality real or constructed?

open-ended interview—An interview in which only the topic to be discussed is known ahead of time. The interview is allowed to follow its own logic with occasional probes to keep on topic.

outcome evaluation—Assesses the degree to which a program achieved an outcome, either that envisioned in the program design or some outcome that achieves a desirable consequence.

paradigm—Set of theories, research questions, assumptions, and definitions that define a scientific community; learned as part of training in a discipline and seldom questioned by its practitioners.

parametric statistics—Statistical methods that seek to build inferences to a defined population by studying a random sample of it.

participant observation—Data collected by observation while participated in some program- or project-related activity; participating in meetings, observing public places, working alongside study subjects.

participatory evaluation—Evaluation in which stakeholders actively work with evaluators in evaluation design, implementation, analysis, and recommendations.

pattern analysis—Method for analyzing case-study data by building comparative matrices within each site and across sites.

policy—Ideas, assumptions, and conditions surrounding ideas of what is appropriate to do in a given situation and why; governs decision making around activities such as programs.

positivism—The belief that there is an external truth out there that is knowable and testable; a philosophical stance that holds that there is an objective reality outside of the observer that can be known by empirical study.

postpositivist—A philosophical stance that holds that there is an objective reality, but it is unknowable because we can only get at it through the filter of human perception.

process evaluation—Assessment of the decisions and actions involved in implementing and operating a program.

practicing anthropology—That branch of anthropology that applies the theories and methods of anthropology outside of academia, either part time or full time.

program—Organized set of activities that seeks to meet some kind of human need.

program theory—The set of ideas underlying how a program should operate to achieve what it set out to do. Program theory is usually the basis of logic models.

protocol—A standard set of procedures that is used to govern some set of activities in a standard way. We are most concerned with evaluation protocols, training protocols, and scientific protocols that protect the quality of evaluations.

qualitative approach—An approach to investigation that relies on description of instances of something and their analysis by comparison.

quantitative approach—An approach to investigation that relies on measurement of the observed and analysis relying on statistics or other mathematical measurements.

quasi-experimental evaluation—An evaluation that seeks to assess program effects by comparing a group of individuals receiving some program exposure (treatment) with a group receiving either no program or an alternative program. Members of the treatment group receive the program. Control groups are assembled by measuring potential members against a set of demographic and/or sociocultural criteria chosen to ensure comparability on characteristics that are likely to be relevant to the desired program outcome.

quintain—A group of similar entities from which cases are drawn for case studies; defines the set to which the case may apply.

rapid assessment—A study or evaluation in which standard methods are applied to a well-defined evaluation question in a short period of time to produce results that are needed urgently; requires clarity and discipline in the choice of methods and their application; usually involves a team of investigators.

recommendations—Data-based suggestions for changes to programs based on an evaluation.

relativism—A philosophical stance that holds all truth to be defined in its own cultural context. At its extreme a relativist will hold that all alternative ways of being are equally valid.

reliability—Would another investigator achieve similar results under similar conditions? Always relative in dealing with human life. However, results that appear out-of-line with others using similar methods in similar contexts require further investigation to determine the reason for the difference.

Responsive evaluation—Approach in which the evaluator begins the evaluation with no pre-conceived notion about the appropriate evaluation design. The design is undertaken only after a understanding of the program is obtained from preliminary work. sampling—Units or respondents are recruited for a survey in such a way that each eligible entity in the population studies has an equal chance of being included. Eligibility is defined by sampling criteria.

sample frame—The defined population from which study units are sampled.

semistructured interview—An interview that is guided by a central topic and a list of subtopics or areas to be covered. Topics can arise in any order and are left to the interviewee to fill in.

stakeholder—An individual or organization that has a personal or professional interest (or stake) in the outcome of an evaluation (not necessarily the program, although they commonly overlap).

structural functionalism—Theory holding that culture is best understood as a system of structures set up to achieve particular functions; first step away from an anthropology that focused on static description.

structured interview—An interview that is guided by a set of specific questions administered in a set order. There is normally room for the interviewee to add material or elaborate. No answer choices must be made.

subculture—Identifiable variant of a cultural pattern; often based on ethnicity or geographic region.

summative evaluation—Evaluation of the effects of a program after implementation.

theory—A systematic set of rules for exploring how things work and why.

thick description—Very detailed description of culture or an event in cultural context.

triangulation—Establishing the validity of a finding by comparing results from multiple data sources.

unobtrusive observation—Information gleaned by looking carefully at study settings and behavior of people in natural interactions. Usually part of notes. No instruments.

utilization-focused evaluation—Evaluation focus and design are chosen to maximize usefulness of the final product to those who will use the results; involves intensive consultation with stakeholders in building the evaluation design.

validity—Are scientific results accurate within a specified frame of reference? Are they an adequate guide for action?

APPENDIX B

THE BUSINESS SIDE

This appendix is included in response to requests of many students who have attended various workshops I have given over the past several years. There is a whole range of business concepts and terms that people in the public and private sectors use as if everyone understood what they meant. Because most of us don't have MBAs, this appendix assembles some of these concepts into what is hopefully a coherent framework.

I work either for consulting firms or as an independent mostly under contract to federal and state agencies and nonprofit organizations. My understanding of business comes from this perspective. Much of what is in this appendix deals with arrangements for working in this capacity. This material will also apply if you work for a government agency or a nonprofit that enters into contracts to conduct evaluations. Outside of these contexts some will be useful and some won't. Take what you can use and leave the rest. I have sought here to help you refine your questions rather than provide any kind of definitive guidance.

LABOR DEFINITIONS

Exempt and nonexempt staff. The "exempt" refers to whether you are subject to the provisions of the Fair Labor Standards Act of 1938. This act specifies the condition under which people are to be paid for their time. Nonexempt staff work to the clock. They must be paid a fixed rate for every hour they work. If they work overtime, they must be paid time and a half. If they work on weekends and holidays, they are paid double. Exempt staff work to the job. They agree to accomplish a specified load of work in a specified number of hours. They then must work as long as it takes to get the job done while (theoretically) charging the agreed-upon hours. They get no overtime pay. Nonexempt staff are those with jobs that are repetitive or predictable in some way (clerical staff, computer programmers, support staff of all kinds). Exempt staff are usually professionals. Your job is likely to be exempt unless you work part time. Part-time staff in any capacity are nonexempt.

Comp time (or compensation time). In some (but not all) organizations, there is a policy that exempt staff can take time off to compensate for time they worked that is beyond their forty hours/week. For example, if you work forty-eight hours straight on a proposal, you can take a day off to recover. The slang term for this is "comp time," and using it is called "comping it out." However, comp time is not legally mandated; it is a policy of individual organizations. You must check to see whether the organization you are working for has this policy.

Time recording. When you start work, you will be given a paper or virtual time sheet or time card. If you are exempt staff, you need to account for forty hours work a week and no more. This time must be allocated to projects and business activities such as staff meetings, talks with your boss, and company-related activities. You must record actual time worked. This is not like the academy or the government, where you just do your work and get paid. And it has nothing to do with how many hours you are budgeted to work on specific projects.

PROCUREMENT INTEGRITY

If you are working for a company, you are competing with other similar companies for work. If you are a government employee managing projects, you are trying to be fair all around. For all of you there are penalties for compromising free and open competition. The government is assiduous in enforcing fairness among its employees, contractors, grantees, and partners. Ignorance is no excuse.

Procurement integrity. This is the overall term for fairness in competition for work with the federal government. Procurement is governed by the Federal Acquisition Regulations (FAR). You will often hear your own colleagues and your clients refer to the FAR.

Audits. Because your company has an agreement with the government, once in a while some very officious people will appear in your office, wanting to see your timesheet. These are auditors, people sent by the federal government to make sure you are honoring your half of the deal. Your part of an audit is your time sheet. They will review your time sheet to make sure everything has been done according to policy. They may ask you questions about what the policy is. They may use scenarios: "What if you leave work for two hours to go to the dentist? How do you charge that?" Answer: I don't.

MARKETING

Marketing is something contractors and academics do to establish themselves as credible sources for specific kinds of services. It refers to meetings, phone conversations, and e-mails with potential clients about what kind of work they have and when it will come out. It's often informal, a collegial conversation. It also includes more official presentations of your company's capabilities. Marketing normally has a budget in companies and a number for you to charge on your time sheet. Some companies have marketing specialists who network and make connections. Unless this is your job, you will find that marketing comes naturally without you thinking all that much about it; it's talking to people about their problems and how they might address them.

Some cautions are in order around marketing. Marketing about specific contracts can only occur *before* a request for proposals or an announcement is released. Once it is released, it is illegal for government employees to talk to you about it. And you should not act. Talking about a procurement that has been released is a violation of procurement integrity.

PROPOSALS

To start a competition, the government or organization releases an RFP (request for proposals). If your organization does good enough marketing, you are likely to know that it's in the works before it's released. Either one of your contacts has told you this or you found it by checking one of the many websites that describes upcoming government work.

After the procurement is released, your company will make a bid decision based on the work requested, the company's capabilities in the area, likely competition, the adequacy of the funding available, the timeline for the proposal, and the likely cost of preparing a proposal. All proposal activity is an unreimbursed cost, that is your company pays for it directly, so you don't want to start one you are not able to complete and don't have a reasonable chance of winning.

There are three mechanisms for proposing and managing research. Your proposal approach will depend on which of these you are applying for:

Grants. These are the least specific of funding mechanisms. The funder proposes a general question to be addressed and gives a range of funding available for grants. These are used for basic research or for a question that is not well enough understood to investigate. Under a grant mechanism the grantee acts as an independent researcher and is free to use whatever theories and methods he or she chooses. The end product is a professional paper or publication. Most academic research is grant funded.

Contracts. Contracts are business arrangements in which a client enters into an agreement with a contractor to conduct research that the client lacks the expertise or the time to complete themselves. The subject to be investigated is quite specific, and the methodology is often specified in the request for proposals. Under contracts, the contractor is an extension of the client, and the research belongs to the client. The end project is usually a final report and often a presentation. Most evaluations are conducted under contract.

Cooperative agreement. These are partnerships between two or more organizations to work together to investigate an issue or to develop and implement a project. The scope of work is negotiated between/among parties to the cooperative agreement. Each party has specified responsibilities, and each of them contributes resources to support the project. Very often cooperative agreements are between the federal government and one or more state or local governments to demonstrate a project. The end project is a report describing what happened and how the project went. This forms guidance as to whether to expand or eliminate or redesign a program. Sometimes evaluators are incorporated into cooperative agreements, most often as an employee or a contractor of one of the parties to the agreement.

The rest of this section applies to proposals for contracts. Grant proposals are usually academic in nature and out of the scope of this book. It is unlikely that most of you will ever participate in a cooperative agreement, although you may evaluate cooperative agreement projects under contract.

Principles for Contract Proposals

- Read the RFP carefully and write down the requirements. In a federal RFP they're pretty clear. In others you may have to search. What things are *required* for this project?
- Propose what they ask for, not what you think they should do. They will probably have specified a method. It may be bad or at least unlikely to do what they need. Feel free to point out the shortcomings of their idea in the proposal, but only after you discuss how you will do what they ask for. They will not consider your proposal unless is it *responsive* to the RFP—that is, proposes what they asked for. The reason for this is that they must rate and compare proposals from different sources using a "grade sheet" developed along with the Request for Proposals.

After they check your proposal for the required elements, they can start assigning credit for your (better) ideas.

Questions. Do not call your client and ask questions after the RFP is out. There will usually be a specification on the front page of the RFP of the deadlines for the proposal itself and an earlier deadline for questions. Questions are things that the RFP leaves uncertain. They must be compiled by the contracts officer for your organization and submitted to the funding organization by the deadline. Both the questions and the client's response to them will be released to all potential competitors. So your competitor knows what was asked and what the responses are for everyone.

In compiling questions think about whether you want to hear the answer. "Does the data collection person need to be a registered nurse?" or "Does the government really want the project design completed in three weeks?" Each of these raises a problem. If it isn't specific in the RFP and if isn't clarified in a question response, they can't penalize you for getting it "wrong." Additionally, don't give away your innovative ideas in questions. "Would the government entertain the idea of telephone focus groups with dispersed project leaders to improve response rate?"

Costing, budgeting and expenses. You will also submit a budget with your proposal showing anticipated labor hours, rates for all people to work on the project, travel expenses, other costs, and, of course, a bottom-line cost. Costing is somewhat of an art, and most companies have one or more people skilled at doing this. Cost is an extremely important part of the competitive edge companies have. It's not that everything goes to the lowest bidder; it goes to the lowest bidder who has demonstrated the best technical capability. However, all things being approximately equal, many good proposals are lost because of cost.

Submitting your proposal. Read the directions in the RFP. There is no flexibility in the time and date proposals are due. If you are late, all of the time and effort spent on the proposals is lost. It's good to have the technical part of the proposal done at least a week before the due date. Also check how the funder wants it submitted—e-mail or snail mail. If snail mail, back up the deadline for the technical proposal by three days.

BUDGETS

You will need someone in the organization you work for to help you with budget. Whether you are a client or a proposer, budgets require specialist input. They are complex and embedded in FAR regulations. However, there are a couple of concepts you might want to know ahead of time.

Direct costs and indirect costs. You may hear someone asking you to maximize direct costs and minimize indirect costs. The kind of time you work is broken up into direct and indirect costs to the organization. Direct costs are costs are billed to a client for productive work you do. Indirect costs are the costs to the company of doing business (staff meetings, management, marketing, professional activity not funded under a grant or contract). If you are working under contract, all of these costs are paid by the client. Indirect costs are simply allocated across all projects. The funding available for indirect costs is negotiated with the government usually under an umbrella authorization to do business with the government. If you work for a private organization under contract, they usually accept the federal standard. Indirect costs are usually lumped together into overhead.

Labor rates. The first time you look at the amount of money your company charges for an hour of your time, you will be shocked. "What's this $150 per hour?" you'll think. "I only get $50." The rate that is requested in a contract or grant is made up of several things. First is how much you are paid. Then your hourly pay is inflated by the cost of vacations, holidays, and sick leave. The cost of your fringe benefits is factored in (health insurance, 401(k), pension). Then they add a portion of the indirect costs directly attributable to you (office space, computer, telephone, marketing charges). At the end you get a "loaded" rate that may be between two and three times what you are actually paid. When people talk about "load" or "labor load," they are talking about the percentage of your base rate that shows up in bids. In the above case the load is 3.0 or three times your base rate

MANAGING YOUR PROJECT

Your job as a project manager is to deliver your projects on schedule and within budget as proposed and funded. This is a big challenge and requires constant tracking of both.

You should draft out your expectations for what will happen when and assign labor accordingly. Don't forget clerical support.

Your contract will specify "deliverables" with due dates. Deliverables are intermediate and final products. Put them in your schedule so you know how to manage time and labor so they show up on time.

Under most contract arrangements the government is committed to pay what the project costs the contractor plus a fee. A contract award is financially a ceiling over which costs should not go. But sometimes, because of poor budget management or unexpected costs, cost overruns occur. These are very bad. If you are an independent contractor, you must normally absorb these. If you work for a company, they must be absorbed as indirect costs. For this reason their first response to a potential overrun is to justify additional funding to the client. If you are a government employee, they put you in the difficult position of having to look for extra funds to get your contract completed .

Try to remember that everyone has a schedule and honor those of others involved in your project. If you are a government person, no matter how much you need interim results for an upcoming meeting, your project director may not be able to produce them early. If you are a project director, keep in mind that your technical officer or contact has their own deadlines. They have promised their own hierarchy results by a specific date. They are really embarrassed if they can't produce them because their contractor failed. Try hard not to put them in this position.

NOTES

CHAPTER ONE

1 The insider-outside perspectives captured in the emic-etic dimension of social research appears in many sources and is discussed in Chapter 3. A straightforward definition of these terms can be found in Stake (2006). For a more philosophical discussion, see Farris (1968, 568–99).

2. Evaluation research is the study of theory and method of evaluation itself. It deals with what evaluation is and how it should be done under varying circumstances. Most evaluation researchers are academics. I present various approaches to evaluation that have resulted from evaluation research in this chapter. However, I do not discuss evaluation research itself.

3. Groups of people to whom programs are addressed are often called "target populations," a terminology I avoid. I find "intended audience" or "designated population" more acceptable. A minor point, but I have observed that some people wince when the "target" terminology is used.

4. This is just a small sample of the large number of contexts in which evaluations are conducted. If you want to see what kinds of jobs there are for evaluators, visit the Career Center at the American Evaluation Association website, www.eval.org/programs "careercenter.asp.⁵ Most students of anthropology have wrestled with the culture concept through undergraduate and graduate school and continue to do so throughout their careers. In my own graduate work I was assigned a classic work of anthropology that presented some 490 definitions of culture (Kroeber and Kluckhohn 1952). The purpose of this assignment was to help us understand that culture is complex and problematic for anthropologists rather than to get us to absorb all of these definitions. It was from this exercise that we learned that the definition of culture is an arbitrary and heuristic exercise for those of us who are not scholars devoted to the philosophical understanding of culture.

6. Ethnography is not new to evaluation. Nor is grounding the investigation in the reality of the participant in the evaluated. Probably the best-known application of ethnography to evaluation comes from the work of David Fetterman. Fetterman is an anthropologist who was once president of the American Evaluation Association. During his presidency and later in his career he developed, with others, the idea of empowerment evaluation, in which it was the responsibility of the evaluator to help community members use evaluation to achieve desired goals (Fetterman 2005). Yvonne Lincoln and Evon Guba (1985) initiated a movement in evaluation toward naturalistic inquiry that rejected science as a means of understanding humans and focused exclusively on grounded approaches to individual situations using ethnographic methods. Case-study evaluators use ethnographic methods as part of mixed-methods case studies. (Stake 2006; Yin 2006).

7. By this I mean that it is often reductionist to apply biological models to the survival of the fittest in human life. People's lives are governed within societies with

culture. The individual is not the unit of selection for sociocultural attributes. Thus, the idea that humans "evolve" altruism or aggression or any other culturally defined characteristic is a misinterpretation of evolutionary theory.

8.   One good example of a program that is maintained by political pressure is the DARE program—a "just say no" substance abuse prevention program for teenagers that has been widely used in middle schools in the United States since its inception in 1983. The key element in DARE involves trained police officers going into schools to explain the risks and consequences of substance use. In 2003 the US General Accounting Office (GAO) published a meta-analysis showing that—according to *six* evaluations, some quasi-experimental—this program does not work to reduce substance use among adolescents. Nonetheless, it thrives still because the police like it, and police have lots of clout in local communities where substance abuse prevention is delivered.

CHAPTER TWO

1.   See Appendix A for a glossary of terms.

2.   In public health evaluation outcome is short-term effect; impact is long-term effect. In other fields these terms may be used the other way around. You need to determine the vocabulary from the context. But note that people use both terms for the same thing. Sometimes you just need to ask.

3.   I'm not sure whether anyone knows when and where Robert Stake came up with it, but it is easily one of the most quoted statements in evaluation.

4.   Different evaluators use different terms to reflect this postmodern view of the world, and each have slight differences from the others. However, they are similar enough that I have chosen fairly arbitrarily to use the word constructivist for consistency. This is in agreement with Lincoln and Guba (2005).

5.   Kuhn is the classic source for a definitive discussion of the role of paradigms in science. Kuhn addresses paradigms mostly in the context of physics and chemistry. However, his way of thinking about them is useful in any examination of the epistemology of any systematic field of study.

6.   Many people have written on the locus of reality ("out there" versus "in here") in both anthropology and evaluation. In anthropology this is reflected in the post-positivist controversies around almost everything. See, for example, Clifford and Marcus (1986) and articles in the edited volume by Richard Fox (1991). Each of these volumes has an influential introduction that deals with this dilemma. In evaluation a somewhat turgid but fairly comprehensible discussion can be found in Lincoln and Guba (1985).

7.   In fact, several years ago, in 2005, the US Department of Education (DOE), the bastion of evaluation orthodoxy, proposed that only evaluations utilizing a control group be considered for DOE funding. This policy statement said that priority for awarding evaluation contracts for DOE programs would be given to projects in which students, teachers, and classrooms were randomly assigned to treatment and non-treatment conditions. In a pinch, quasi-experimental designs could be considered.

8.   This book is helpful in applying the KEC to evaluations. I once used this book as

a text for an Evaluation Anthropology course but found it inappropriate for the purpose. But you may run into the KEC if you are working with some of the more quantitatively inclined evaluators.

9. Government and Results Act of 1993, www.whitehouse.gov/omb/mgmt-gpra /gplaw2m#h1. Also relevant here is the GPRA Modernization Ace of 2010, www .whitehouse.gov/omb/performance/gprm-act.

CHAPTER THREE

1. If you want to read the five thousand pages of Boas's ethnographic writings on the Kwakiutl, check out your university library. If you would like to do this, start with Boas (1974). This is an edited collection of Boas's work. If you want to go further into his work, I recommend Boas (1925) . I take this material from Harris (1968, 314–15).

2. There is a vast literature on the relationship of anthropology to the emergence of colonialism and the policies of the US government relative to American Indians. For Britain, George Stocking's work *Victorian Anthropology* (1987) describes the emergence of anthropological fieldwork in the British colonies, especially in Africa and its relationship to colonial administration. See also Assad's (1973) edited volume, *Anthropology and the Colonial Encounter.* For an interesting take on the tumultuous relationship between US policy and the American Indian, see Meyer and Royer (2001) and the final three chapters in Castile (1979).

3. Radcliffe-Brown used an organic metaphor to understand the systemic functioning of societies. Anthropological thinking has now moved far from this simple conception of sociocultural systems. Still, sometimes in evaluation, parsimonious is best. To see Radcliffe-Brown's own description of this, see ch. 4, "On the concept of function in the social sciences" (Radcliffe-Brown 1965).

4. Today many practicing and applied anthropologists have returned to AAA, as the association has made an effort to bring them back. Many practitioners today hold memberships in both AAA and SfAA.

5. No one knows precisely how many anthropologists are working in practice as a percent of degrees granted at the master's and/or doctorate level. There are several reasons for this. Anthropologists who have made careers outside of the academy are hard to identify unless they maintain membership in national professional organizations. Many of them no longer identify as anthropologists. Others may still use anthropological skills in their work but maintain no connection with the profession.

6. Anthropologists sometimes quibble with the idea of cultural competence because, for them, human beings are culturally competent by definition. I myself would probably have come up with a different term if anyone had asked. However, the term has currency. We use it because many different kinds of colleagues know what we mean when we say it. The literature abounds with discussions of poor cultural competence leading to program or product malfunction and insensitive management of service encounters in various settings. Most especially cultural competence becomes critical in health care settings where failure to communicate across the boundary between patients and health care providers may result in serious health consequences. One of the best known of these

in recent years is Ann Fadiman's account of the mismanagement of a case of epilepsy in a Hmong child in the United States (Fadiman 1997).

7. This perspective of culture change as a source of difficulty or a pathology is nowhere clearer than in discussions of revitalization movements like the ghost dance and cargo cults. These movements were depicted as ways of trying to restore the past balance. In fact, they were undoubtedly responses to new sources of economic and political power unprecedented in their past. As explanations of what was happening to them under oppressive conditions of contact, they weren't bad. For an interesting account of cargo cults, try Worsley (1968).

8. Choosing a community for an evaluation because it is a known failure almost always results in an inconclusive results because failures of a basically sound program usually occur for idiosyncratic reasons like staff turnover, loss of funding, individual leadership failures. These events generate a lot of interesting stories and may reinforce what you already know about failure. (Did you really need to be reminded that high staff turnover causes program failure?) To learn what the program can do—its effectiveness—select communities where the program is succeeding.

9. The word "evaluation" is such a turn-off to many program people that government agencies often prefer to call these "program assessments." A rose by any other name...

10. In this section I describe what anthropological methods are the most useful in evaluation. I provide detailed information on how to do them in Chapter 6.

CHAPTER FOUR

1. Not all evaluations are value driven. There is a whole school of value-free evaluation that avoids this issue in favor of behavior, knowledge, or some other outcome. See Alkin (1990).

2. For a very interesting discussion of the "new immigrants," see the work of Arjun Appadurai (1996). An immigrant himself, Appadurai captures this experience in an especially poignant way.

3. When I first began working in public health, especially at the CDC, I was impressed at how open they were to ethnography in spite of their grounding in epidemiology, a very empiricist approach. I finally began to understand that, although they were trained in epidemiology, many of them had an MD under their master's in public health. They learned in medical school that when you have seen one case, you have seen one case and to be wary of generalizations based on previous experience until they have considered the individual case. This training makes them vaguely uncomfortable with the certainties implied by the epidemiological approach. They believe that epidemiological results are true but not that they have enough information to act on them. Ethnography gives them this additional information.

4. Actually, if you talk to anthropologists from different "schools," you will discover that they don't agree on the definition of culture either.

5. Face validity means that a set of results is plausible, i.e. it makes sense to an intelligent observer. For example, a result demonstrating that all of the women in a

population sample are employed in the auto industry would lack face validity (unless the sample was chosen to demonstrate this). A finding that lacks face validity is not necessarily untrue. Strange things happen. However one should always delve into what seem to be unlikely results. Nonetheless, results that don't pass this believability test often turn out to be misinterpretations of data, whether quantitative or qualitative.

6. I always find it a bit of a chore to sort out the various "disciplinaries." Terms commonly used include "interdisciplinary," "multidisciplinary," and "transdisciplinary." I once had to distinguish them for a proposal I was writing. Multidisciplinary is research that brings scientists from multiple fields to study something. They may or may not collaborate, but their expertise is available to everyone. Interdisciplinary teams collaborate on some issue, bringing their own disciplines to bear on the problem, but they maintain disciplinary autonomy in doing so. Transdisciplinary research is the pursuit of an integrated approach from interdisciplinary teams that is synergistic and not fully a product of any specific discipline, not even anthropology. It is a highly collaborative process. It is, of course, a continuum with multidisciplinary research at one end and transdisciplinary research at the other.

CHAPTER FIVE

1. The summary of the Tuskegee Study was abstracted from Wikipedia. See wikipedia.org/wiki/Tuskegee_syphilis_experiment.

2. It was surprising to me that the Belmont Report wasn't published until April 18, 1979, over thirty years after the Nuremberg Trials.

3. The American Evaluation Association has prepared a statement on cultural competence in evaluation that lays out its own strong position in support of building cultural sensitivity to all evaluation stakeholders. This statement is updated regularly. The original was published in April 2011 and was last updated in 2013. See www.eval.org/ccstatement.

4. This article describes a worst-case scenario of what can happen when you turn a final report in. In this case uncertainty about the future of the program and about whether an evaluation led to a reaction to the final report in which the competence of the evaluators was brought into question. The authors recommend a written contract between the clients and the evaluator in which expectations for the evaluation are made explicit.

5. Many issues in the relationship of evaluators to the community and to social justice revolve around and the critique of empowerment evaluation. For a review of the critique, see Miller and Campbell (2006) and Smith (2007). Also see a 2007 response from David Fetterman and Abraham Wandesman to the critique.

6. The application of ethical guidelines to individual evaluations is widely discussed in the evaluation literature. David Fetterman (1986) discusses the need for "ethical dexterity' in individual ethnographic evaluations. Linda Mabry (1999) argues for mediating conflicts between ethical guidelines and judgment in specific situations in circumstantial ethics. For a discussion of influences that may affect the interpretation of the AEA Ethical Guidance, see Smith (2002).

7. See the Misuse of Evaluation in *New Directions in Evaluation* (Winter 1994)

for a discussion of evaluation misuse along a variety of dimensions. Especially see the introduction, "What Constitutes Misuse?" by Stevens and Dial (1994, 3–13) for a good summary of the issue.

8. Some important anthropological "classics" are part of the national character studies done in those days, most notably Ruth Benedict's book on Japanese character, the *Chrysanthemum and the Sword* (1946).

9. For a good discussion of the role of government in the anthropology and its problematic aspects, see *Anthropology and the Colonial Encounter* by Asad (1975). I would recommend Forster (1975).

10. For a full discussion of this issue, see APA (2009).

11. Blogs are a very good source of information on emerging ethical issues. For example, AAA maintains an ethics blog that discusses issues that arise in connection with new modalities of research (http://ethics.aaanet.org). I even found a Bloggers Code of Ethics (see www.cyberjournalist.net/news/000215.php). The Blogger Code comes up with familiar categories: be honest and fair, minimize harm, and be accountable.

12. It is important to understand that for any project, you may end up getting multiple IRB clearances if the study is a complex one. Every organization connected with your research will require that IRB be considered in government-supported research. Sometimes multiple organizations will accept the IRB clearance of a partner organization. For example, partners will often accept CDC IRB clearance rather than requiring their own.

13. IRB requirements sometimes don't consider evaluation to be research because it is not intended to generalize. However, I have never worked for a company that would let their staff do evaluation without IRB clearance. It's a matter of legal coverage.

14. Sometimes it may surprise you what a diligent IRB will consider "identifiers." For example, I was once prohibited from using dates of procedures for a clinical study because the data also contained respondents' birth dates. They argued that it would be possible to link procedures to individuals if you know their birth data.

CHAPTER SIX

1. The following resources provide good guidance in ethnographic methods and have been very useful to me in building and justifying evaluations. Bernard (2011) is probably the most widely used methodology guide in anthropology and my personal favorite. I have gone through three copies already. It doesn't matter what edition you use (use the one you have if you have one!). The latest edition includes lots of valuable tips on how to use new technologies to widen your data. Also check out LeCompte and Scheunsel (2010), a very nice take on ethnography in practice. The authors are well-known practitioners and developed a lot of the ethnographic methods that many of us use in practice—handy and usable.

2. In my own work I used the CDC Program Evaluation Framework (CDC 1999) and used it in earlier drafts of this chapter. I found that it was too specific to government decision-making strategies to be adequate for use here. The CDC Program Evaluation Framework was developed in 1999 by a group of evaluators at the CDC in an effort to standardize the way the various centers, institutes, and offices there did evaluation.

3. I do not love the word "evaluand" and try hard not to use it. Alas, I cannot find another term sufficiently broad to accommodate programs, products, and projects yet precise enough to capture "the thing that is being evaluated." So evaluand it is!

4. RE-AIM is an acronym for Reach, Effectiveness, Adoption, and Implementation Model. RE-AIM is often used to assess public health programs conceptualized by a federal agency or private funder, designed by some intermediate agency or organization, and implemented in communities in an attempt to modify the health behaviors of individuals. See Glasgow, Vogt, and Boles (1999).

5. The ability to figure out what your study is about is the most important and most difficult of all stages of any social research. If you can't arrive at this, you probably haven't learned enough about the thing you are evaluating or haven't yet thought about it enough. A lot of work—evaluation as well as other modes of social research—fails to produce the anticipated results because the social researcher never decided what to investigate clearly enough. It is an extremely valuable skill. And it is certainly not obvious when you start, even if your client thinks it is.

6. It is amazing how often people fail to distinguish these two parts of evaluation preparation and how much grief it causes. For example, both evaluators and clients may push to evaluation planning without an a priori evaluation design. The result of this is too often confusion during data collection because the linkage of data to the goals of the evaluation is unspecified.

6. I hate the term "convenience sample" and never use it. To me it implies that you sort of picked some people you happened to run into rather than choosing them based on what you need to know.

7. Krueger and Casey (2000). This is a kind of "bible" on focus groups. Krueger conducts well-known focus group training that a lot of the people I know have taken. It is a very useful guide, worth buying when you find yourself doing these. No hurry, though. Just look at it to see what these are about.

8. One of the basic skills that psychological counselors and anthropologists pick up is the ability to listen carefully and remember what they heard. This is why it is very important to write notes as soon as possible after you come out of the interview. I try to schedule at least a half-hour of down time after interviews, but this isn't always possible. This is why we use tape recorders. I have found that people get used to these much more easily than they get used to someone writing down what they say.

9. If you just e-mail the evaluation to the client, it may be archived immediately, especially if the findings are unacceptable in some way., I always try to negotiate dissemination at the beginning of the evaluation. However, if the client really hates it, there isn't much you can do.

CHAPTER SEVEN

1. I'm sure many would disagree with me on this point. And I'm sure there are contexts in which doctorates are required for credible evaluation. Just not where I've been.

2. For a full discussion of project and cost management, see Appendix B.

3. There are many books and websites with advice on building a short résumé. I guess one of the best known is Richard N. Bolles's *What Color Is Your Parachute?* (2014). The anthropologists among you may be interested in Carol Ellick and Joe E. Watkins (2011).

4. In connection with this, there are two kinds of jobs in most business organizations having to do with the Fair Labor Practices Law. Nonexempt jobs are jobs where people work to the clock and must be paid overtime if they work more hours than they should. Exempt staff work to the job; they are expected to do what needs to be done to finish the job in a timely fashion. Although you may have to account for a certain number of hours per week, if you are exempt, you only charge forty hours, no matter how many hours you work. So if you work sixty hours in one week to finish a proposal, you don't get paid overtime. You may be able to take time off to compensate yourself for overwork hours, but there is no guarantee you can do this. Professionals almost always work exempt if they are full time. As a professional, you should be curious about what is going on if you are offered a nonexempt job: Is it a full-time job? Does it have fringe benefits? Why is it nonexempt?

5. See Bureau of Labor Statistics, Overview of BLS Statistics on Pay and Benefits, www.bls.gov/bls/wages.htm.

REFERENCES

Abma, T. A., and R. E. Stake. 2001. "Stake's Responsive Evaluation: Core Ideas and Evolution." *New Directions in Evaluation* 92: 7–21.

Alkin, Marvin C. 1990. *Debates on Evaluation.* Newbury Park, CA: Sage.

American Anthropological Association. 2009. "CEAUSSIC Final Report on the Army's Human Terrain System Proof of Concept Program." www.aaanet.org/cmtes/commissions/CEAUSSIC/upload/CEAUSSIC_HTS_Final_Report.pdf.

American Evaluation Association. 2011. "Public Statement on Cultural Competence in Evaluation." www.eval.org/ccstatement.

Appadurai, Arjun. 1996. *Modernity Writ Large: Cultural Dimensions of Globalization.* Minneapolis: University of Minnesota.

Arensberg, Conrad. 1947. "Prospect and Retrospect." *Applied Anthropology* 6: 1–7.

Asad, Talal. 1973. *Anthropology and the Colonial Encounter.* London: Ithaca Press.

Bechar, Shlomit, and Irit Mero-Jaffe. 2013. "Who's Afraid of Evaluation? Ethics in Evaluation as a Way to Counter Excessive Evaluation Anxiety: Insights from a Case Study." *American Journal of Evaluation.* Published online. December 27.

Beebe, James. 2001. *Rapid Assessment Process: An Introduction.* Walnut Creek, CA: Altamira Press.

Benedict, Ruth. 1946. *The Chrysanthemum and the Sword.* Boston: Houghton-Mifflin.

Bernard, H. Russell. 2011. *Research Methods in Anthropology: Qualitative and Quantitative Approaches.* 5th ed. Plymouth, UK: Altamira Press.

Boas, Franz. 1925. Contribution to the Ethnology of the Kwakiutl. Columbia Contributions to Anthropology, vol. 3. New York: Columbia University.

———. 1974. *A Franz Boas Reader: The Shaping of American Anthropology, 1883–1911.* G. Stocking (Ed.) Chicago: University of Chicago.

Bolles. Richard N. 2014. *What Color Is Your Parachute?* New York: Random House.

Butler, Mary O. 2006. "Random Walk." In *Making History at the Frontier,* edited by C. Wasson, 20–31. *NAPA Bulletin* 26.

———. 2012. "Global Localities and the Management of Infectious Diseases." In *Applying Anthropology in the Global Village,* edited by C. Wasson, M. O. Butler and J. Copeland-Carson, 21–56. Walnut Creek, CA: Left Coast Press.

Butler, Mary O., and Jacqueline Copeland-Carson, eds. 2005. *Creating Evaluation Anthropology: Introducing an Emerging Subfield. NAPA Bulletin* 24.

Butler, Mary O., Jacqueline Copeland-Carson, and Peter Van Arsdale. 2005. "Career Planning for Evaluation Anthropology." In *Creating Evaluation Anthropology: Introducing an Emerging Subfield,* edited by Mary O. Butler and Jacqueline Copeland-Carson, 165–78. *NAPA Bulletin* 24.

Campbell, Donald T. 1969. "Reforms as Experiments." *American Psychologist* 24: 409–29.

———. 1974. "Evolutionary Epistemology." In *The Philosophy of Karl Popper,* edited by P. A. Schilpp, 413–65. LaSalle, IL: Open Court.

Campbell, Donald T., and Julian C. Stanley. 1963. *Experimental and Quasi-Experimental Designs for Research.* Chicago: Rand-McNally.

Castile, George P. 1979. *North American Indians: An Introduction to the Chichimeca.* New York: McGraw Hill.

Centers for Disease Control and Prevention. 1994. "Final Report—Contract No. 200-93-0626, Task 7. Syphilis in the South: A Case Study Assessment in Eight Southern Communities." www.cdc.gov/std/syphilis-in-the-south.

———. 1999. "A Framework for Program Evaluation in Public Health." *Morbidity and Mortality Weekly Report* 48: RR-11. www.cdc.gov/mmwr/pdf/rr/rr4811.pdf.

Chelimsky, Eleanor. 2008. "The Clash of Cultures: Improving the 'Fit' between Evaluative Independence and the Political Requirements of a Democratic Society." *American Journal of Evaluation* 29 (4): 400–15.

———. 2012. "Valuing, Evaluation Methods, and the Politicization of the Evaluation Process." *New Directions in Evaluation* 133: 77–83.

Clifford, James, and George Marcus, eds. 1986. *Writing Culture: The Poetics and Politics of Ethnography: A School of American Research Advanced Seminar.* Berkeley: University of California.

Cook, Thomas D., and Donald T. Campbell. 1979. *Quasi-Experimentation: Design and Analysis Issues in Field Settings.* Boston: Houghton-Mifflin.

Cousins, B. J. 2005. "Will the Real Empowerment Evaluation Please Stand Up?" In *Empowerment Evaluation Principles in Practice,* edited by David M. Fetterman and Abraham Wandesman, 183–208. New York: The Guilford Press.

Davidson, E. Jane. 2005. *Evaluation Methodology Basics.* Thousand Oaks, CA: Sage.

Eddy, E. M., and W. L. Partridge. 1978. *Applied Anthropology in America.* New York: Columbia University.

Ellick, Carol, and Joe E. Watkins. 2011. *The Anthropology Graduates Guide: From Student to a Career.* Walnut Creek CA: Left Coast Press.

Fadiman, Anne. 1997. *Spirit Catches You and You Fall Down.* New York: Farrar, Straus and Giroux.

Fetterman, David M. 1986. "Conceptual Crossroads: Methods and Ethics in Ethnographic Evaluation." *New Directions in Evaluation* 30: 23–36.

———. 1994. Empowerment Evaluation. *Evaluation Practice,* 15(1): 1–15.

———. 1999. Reflections on Empowerment Evaluation: Learning from Experience. *Canadian Journal of Program Evaluation* [Special Issue], pp. 5–37.

———. 2001a. "Empowerment Evaluation and Self-Determination: A Practical Approach to Program Evaluation." In *Integrating Behavioral and Social Sciences with Public Health,* edited by N. Schniederman and M. A. Speers. Washington, DC: USical Association.

———. 2001b. *Foundations of Empowerment Evaluation: Step-by-Step.* Thousand Oaks, CA: Sage.

———. 2002. "Empowerment Evaluation: Building Communities of Practice and a Culture of of Learning." *American Journal of Community Psychology* 3091): 89–102.

———. 2005. Empowerment and Ethnographic Evaluation: Hewlett-Packard's $15 Million Digital Divide Project (A Case Example). In *Creating Evaluation Anthropology,* edited by M. O. Butler and J. Copeland-Carson. NAPA Bulletin 24: 71–78.

———. 2013. *Empowerment Evaluation: Learning to think like an Evaluator. In Evaluation Roots: A Wider Perspective of Theorists Views,* edited by M. A. Alkin. Thousand Oaks, CA: Sage.

Fetterman, David M., Shakeh J. Kaftarian, and Abraham Wandesman, eds. 1996. *Empowerment Evaluation: Knowledge and Tools for Self-Assessment and Accountability.* Thousand Oaks, CA, Sage.

Fetterman, David M., and Abraham Wandesman. 2007. "Empowerment Evaluation: Yesterday, Today and Tomorrow." *American Journal of Evaluation* 28 (2): 179–98.

Fluehr-Lobban, Carolyn. 2003. "Ethics and Anthropology: 1890–2000." In *Ethics and the Profession of Anthropology: Dialogue for Ethically Conscious Practice*, edited by Carolyn Fluehr-Lobban, 1–28. Walnut Creek, CA: Altamira.

Forster, Peter. 1975. "Empiricism and Imperialism: A Review of the New Left Critique of Social Anthropology." In *Anthropology and the Colonial Encounter*, edited by T. Asad, 23–38. London: Ithaca Press.

Foster, George M. 1962. *Traditional Cultures, and the Impact of Technological Change*. New York: Harper.

Foucault, Michel. 1994. "Govermentality." In *The Essential Foucault*, edited by Paul Rabinow, 229–45. New York: The New Press.

Fox, Richard, ed. 1991. *Recapturing Anthropology*. Santa Fe, NM: School of American Research.

Hoover K. W., Butler M., Workowski K. A., Carpio F,. Follansbee S., Gratzer B., Hare B., Johnston B., Theodore J. L., Wohlfeiler M., Tao G., Brooks J. T., Chorba T., Irwin K., Kent C. K., and the Evaluation Group for Adherence to STD and Hepatitis Screening. 2010. "STD screening of HIV-infected MSM in HIV clinics." *Sexually Transmitted Diseases* 37(12): 771–6.

Geertz, Clifford. 1973. "Thick Description: Toward an Interpretive Theory of Culture." In The Interpretation of Culture, edited by C. Geertz, 3–30. New York: Basic Books.

Glasgow, Russell E., Thomas M. Vogt, and Shawn M. Boles. 1999. "Evaluating the Public Health Impact of Health Promotion Interventions." *American Journal of Public Health* 89 (9): 1322–27.

Goodman, Charity, Brad Trainor, and Stan Divorski. 2005. "Using Ethnographic Methods to Evaluate the Department of Veterans Patient Safety Program." In *Creating Evaluation Anthropology: Introducing an Emerging Subfield*, edited by Mary O. Butler and Jacqueline Copland-Carson, 57–70. *NAPA Bulletin* 24.

Greene, Jennifer. 1997. "Evaluation as Advocacy." *American Journal of Evaluation* 18 (1): 25–35.

Greene, Jennifer C., and Valerie J. Caracelli. 1997. "Defining and Describing the Paradigm Issue in Mixed Method Evaluations." *New Directions for Evaluation* 74: 5–17.

Gouinlock, James S. 2014. "John Dewey." In Encyclopedia Britannica. www.britannica.com/EBchecked/topic/160445/John-Dewey.

Harris, Marvin. 1968. *The Rise of Anthropological Theory*. New York: Crowell.

Hawking, Stephen J. 1988. *A Brief History of Time*. New York: Bantam Books.

Holmberg, Allan R., and Henry Dobyns. 1965. "The Transformation of Peasant Societies." *Science* 147 (3661): 1062–66.

House, Ernest R. 1997. "Evaluation in the Government Marketplace." *Evaluation Practice* 18 (1): 37–48.

———. 2001a. "Responsive Evaluation (and Its Influence on Deliberative Democratic Evaluation)." *New Directions in Evaluation* 92: 23–30.

———. 2001b. "Unfinished Business: Causes and Values." *American Journal of Evaluation* 22 (3): 309–15.

———. 2008. "Blowback: Consequences of Evaluation for Evaluation," *American Journal of Evaluation* 29 (4): 416–26.

House, Ernest R., and Kenneth R. Howe. 1999. *Values in Evaluation and Social Research.* Thousand Oaks, CA: Sage.

Kroeber, Alfred, and Clyde Kluckhohn. 1954. "Culture: A Critical Review of Concepts and Definitions." Harvard University. *Papers of the Peabody Museum of American Archaeology and Ethnology,* vol. 47.

Kreuger, Richard A., and Mary Anne Casey. 2009. *Focus Groups: A Practical Guide for Applied Research,* 4th ed. Thousand Oaks, CA: Sage.

Kuhn, Thomas S. 1962. *The Structure of Scientific Revolutions.* Chicago: University of Chicago Press.

Lansing, J. S. 2003. "Complex Adaptive Systems." *Annual Reviews of Anthropology* 32: 183–204.

LeCompte, Margaret D., and Jean J. Scheunsel. 2010. *Designing and Conducting Ethnographic Research: An Introduction. Ethnographers Toolkit, Book 1.* Plymouth, UK: Altamira Press.

Lincoln, Yvonna S., and Evon G. Guba. 1985. *Naturalistic Inquiry.* Newbury Park, CA: Sage.

Linney, Jean Ann, and Abraham Wandersman. 1991. *Prevention Plus III: Assessing Alcohol and Other Drug Prevention Programs at the School and Community Level: A Four-Step Guide to Useful Program Assessment.* Rockville, MD: US Department of Health and Human Services, Office of Substance Abuse Prevention.

Mabry, Linda. 1999. "Circumstantial Ethics." *American Journal of Evaluation* 20 (2): 199–212.

———. 2010. "Critical Social Theory Evaluation: Slaying the Dragon." *New Directions in Evaluation* 127: 83–98.

Marcus, George. 1995. "Ethnography in/of the World System: The Emergence of Multi-Sited Ethnography." *Annual Review of Anthropology* 24: 95–117.

McNall, M. and P. G. Foster-Fishman. 2007. "Methods of Rapid Evaluation, Assessment and Appraisal." *American Journal of Evaluation* 28 (2): 151–68.

Meyer, Carter J., and Diana Royer, eds. 2001. *Selling the Indian.* Tucson: University of Arizona.

Miles, Matthew B., A. Michael Huberman, and Johnny Saldaña. 2014. *Qualitative Data Analysis.* 3rd ed. Thousand Oaks, CA: Sage.

Miller, R. L., and R. Campbell. 2006. "Taking Stock of Empowerment Evaluation: An Empirical Review." *American Journal of Evaluation* 27 (3): 296–319.

Morris, Michael. 2011. "The Good, the Bad and the Evaluator." *American Journal of Evaluation* 32 (1): 134–51.

National Commission for the Protection of Human Subjects of Biomedical and Behavioral Research. 1978. "The Belmont Report: Ethical Principles and Guidelines for the Protection of Human Subjects of Research DHEW Publication (OS)78-0012." Washington, DC: US Government Printing Office.

Patton, Michael Q. 2005. "The View from Evaluation." In *Creating Evaluation Anthropology,* edited by Mary O. Butler and Jacqueline Copeland-Carson, 31–40. *NAPA Bulletin* 24.

———. 2008. *Utilization-Focused Evaluation.* 4th ed. Thousand Oaks, CA: Sage.

Pike, Kenneth. 1954. *Language in Relation to a Unified Theory of the Structure of Human Behavior,* vol. 1. Glendale, CA: Summer Institute of Linguistics.

Price, David. 2003. "Anthropology Sub Rosa: The CIA, the AAA and the Ethical Problems Inherent in Secret Research." In *Ethics and the Profession of Anthropology: Dialogue for*

Ethically Conscious Practice, edited by Carolyn Fluehr-Lobban, 29–49. Walnut Creek, CA: Altamira.

Radcliffe-Brown, A. R. 1965. *Structure and Function in Primitive Society.* New York: Free Press.

Rouse, R. 1991. "Mexican Migration and the Social Space of Post-Modernity." *Diaspora* 1: 8–23.

Schensul, Jean, and Mary O. Butler. 2012. "Toward a Practice-Based Ethnography in the Global Village." In *Applying Anthropology in the Global Village,* edited by Christina Wasson, Mary O. Butler, and Jacqueline Copeland-Carson, 289–302. Walnut Creek, CA: Left Coast Press.

Safran, M. A., Hoover K. W., Tao G., Butler M. O. 2013. "Sexual behavior and desire to discuss mental health as reported by HIV-infected men who have sex with men." Published on-line on 20 March 2013. *International Journal of STD & AIDS.*

Scriven, Michael. 1967. "The Methodology of Evaluation." In *Perspectives of Curriculum Evaluation,* edited by Ralph W. Tyler, Robert M. Gagné, and Michael Scriven, 39–83. Chicago: Rand-McNally.

———. 1991. "Beyond Formative and Summative Evaluation." In *Evaluation and Education: At Quarter Century,* edited by Milbrey Wallin McLaughlin and D. C. Phillips, 19–64. Ninetieth Yearbook of the National Society for the Study of Education. Chicago: University of Chicago Press.

———. 2012. "Key Evaluation Checklist." www.umich.edu/evalctr/archive_checklists /kec_feb07.pdf.

Shadish, William R., Thomas D. Cook, and Laura C. Leviton. 1991. *Foundations of Program Evaluation: Theories of Practice.* Newbury Park, CA: Sage.

Sieber, Joan E. 1980. "Being Ethical: Professional and Personal Decisions in Program Evaluation." *New Directions for Evaluation* 7: 51–61.

Smith, N. L. 2002. "An Analysis of Ethical Challenges in Evaluation." *American Journal of Evaluation* 23 (2): 199–206.

———. 2007. "Empowerment Evaluation as Evaluation Ideology." *American Journal of Evaluation* 28 (2): 169–78.

Squires, Susan. 2005. "Telecommunication—Product Meaning and Use: Two Examples of Needs Assessment." In *Creating Evaluation Anthropology: Introducing an Emerging Subfield,* edited by Mary O. Butler and Jacqueline Copeland-Carson, 79–88. *NAPA Bulletin* 24.

Stake, Robert E. 1995. *The Art of Case Study Research.* Thousand Oaks, CA: Sage.

———. 2006. *Multiple Case Study Analysis.* New York: Guilford.

Stevens, Carla, and Micah Dial. 1994. "What Constitutes Misuse?" *New Directions in Evaluation* 64: 3–13.

Stocking, George. 1974. *A Franz Boas Reader: The Shaping of American Anthropology 1883–1911.* Chicago: University of Chicago.

———. 1987. *Victorian Anthropology.* New York: The Free Press.

Strauss, Anselm, and Juliet Corbin. 1990. *Basics of Qualitative Research: Grounded Theory Procedures and Techniques.* Thousand Oaks, CA: Sage.

Tax, Sol. 1975. "Action Anthropology." *Current Anthropology* 16(4): 514–7. December 1975.

Trimble, Joseph, Ed Trickett, Celia Fisher, and Leslie Goodyear. 2012. "A Conversation on Multicultural Competence in Evaluation." *American Journal of Evaluation* 33 (1): 112–23.

Tyler, R. W. 1991. "General Statement on Program Evaluation." In *Evaluation and Education: At Quarter Century,* edited by Milbrey Wallin McLaughlin and D. C. Phillips, 3–17. Ninetieth Yearbook of the National Society for the Study of Education. Chicago: University of Chicago Press.

US Government Accountability Office. 2003. "Youth Illicit Drug Use Prevention: DARE Long-Term Evaluations and Federal Efforts to Identify Effective Programs." GAO-03-172R. January 15.

US Government Printing Office. 2010. GPRA Modernization Act of 2010. Washington, DC. www.gpo.gov/fdsys/pkg/PLAW-111publ352/pdf/PLAW-111publ352.pdf.

Webb, Eugene J., Donald T. Campbell, Richard D. Schwartz, and Lee Sechrest. 2000. *Unobtrusive Measures: Nonreactive Research in the Social Sciences.* Revised Edition. Thousand Oaks CA: Sage.

Wholey, Joseph S. 2010. "Use of Evaluation in Government: The Politics of Evaluation." In *Handbook of Practical Program Evaluation,* edited by Joseph S. Wholey, Harry P. Hatry, and Kathryn E. Newcomer, 651–67. San Francisco: Jossey-Bass.

Whyte, William Foote. 1978. "Organizational Behavior Research." In *Applied Anthropology in America,* edited by Elizabeth W. Eddy and William L. Partridge, 129–43. New York: Columbia University Press.

Worsley, Peter. 1968. *The Trumpet Shall Sound: A Study of "Cargo" Cults in Melanesia.* New York: Schocken.

Yin, Robert K. 1993. *Applications of Case Study Research.* Newbury Park, CA: Sage.

———. 2006. *Case Study Research.* 4th ed. Thousand Oaks, CA: Sage.

INDEX

ABOUT THE AUTHOR

Mary Odell Butler is an anthropologist-evaluator with thirty-five years of experience in research design, management, and evaluation, along with twelve years of university teaching at the graduate and undergraduate levels. She has special expertise in program evaluation, evaluation research, and case-study methods and has conducted numerous projects for the Center for Disease Control, the Health Resources and Services Administration, the Environmental Protection Agency, the National Institutes of Health, and private foundations. She has been chair of the Committee for Practicing, Applied and Public Interest Anthropology, a standing committee of the American Anthropological Association, and a past president of the National Association for the Practice of Anthropology. In addition to her academic responsibilities, she is employed by Westat, a consulting firm in Rockville, Maryland, as a senior analyst supporting work in evaluation of public health programs. Butler is co-editor of *Applying Anthropology in the Global Village* (Left Coast Press, 2011) and *Creating Evaluation Anthropology: Introducing an Emerging Subfield* (Wiley-Blackwell, 2005).